BLACK SOCIALIST PREACHER

ALSO BY PHILIP S. FONER

History of the Labor Movement in the United States (6 vols.)
The Life and Writings of Frederick Douglass (5 vols.)
British Labor and the American Civil War
On Art and Literature: Writings of José Martí
A History of Cuba and its Relations with the United States (2 vols.)
The Complete Writings of Thomas Paine (2 vols.)
Business and Slavery: The New York Merchants and the Irrepressible Conflict
W.E.B. Du Bois Speaks (2 vols.)
Paul Robeson Speaks
The Fur and Leather Workers Union
Jack London: American Rebel
Mark Twain: Social Critic
The Jews in American History, 1654-1865
The Case of Joe Hill
The Letters of Joe Hill
The Bolshevik Revolution: Its Impact on American Radicals, Liberals and Labor
American Labor and the War in Indochina
Helen Keller: Her Socialist Years
The Autobiography of the Haymarket Martyrs
The Black Panthers Speak
The Voice of Black America: Major Speeches of Negroes in the United States, 1797-1973 (2 vols.)
Women and the American Labor Movement: From Colonial Times to the Eve of World War I
Women and the American Labor Movement: From World War I to the Present
The Spanish-Cuban-American War and the Birth of American Imperialism, 1895-1902 (2 vols.)
Organized Labor and the Black Worker, 1619-1981
American Labor Songs of the Nineteenth Century
Labor and the American Revolution
We, the Other People: Alternative Declarations of Independence by Labor Groups, Farmers, Women's Rights Advocates, Socialists, and Blacks
Formation of the Workingmen's Party of the United States
The Democratic-Republican Societies, 1790-1800
The Factory Girls
The Great Labor Uprisings of 1877
History of Black Americans: From Africa to the Emergence of the Cotton Kingdom
American Socialism and Black Americans' From the Age of Jackson to World War II
Inside the Monster: José Martí on the United States and American Imperialism
Our America: José Martí on Latin America and the Struggle for Cuban Independence
On Education: José Martí on Educational Theory and Pedagogy
The Black Worker: A Documentary History (with Ronald Lewis) (6 vols.)
Proceedings of Black State Conventions, 1840-1865 (with George Walker) (2 vols.)
Wilhelm Liebknecht: Letters to the Chicago Workingman's Advocate
Mother Jones Speaks: Collected Writings and Speeches
History of Black Americans (vols. 1-3)
Karl Marx Remembered: Comments at the Time of His Death
First Facts of American Labor

*To the memory
of my beloved Roslyn*

By one who was once a chattel slave freed by the proclamation of Lincoln and now wishes to be free from the slavery of capitalism.
From the dedication to a pamphlet by Rev. Woodbey.

The Teachings of Reverend George Washington Woodbey
and his Disciple, Reverend G. W. Slater, Jr.

BLACK SOCIALIST PREACHER

Edited and with an Introduction by
Philip S. Foner

Foreword by Congressman Ronald V. Dellums

HX
536
.W72
1983

SYNTHESIS PUBLICATIONS   SAN FRANCISCO, CALIFORNIA

ACKNOWLEDGEMENTS

I am indebted to the following institutions for kind assistance in the preparation of this work: Tamiment Institute; Elmer Bobst Library; New York University; Langston Hughes Memorial Library; Lincoln University, Pennsylvania; Chicago Historical Society; Chicago Public Library; Library of Congress; New York Public Library; New York Public Library— Schomburg Collection; Howard University Library; Omaha Public Library; University of Nebraska Library; Nebraska Weslyan University Library; Nebraska State Historical Society; San Diego Historical Society; University of California, Los Angeles Library; University of California, Berkeley Library; Duke University Library; Clinton (Iowa) Public Library; Columbia University Library; University of Pennsylvania Library.

Copyright © 1983 by Philip S. Foner

All rights reserved. No portion of this book may be reproduced, by any process or technique, without the express written consent of the publisher.

Photograph of Woodbey courtesy of State Historical Society of Wisconsin.

Library of Congress Cataloging in Publication Data

Woodbey, George Washington, b. 1854
   Black socialist preacher.

   Includes bibliographical references and index.
   1. Socialism and religion—United States—Addresses, essays, lectures.
2. Afro-Americans—Social conditions—To 1964—Addresses, essays, lectures.
3. Socialism—United States—Addresses, essays, lectures. I. Slater, George W.
II. Foner, Philip Shelden, 1910-   III. Title.
HX536.W72   1983   261.2'1   83-17927
ISBN 0-89935-026-7
ISBN 0-89935-025-9 (pbk.)

Published by Synthesis Publications
2703 Folsom Street, San Francisco, CA 94110

Printed in the United States of America
10 9 8 7 6 5 4 3 2 1

CONTENTS

i	Foreword by Congressman Ronald V. Dellums
1	Introduction by Philip S. Foner

PART ONE   WRITINGS AND SPEECHES OF
REVEREND GEORGE WASHINGTON WOODBEY

39	What to Do and How to Do It: or, Socialism vs. Capitalism
87	The Bible and Socialism: A Conversation Between Two Preachers
203	The Distribution of Wealth
240	Woodbey's Arrest in Long Beach
242	Remarks of Rev. Woodbey at the 1908 Socialist Party Convention
245	Socialist Agitation
247	The New Emancipation
251	Why the Negro Should Vote the Socialist Ticket
256	What the Socialists Want
260	Why the Socialists Must Reach the Churches with Their Message
263	Notes to Part One

PART TWO   **WRITINGS OF WOODBEY'S PREDECESSORS**
- 269   Socialism from the Biblical Point of View by Rt. Rev. James Theodore Holly, D.D., LL.D.
- 282   The Negro and Socialism by Rev. R.C. Ransom
- 290   Notes to Part Two

PART THREE   **ARTICLES OF REVEREND GEORGE W. SLATER, JR.**
- 293   Introduction
- 296   How and Why I Became a Socialist
- 299   Negroes Becoming Socialists
- 302   Booker T. Washington's Error
- 305   The Cat's Out
- 309   Abraham Lincoln a Socialist
- 312   Taft, the Republican Party, and the Negro
- 315   The Hell of War
- 317   Reaching the 1,000,000
- 319   Mine Eyes Have Seen It
- 321   Know the Truth
- 325   Roosevelt and the Race Problem
- 328   Emancipation
- 331   Pullman Porter Pity
- 334   The New Abolitionists
- 336   The Colored Man Welcome
- 339   The Colored Strike Breaker
- 342   Tillman vs. Till-Men
- 344   Race Problem's Socialist Cure
- 346   The Negro and Socialism
- 348   Lincoln and the Laborer
- 351   Socialism and Social Service
- 355   Notes to Part Three

- 359   Index

Foreword

The writings and speeches of Reverend George Washington Woodbey have clear relevance today. He understood that racism is not the only enemy of the minority communities. The economic system that perpetuates poverty, illiteracy, sickness, and despair is also our enemy. Reverend Woodbey saw that it was not enough to seek entry into the system. We must change the system. The basic underpinning of the system is economics. It is here that our struggle for change should begin.

The tremendous changes needed will mean a tremendous political struggle, requiring courage, tenacity, and strength to endure. The minority communities have all these qualities, which are the qualities needed for national and world leadership in the months and years ahead.

The minorities, particularly Blacks, are well suited to understanding the necessary economic changes that must be made in our system. Blacks are the constant, probably the leading, victims of an economic system which relies on a certain amount of built-in unemployment. We understand not only political oppression and injustice, but economic oppression and injustice as well. We all know about Blacks being "last-hired, first-fired." The Black middle class notwithstanding, the overwhelming majority of Black people in this country are have-nots, and to the degree that our politics has not addressed that reality, our politics do not address the Black condition in this country. The ravages of racism are devastating, the untold number of Blacks in this country who are victims of poverty and hunger and disease is devastating; the fact that millions of our people continue to be unemployed is devastating. We have seen how poverty breaks down our families, how our children get into drugs, how so many lives are wasted and ruined.

Human rights include economic rights as well as political rights. True political democracy will never be possible without economic democracy. This is because heavily unequal control of property can offset the equality of such political processes as each person having an equal vote, since money can control or influence votes disproportionately. In addition, since many decisions which are the most basic and life-affecting are made by private businesses, by bosses or corporate boards, when people have no control over that decision-making process, they have no control over large areas of their lives. Clearly, no brand of economics is written into our Constitution. More and more, peoples throughout the world, especially the Third World, are seeking ways to control the productive processes of their countries. The United States should study both their successes and their failures, to evolve a new economy. We should examine the old concept that a town of 500 people is "public" while a corporation such as General Motors, which has revenues larger than two thirds of the countries in the world, is "private." We must recognize as well that certain industries affect our lives so deeply that they can no longer be considered private in the traditional sense of the word. What is so radical in the wealthiest nation in the world to say that we should now move that wealth be a right, that education be a right, that housing be a right, that food be a right, that shelter be a right, that all these things be a right?

Over the past generation, many movements for liberty, equality, justice and human rights and human dignity have emerged around the world. Progressives, and particularly Black progressives, with our special understanding of oppression and of Third World peoples, should be open to relationship with these movements and to an exchange of ideas. Blacks are uniquely suited to be in the vanguard of this.

There is a special brotherhood of the oppressed of the world, between Third World people in the United States and the rest of the poor and oppressed of the world, and there is a special responsibility of American Blacks to help all people understand together the changes that must be made together.

RONALD V. DELLUMS

Having an extended personal acquaintance with the Reverend Woodbey, I do not hesitate to recommend that those who inform themselves upon the economic questions of the day, and their scientific and practical solution, should hear this logical advocate of the cause of labor.

Rev. G.W. Woodbey is worthy in every respect of the confidence of all members of Trades Unions and the laboring class in general.

                      Louis V. Guye, Editor *Trans-Mississippi Barber*,
                                      Omaha, Neb., Nov. 12, 1901.

G.W. Woodbey has been greatly appreciated in Kansas City, Mo. He thoroughly understands his subject and has a happy way of making his audiences understand him.

                      Garnet Futvoye, Sec. Socialist Club of Jackson Co.,
                                      Kansas City, Mo., Dec. 12, 1901.

It has been my good fortune to hear the Rev. G.W. Woodbey on "The Social Economics of Jesus," "The Golden Rule in Politics," and other topics. I heartily recommend him to all who study social problems and the Bible's remedy therefor. He is an able, logical, sincere and eloquent Christian, and his work in the labor movement has marked him as a man of courage and honesty.

                      Will J. Stevens, of the Nebraska Oxygenor Co.,
                                      Omaha, Neb., Nov. 18, 1901.

I have known G.W. Woodbey for over a year and know him to be an earnest worker for the cause of Socialism. He is one of the most forcible and eloquent speakers we have in this locality; has done excellent work in the campaign, and is worthy of anything you can do for him. I highly recommend him to all in our great movement.

                      Geo. E. Baird, Sec. State Com. Socialist Party,
                                      Omaha, Neb., Nov. 17, 1901.

**Tributes from material advertising
Woodbey's lectures in Omaha, Nebraska, where
he began his work for the Socialist Party.**

Introduction

Although several articles[1] and one book[2] have dealt with the relationship between American socialism and black Americans, this present work marks the first time that the writings of black socialists have been published in book form. For this first collection, I have chosen the writings of a specific group of black socialists, black socialist preachers, and especially those of the leading black socialist preacher, George Washington Woodbey of San Diego, California. Woodbey was the leading black socialist in the United States during the first decade of the twentieth century, and fortunately his major publications on socialism have been preserved. They are now reprinted for the first time.

Along with the writings of Reverend Woodbey, I have included writings of two other black ministers on socialism (Rt. Rev. James Theodore Holly and Rev. R.C. Ransom) in order to present an earlier view of this subject before Woodbey appeared on the scene. This is followed by a series of articles by Woodbey's disciple, Reverend George W. Slater, Jr., of Chicago, which appeared in the *Chicago Daily Socialist* and *The Christian Socialist*. Together they provide a full presentation of the views of the leading black socialist preachers in the United States during the opening decades of the twentieth century.

In several ways, these writings and speeches reflected the Socialist Party position on the Negro question. They reflected, for example, the party's view that it had nothing special to offer the Negro except the same opportunities as those enjoyed by whites, and that, in the main, the plight of blacks under capitalism, like that of the whites, would be solved automatically under socialism. None of the black socialist preachers, moreover, criticized the Socialist Party for failing to mount a campaign against disfranchisement, segregation, lynching, and peonage in the South. They appear to have accepted the fact that the party viewed the grievances of black workers as identical to those of white workers, and that the socialists had no special message for them.

But the black socialist preachers did repeatedly emphasize that blacks would have the most to gain from a socialist victory because the "colored man is the worst off of all the working class of people," and received "less wages, less protection, less education, pays more for food, clothing, house rent, etc."[3] Hence it was in the basic interest of black Americans, "as poor people," to support the Socialist Party—"the party which will solve the problems of the black man, as well as those of his white brother."[4] And Reverend Woodbey added that it was in the interest of "the women, more than the men, . . . if possible, to be Socialists because they suffer more from capitalism than anyone else."[5]

The writings and speeches in this volume were addressed to black Americans all over the United States. Since the church was a dominant influence in the black community, more black Americans learned of socialism through the writings included in this volume than all the publications of the various socialist groups combined.

* * *

In the *Ohio Socialist Bulletin* of February, 1909, Reverend Richard Euell, a black minister of Milford, Ohio, published "A Plan to Reach the Negro." The Negro, he wrote, "belongs to the working class and must be taught class consciousness." Blacks could be more rapidly recruited into the party if socialists would go to them in their churches and point out "the way to freedom and plenty." Most of them had no experience with any organization other than the church and could think of committing themselves to action only in religious terms. The Bible, and even motion pictures about the "Passion Play," could be used effectively to imbue religion with radicalism and convince the black working class of the evils of the capitalist system and the virtues of socialism.[6]

The first black socialist to conduct the type of work Reverend Euell recommended was Reverend George Washington Woodbey (sometimes spelled Woodby), and he had already been performing this function for the socialist cause for several years before "A Plan to Reach the Negro" was published.

Woodbey was not the first black minister to espouse the cause of socialism. In 1889, a small group of white ministers, led by William D.P. Bliss and George D. Herron, formed the Society of Christian Socialists. The Declaration of Principles of the Christian Socialist Movement, adopted on April 15, 1889, asserted that its object was "to show that the aim of Socialism is embraced in the aim of Christianity." It called for the establishment of a system of "social, political, and industrial relations... based on the Fatherhood of God and the Brotherhood of man, in the spirit and according to the teachings of Jesus Christ." All who agreed with this outlook were invited to join and form chapters of the Society of Christian Socialists.

Chapters did spring up in various parts of the country, with their members dedicated to the peaceful establishment of a socialist society. They subscribed to *Dawn,* the movement's official publication edited by Bliss, and distributed copies of Bliss's pamphlet, *What is Christian Socialism?,* which called for municipal ownership of light, heating, and transit companies; the nationalization of the telegraph and railroads; and the establishment of postal savings banks—all as preparatory steps to the complete socialization of all industries. It also advocated levying taxes as an interim measure to reduce the glaring inequalities of wealth. But as a solution for the evils of American capitalism, Christian Socialism gained few adherents. By the late 1890s, it was all but dead; *Dawn* had ceased publication in

1896, and soon afterwards, the chapters closed their doors.

The Christian Socialist movement was short-lived and fleeting, but it left a deeper mark on black Americans than did any of the other organized groups seeking to achieve socialism. This was not because the Christian Socialists made greater appeals to blacks or discussed the Negro question more frequently. On the contrary, neither in the Declaration of Principles nor in *Dawn*, nor any of its widely distributed pamphlets, was the "Negro question" ever discussed by the Christian Socialist movement. Rather, it was by harking back to the principles of the early Christians, by viewing the cooperative commonwealth as the material expression of the teachings of Christ, and by emphasizing the gradualist, peaceable approach to socialism that these movements appealed to a number of black ministers.

It was through the debates in the columns of *The Christian Recorder* and the *AME Church Review* that many black Americans learned of socialism. Both were organs of the African Methodist Episcopal Church, a major church in the black community, and thus their influence was far greater than that of the socialist publications. Those who wrote on the subject in *The Christian Recorder* upheld the view that blacks should shun socialism as a "pernicious doctrine" akin to anarchism, and rejected the notion, dear to Christian Socialists, that Christ was the "original socialist." On the other hand, those who wrote in the *AME Church Review* argued forcefully that socialism was the proper form of society for all workers, including blacks, and cited the Bible and contemporary social scientists to reinforce their arguments. Yet, even those black leaders who condemned socialism conceded that, theoretically, blacks had the best reason to demand a fundamental change in American society along the lines proposed by the socialists. As one of them, Alexander Clark, stated: "They might be excused for listening to the siren voices of the Socialists."[8]

"Socialism is the subject now uppermost in all minds, almost to the exclusion of every other thought in this closing decade of the nineteenth century," Reverend James T. Holly wrote at the beginning of his article "Socialism from the Biblical Point of

View" (reprinted in this volume). The former shoemaker, an ardent advocate of the emigration of black Americans to Haiti, had sent the article to the *AME Church Review* from Port-au-Prince where he lived. In a far-ranging discussion, Reverend Holly called for the application of "biblical socialism" to cure the evils of modern capitalist society.[9] Several years later, the talented Reverend Reverdy C. Ransom, later elected bishop of the AME Zion Church, published "The Negro and Socialism" in the *AME Church Review* (also reprinted here). After painting a picture of the "spirit of unrest" which pervaded every avenue of American life, he declared: "The present social order with its poverty and vast reserve army of unemployed cannot be accepted as final, as the ultimate goal for which ages have been in travail." According to Ransom, socialism was both the logical and inevitable answer. It was a form of society especially suited for the American Negro who, although belonging "almost wholly to the proletarian or industrial class," was finding it increasingly difficult to obtain work because of opposition from both employers and labor unions. Reverend Ransom predicted that when the Negro "comes to realize that socialism offers him freedom of opportunity to cooperate with all men upon terms of equality in every avenue of life, he will not be slow to accept his social emancipation."[10]

Editorially, the *AME Church Review* urged its readers to give Reverend Ransom's defense of socialism the "careful reading" it deserved.[11] When Reverend W.H. Coston of Ohio, in a critical review of Reverend Ransom's article in *The Christian Recorder,* confused socialism and anarchism, the *AME Church Review* criticized Coston for having distorted what Reverend Ransom had actually said. It pointed out that Ransom had made it clear that the two movements were quite different in theory, methods, and objectives.[12]

While Reverend George Washington Woodbey was not the first black minister to advocate socialism, he was the first to join the party of socialism in the United States and to play a leading role in its activities. Unquestionably the most outstanding black socialist in the first decade of the twentieth century, George

Washington Woodbey was born a slave in Johnson County, Tennessee, on October 5, 1854, the son of Charles and Rachel (Wagner) Woodbey. Of his early life nothing is known other than that he learned to read after freedom came, was self-educated except for two terms in a common school, and that his life was one of "hard work and hard study carried on together." A fellow socialist who knew him wrote: "He has worked in mines, factories, on the streets, and at everything which would supply food, clothing and shelter."

Woodbey was ordained a Baptist minister at Emporia, Kansas, in 1874. He was active in the Republican Party of Missouri and Kansas. Also a leader in the Prohibition Party, when he moved to Nebraska he became a prominent force in the prohibition movement in that state. In 1896, Woodbey ran for lieutenant governor and Congress on the Prohibition ticket in Nebraska.[13]

That same year, he made his first acquaintance with the principles of socialism when he read Edward Bellamy's *Looking Backward,* and his interest was further aroused by copies of the *Appeal to Reason* which came into his hands. Although he subscribed to the *Appeal,* he did not join the Socialists. Instead, he joined the Populist Party, and in 1900, he supported William Jennings Bryan, the Democratic and Populist candidate for President. But he also heard Eugene V. Debs speaking during the presidential campaign and was so impressed that when the Democratic Party asked Woodbey to speak for Bryan, he agreed but delivered speeches which were geared more to the ideas advanced by Debs than those by the Democratic candidate. After several such speeches, the Democrats stopped scheduling dates for Woodbey's speeches, and the black minister came to the conclusion that his place was in the Socialist camp. He resigned his pulpit and announced to his friends that henceforth his life "would be consecrated to the Socialist movement." A Nebraska Socialist recalls:

> We remember him in the stirring days of the inception of the Socialist movement in Omaha. Night after night he spoke on the streets and in the parts of that city. Omaha had never had the crowds that attended Woodbey's meetings.[14]

Woodbey visited his mother in San Diego during the spring of 1902, and immediately made an impression on the comrades in Southern California. A dispatch to the *Los Angeles Socialist* on May 31, 1902, expresses this clearly:

> Socialism is on the boom here in this county and city. We have had Rev. G.W. Woodbey, the Colored Socialist orator of Nebraska with us for nearly a month during which time he has delivered 23 addresses and will speak again tonight, and then he will do some work in the country districts where he has been invited to speak. . . .
> Comrade Woodbey is great and is a favorite with all classes. He came here unannounced ostensibly to see his mother who resides here but as he says that he is "so anxious to be free," that he feels impressed to work for the cause constantly. He has had very respectable audiences both on the streets and in the halls. He likes to speak on the street and it is the general verdict that he has done more good for the cause than any of our most eloquent speakers who have preceded him. He is full of resources and never repeats his speeches, but gives them something new every time. He requested me to state in my notes to the "Socialist" that he desires to visit Los Angeles later on if you folks can find a place for him. He makes no charges but depends entirely on passing the hat for his support. . . .[15]

Los Angeles did find a place for Woodbey, and he delivered a series of soapbox speeches and lectures in the leading hall. When after one of his speeches, Woodbey was denied admittance to the Southern Hotel and Northern Restaurant because of his color, the Los Angeles Socialist Party organized a successful boycott of the establishments and distributed leaflets reading:

> We demand as trade unionists and socialists, that every wage-worker in Los Angeles bear well in mind these two places that depend on public patronage—the Northern Restaurant and the Southern Hotel—keep away from them. They draw the color line.

Woodbey accepted an offer to become minister of the Mount Zion Baptist Church in San Diego and made his home in California for the next two decades. He was elected a member of the state executive board of the Socialist Party, and soon became widely known in the state as "The Great Negro Socialist Orator." In a Los Angeles debate with Archibald Huntley, Ph.D., where Woodbey took the affirmative of the topic, "Resolved that Socialism is the True Interpretation of Economic Conditions and that it is the Solution of the Labor Problem," he was listed as a "well-known Socialist Lecturer."

An announcement that Woodbey would deliver a reply to Booker T. Washington's "Capitalist Argument for the Negro" packed Los Angeles's leading hall on May 1, 1903. He paid tribute to Washington "as a gentleman" and educator, but added: "He has all the ability necessary to make a good servant of capitalism by educating other servants for capitalism." Woodbey charged that whether consciously or not, Tuskegee Institute fulfilled the role of providing black workers to be pitted against white workers so as to bring about a general lowering of wage scales. What Washington failed to understand was that there was basically no unity between capitalists, white or black, and workers, white or black. "There is no race division industrially, but an ever-growing antagonism between the exploiting capitalists, black or white, and the exploited workers, black or white." In this "industrial struggle," the working class was bound to "ultimately triumph."

> And then the men of all races will share in the results of production according to their services in the process of production. This is Socialism and the only solution to the race problem.

A frequent target of the police of San Diego, Los Angeles, San Francisco, and other California communities, Woodbey was in and out of jail several times between 1902 and 1908, and was hospitalized more than once as a result of police brutality. But he gave as well as received. When he was attacked and driven off a street corner in San Diego in July, 1905, by Police Officer George H. Cooley, Woodbey led a group of protestors to the police station to lodge a complaint. There Cooley again attacked the black socialist, "using at the same time oaths and language too mean and vile to print." Woodbey was literally thrown bodily out of the station house. He immediately brought charges against the police officer for assault and battery and informed his California comrades:

> In the days of chattel slavery the masters had a patrol force to keep the negroes in their place and protect the interests of the masters. Today the capitalists use the police for the same purpose.

But slaves had rebelled despite the patrols, and he was following that tradition by telling the police that they could not get away with their brutality against enemies of the capitalist system.

Although Woodbey's case against the police was prosecuted by the County Attorney, assisted by Job Harriman, California's leading socialist attorney, and although all witnesses testified that the black socialist's conduct had been "perfectly gentlemanly," and that he had a perfectly lawful right to be at the station house, the jury, composed of conservative property owners, took only 15 minutes to find the defendant not guilty. Woodbey was furious and published the names of the jurymen, calling upon all decent citizens to have nothing to do with them. He followed this up by returning immediately to the soapbox in San Diego and held one of the biggest street corner meetings in the city up to this time. As he wrote:

> The case has made more Socialists than I could possibly have made in many speeches. Had I not gone to the court with the matter the public would forever have contended that I was doubtless doing or saying something that I had not right to do or say. And when I complained I would have been told that if I had gone to the courts I would have got justice. Now, as it is, nothing of the kind can be said, and the responsibility is placed where it rightly belongs.

Many nonsocialists in San Diego, Woodbey noted, were learning the truth of the socialist contention that "the police force are the watch dogs of capitalism."[16]

In more than one California city, Woodbey was arrested and hauled off to jail for trying to sell copies of his socialist booklets.

The writings made Woodbey's name known throughout the entire Socialist Party in the United States and even internationally. Woodbey's ability to explain socialism in simple terms led to the demand that he "embody some of the things he has said to the thousands who have listened to his talks, in a written form...." The response was the pamphlet *What to Do and How to Do It or Socialism vs. Capitalism.* A copy of a small edition, privately printed, fell into the hands of A.W. Ricker, a socialist organizer in the West and South. While at the home of socialist publisher Julius A. Wayland, in Girard, Kansas, he read it aloud to the Wayland family. "At the conclusion," Ricker wrote, "we decided that the book ought to be in the hands of the millions of American wage slaves, and we forthwith wrote to Rev. Mr. Woodbey for the right to bring it out."

It was published as No. 40 of the widely distributed *Wayland's Monthly* in August, 1903. Ricker gave it a sendoff in the *Appeal to Reason* writing:

> The book in many respects is the equal of "Merrie England," and in the matter of its clear teaching of the class struggle, it is superior. It has been read by every negro in Girard, (Kansas), and has made Socialists of those who were susceptible of understanding after every other effort had failed to shake their unreasoning adherence to the Republican Party. A good supply should be ordered by every local in the land, there is no book in the language that will excel it in propaganda value, and we expect to see it pass through one edition after another, as soon as it is read by the comrades.[17]

Since Robert Blatchford's *Merrie England,* published in England in 1894 and in the United States in 1900, was considered one of the best of the socialist educational publications, the tribute to Reverend Woodbey's pamphlet was well understood by readers of the *Appeal to Reason.*

Woodbey's 44-page booklet carried the touching dedication:

> This little book is dedicated to that class of citizens who desire to know what the Socialists want to do and how they propose to do it. By one who was once a chattel slave freed by the proclamation of Lincoln and wishes to be free from the slavery of capitalism.[18]

In his preface, Reverend Woodbey acknowledged that there was "nothing original" in his little book, his aim being simply to make the subjects treated "as plain as possible to the reader." It was not directed to those who were already convinced of the superiority of socialism over capitalism, but to "meet the demands of that large and increasing class of persons who have not yet accepted Socialism, but would do so if they could see any possible way of putting it into practice." Within this framework, Reverend Woodbey's booklet is an effective piece of socialist propaganda, and was so highly thought of in socialist circles that by 1908 it had been translated into three languages and gained for its author an international reputation.[19]

Basically, the booklet consists of a dialogue between the author and his mother whom he has rejoined after nearly 17 years of separation. She expresses her astonishment at having learned that her son had become a socialist. "Have you given up the Bible and the ministry and gone into politics?" she asks. Her son attempts to convince his mother that it is precisely because of his devotion to the principles enunciated in the Bible that he became a socialist, and that as the years passed, he became more and more convinced of the correctness of his decision. When his mother points out that among his comrades were a few who believed neither in God nor in the Bible, her son readily agrees, but reminds her that he found "a still larger number of unbelievers in the Republican Party before I left it some twenty years ago," and that other parties had their "equal portion" of nonbelievers. More important, while he believed in the Biblical account of God, the origin of earth and man, and members of his party did not, he and they were able to agree that "man is here, and the earth is here, and that it is the present home of the race, at least." They did not, to be sure, see eye to eye about the "hereafter." Since socialism was "a scheme for bettering things here first," he could be a "good socialist" without surrendering his belief in God or in the Bible. There was room in the Socialist Party for those who were interested only in what it could do for mankind in the present world and for those who, like himself, were "Socialists because they think that mankind is entitled to the best of everything in both this world and the next. Finally, his mother accepts the idea that under socialism persons would be free to have "their own religion or none, just as they please, so long as they do not interfere with others."

Having laid to rest his mother's anxiety and made her willing to listen to the fundamental principles of a movement which obviously had not destroyed her son's religious convictions, Reverend Woodbey proceeds to explain to her the evils of capitalist society and the way by which socialism, gaining power through the ballot box, would set out to eliminate these evils. After he takes his mother through such subjects as rent, interest, and profits, all gained from labor's production, and value which is created only by labor but the fruits of which are appropriated entirely by the capitalists, she expresses bewilderment at the meaning of such words. Her son then illustrates what they mean in simple language and in terms of daily experience. Here, for example, is how he explains surplus value:

> Why didn't the slave have wealth at the close of the war? He worked hard.
> "Because his master got it," mother replied.
> "The wage worker's master got what he produced, too."
> "But wasn't he paid for his work?" asked mother.
> "Yes, about seventeen cents on every dollar's worth of wealth he created...."

Under socialism, he continues, the capitalist would have to turn over to the state a "large amount of capital created by labor" which he had taken from the worker; while the latter, having been deprived of all he produced under capitalism, would have nothing to turn over. The very rich would have no reason to complain "since he and his children, who have done nothing but live off the labor of those who have nothing to turn over, are to be given an equal share of interest with those who have produced it all. So you see we Socialists are not such bad fellows as you thought. We propose to do good unto those who spitefully use us, and to those who curse us, by giving them an equal show with ourselves, provided that they will here-after do their share of the useful work."

But his mother expresses concern that the capitalists will not

Introduction 13

yield peacefully to having the "land, factories and means of production" turned over to the cooperative commonwealth by a socialist Congress elected by the people, and that they would start a war to retain their holdings. Her son concedes that this would quite likely occur, just as the slaveholders had refused to abide by Lincoln's electoral victory and precipitated a civil war. But the capitalists would never succeed in the war they would seek to stimulate, for the majority of the people had clearly become convinced that socialism was the only solution to their problems, or else the socialists could not have won their electoral victories. Hence, the capitalists would have no one to do the fighting for them:

> The slaveholder did not dare to arm the negro, on his side, without proclaiming emancipation, and to do that was to lose his cause; so with the capitalist, if he dares to offer all to the poor man who must fight his battles, he has lost his cause; and with this condition confronting the capitalist, there is no danger in taking over the entire industrial plant as soon as the Socialists can be elected and pass the necessary laws. And the Socialist party will go into power just as soon as the majority finds that the only way to secure to itself its entire product is to vote that ticket.[20]

Mother has only one question left about the transition from capitalism to socialism: "Have the people a right to do this?" Her son reminds her of the Declaration of Independence which clearly affirmed the right of the people, when any form of government became destructive of the rights of life, liberty, and the pursuit of happiness, "to alter and abolish and institute a new government" which would be most likely to affect "their safety and happiness." On this the socialists stand, the son declares firmly. Moreover, it was none other than Abraham Lincoln who, in his speech of January 12, 1840, in the House of Representatives, had said "just what the Socialists now say." He had then declared: "Any people anywhere being inclined and having the power have the right to rise up and shake off the existing government and form a new one that suits them better. . . ."[21]

His mother now fully satisfied, the son proceeds to describe how different departments of government—agriculture, transportation, distribution, intelligence, education, and health—will operate under socialism providing for the needs of the people rather than under capitalism, for the profits of the capitalist. Occasionally, the mother interrupts the narrative with questions that bring answers that satisfy her. Thus, when she asks whether the workers who would own and operate the factories under socialism "would know how to do the work," the answer reassures her:

> Why, the workers are the only ones who do know how to run a factory. The stockholders who own the concern know nothing about doing the work. If the girl who weaves in the factory should be told that Socialism is now established, and that henceforth she is to have shorter hours of labor, a beautiful sanitary place to work in, and an equal share of all the wealth of the nation, to be taken in any kind of thing she wants, do you think she would forget how to work? And if on the other hand, all she produces is to go to the girl who does nothing but own the stocks, then she can work right along. Seems to me, you might see the absurdity of that, mother. "I believe I do see, now," she said, after a moment's hesitation. Then apply that illustration about the girls, to all the workers, and you will get my meaning.[22]

As might be expected, mother asks, "Like all other women, I want to know where we are to come in." Her son assures her that it was in the interest of "the women, more than the men, if possible, to be Socialists because they suffer more from capitalism than anyone else." For one thing, the Socialist platform demands "the absolute equality of the sexes before the law, and the repeal of the law that in any way discriminates against women." Then again, under socialism each woman would, like each man, have her own independent income and would become "an equal shareholder in the industries of the nation." Under such liberating conditions, a woman would have no need "to sell herself through a so-called marriage to someone she did not love, in order to get a living," and, for the first time in history, could marry only for love. Under capitalism, the working man was a slave, "and his wife is the slave of a slave." Socialism would liberate both, but since it would give women political equality and economic freedom, it would actually do more for women than ever for men.[23]

By now mother has been converted, and the booklet ends with the comment: "Well, you have convinced me that I am about as much of a slave now as I was in the South, and I am ready to accept any way out of this drudgery," mother remarked as the conversation turned on other subjects.[24]

Here and there *What to Do and How to Do It* reflected Edward Bellamy's influence on Reverend Woodbey, and sections of the 1903 pamphlet are shortened versions of the 1887 *Looking Backward*.[25] In the main, however, the pamphlet revealed that the black minister had broken with Bellamy's utopianism. While Bellamy emphasized "equitable" distribution of wealth under nationalism, Woodbey was convinced that the solution lie closer to Marx's maxim, "From each according to his abilities, to each according to his needs." Bellamy rejected the label "socialism" as dangerous and un-American.[26] But Woodbey welcomed it and believed its principles were in keeping with the best in the American tradition. Like many in the Socialist Party, Woodbey believed that with the capture of sufficient political offices through the ballot box, socialism could be rapidly achieved. But he was one of the very few in the party in 1903 who took into account the danger that the capitalists would not sit by and calmly watch their control of society eliminated by legislative enactments, and instead would, like the slave owners in 1860, resort to violence to prevent the people's will from being carried into effect. To be sure, unlike Jack London, who in his great 1908 novel, *The Iron Heel,* predicted that the oligarchy of American capitalists would seize power from the socialists and destroy the democratic process by violence, Woodbey was confident that the capitalists would fail.[27] While London predicted that the capitalists would create a special armed force "out of the old regular army," called "the Mercenaries" who, a million strong, would be used to maintain the oligarchy in power, Woodbey rather naively believed that once the people voted for socialism, the capitalists would be unable to make use of the armed forces.

Nevertheless, by equating socialism with the American tradition, Woodbey was in advance of nearly all Christian Socialists. Early in *What to Do and How to Do It,* Reverend Woodbey assured his mother that he would at a future date tell her "more about what the Bible teaches on this subject" of socialism.[28] He fulfilled his promise a year later with *The Bible and Socialism: A Conversation Between Two Preachers,* published in San Diego, California, by the author. The 96-page booklet was dedicated to

> ...the Preachers and members of the Churches, and all others who are interested in knowing what the Bible teaches on the question at issue between the Socialists and the Capitalists, by one who began preaching twenty-nine years ago, and still continues.[29]

As the subtitle indicates, *The Bible and Socialism* consists of a dialogue between Woodbey and another clergyman. The latter is a local pastor to whom Woodbey's mother has given a copy of the 1903 pamphlet and invited to her home to hear her son convince him that he was wrong in contending that "there is no Socialism in the Bible." When the skeptical pastor questions Woodbey about the socialist claim that Karl Marx discovered the principles of Scientific Socialism, and points out that this was centuries after the Bible was written, Woodbey notes, first, that no new idea is ever entirely new and is in some way based on what went before, and, second, that

> Marx, the greatest philosopher of modern times, belonged to the same wonderful Hebrew race that gave to the world Moses, the Lawgiver, the kings and prophets, and Christ the Son of the Highest, with his apostles, who, together, gave us the Bible that, we claim, teaches Socialism. Doubtless Marx, like other young Hebrews, was made acquainted with the economic teachings of Moses, and all the rest of the old Testament sages and prophets, whatever we find him believing in after life.
> If we are able to show that the Bible opposes both rent, interest, and profits, and the exploiting of the poor, then it stands just where the Socialists do.[30]

.

After agreeing that Marx was not a Christian, but noting that this was of no significance since socialism had nothing to do with a man's religion or lack of it, Reverend Woodbey devotes the rest of his pamphlet to detailed references, quotations, and citations to convince the pastor that since the Bible—both the Old and New Testaments—did actually oppose "rent, interest, and profits, and the exploiting of the poor," it was a socialist document with close affinity to such classics as *The Communist Manifesto, Capital* and other writings of Marx. As a Jew, Woodbey emphasizes, Marx was able to do "the greatly needed work of reasoning out from the standpoint of the philosopher what his ancestors, the writers of the Old and New Testaments, had already done from a moral and religious standpoint."[31] This is not to say, he continues, that there is no difference between a socialism based merely on a "moral and religious standpoint" and Scientific Socialism; just as there was a fundamental difference between the socialism advanced by utopian reformers prior to Marx and that set forth by the father of Scientific Socialism. For Scientific Socialism was based on the class struggle which had dominated all history and dominated existing relationships in capitalist society. When the pastor asks Woodbey if the class struggle also exists in the church, there is the following discussion in which his mother joins:

> Master and slave, before the war, all belonged to the same church. They met on Sunday and prayed together, and one church member sold the other the next day. So now, in many cases, master and wage slave belong to the same church, meet on Sunday and pray together, and the one turns the other off from even the pittance he allowed him to take out of his earnings as wages or sets him out of house and home for nonpayment of rent, or under mortgage, the next day. All that notwithstanding, the Bible says love brother and the stranger as oneself.
>
> It took the abolitionist, in and out of the church, to show the inconsistency of slavery and force a division, as the Socialists are now doing.
>
> "Yes," said mother, I belonged to one of that kind of churches, myself, before the war."[32]

Just as his mother was converted at the end of the 1903 pamphlet, so, too, the pastor by the close of *The Bible and Socialism*. He confesses he had learned little of economics while in college, and since he joined the ministry, he had been too busy to give more than a casual thought to the Bible's "economic teachings" and whether or not the churches adhered to them. But as a result of the "interesting evening conversations," he was a changed man,

> ...being convinced that Socialism is but the carrying out of the economic teachings of the Bible, I shall endeavor to study it and lay it before my people to the best of my ability.[33]

Woodbey's pamphlet may have provided little that was new for white, religiously inclined socialists, since the Christian Socialists had already published a considerable body of literature demonstrating to their satisfaction that the Bible and socialism were compatible. But to black churchgoers much of what was in the pamphlet was new and certainly must have made an impressive impact. Moreover, while many Christian Socialists preached an emotional propaganda replete with Christian ethics, they tended to ignore the class struggle or to relate their Biblical references to the contemporary scene. Not so Woodbey: he was a firm believer in the class struggle, had read Marx, and was not in the least reluctant to couple discussions of the Old and New Testaments with specific evils in twentieth-century American society.

Woodbey's third and last socialist pamphlet was *The Distribution of Wealth*, published in 1910 in San Diego by the author. The 68-page booklet consists of a series of letters to J. Jones, a California rancher friend of the author, in which Woodbey describes how the distribution of wealth created by productive labor would operate "after Socialism has overthrown the capitalist method of production." Pointing out in his preface that there was little in socialist literature on how the future cooperative commonwealth would function, Woodbey, without the slightest hesitation, declared he would attempt to fill the gap. Affirming his right to do so, he noted:

If the socialist movement is based upon truth, it cannot be destroyed by the utmost freedom of discussion, nor is the movement or the party necessarily in danger, because your views or mine are not at once adopted even should they be corrected. All I ask of the reader is a fair, honest consideration of what I have written.[34]

What he wrote is an interesting elaboration of how the different institutions under capitalism would operate in the new socialist society. Some of this had already been set forth in his 1903 *What to Do and How to Do It*, but here he develops it further. In 1903, it will be recalled, Woodbey had conceded that the capitalists would resort to armed resistance to prevent the socialist society from coming into being. Now, however, he appears to believe that while capitalists would resist the transition to socialism with "tremendous opposition," it would not necessarily lead to war. In a clear reversion to the utopianism of *Looking Backward*, Woodbey here argues that once socialism had proven its superiority over capitalism even the capitalists and their children would acquiesce and decide to live under it. He writes:

Let us go back, for instance, to the slaveholder, by the way of illustration. He declared that he would go to war before he would permit himself and family to labor like the negro slave and live in poverty, rags, and ignorance. He had been taught to believe that that was the necessary outgrowth of labor. And I submit that the condition of labor under chattel slavery was a poor school in which to teach the child of the master a desire to labor. So the capitalist of today and his children look upon the workers as he has them in the sweatshops, mines, and factories of the country, putting in long hours for a bare existence, under the most unsanitary conditions, living in the worst of places, and eating of the worst of food; and, like his brother, the slaveholder, he is determined that he and his shall not be reduced to such straits. It has not yet dawned upon him that when the people who work own the industries in place of him, all of these disagreeable conditions will at once disappear. . . . It is my opinion that, notwithstanding the false education of the children of the wealthy, even they in the first generation will have so much of their distaste for labor taken away that we will have little or no trouble with them when the majority have changed conditions.[35]

Woodbey's rancher friend keeps asking whether people would work under socialism once the fear of poverty and unemployment were removed. Woodbey's answer is interesting:

> . . .when chattel slavery prevailed, as we said, men thought that labor must continue to be always what it was then, and that because the slave sought to escape he wouldn't work for wages. So now the capitalist, and those who believe in capitalism, think that labor must continue always to be just what it is now; and as some people won't work under the new and better conditions.
>
> It is a wonder to me that men are so willing to work as they are under the present conditions. The fact is, the mind of the child is such that it accepts what it is taught now, and will do the same then.
>
> The boy that was born a slave thought that it was natural for him to be one, and the young master took it for granted that he was intended to be master. But the boy that is born free never thinks that anyone ought to own him; nor does the youngster born at the same time with him think that he ought to own him. But instead, they both go to school often in the same class. They at once accept the conditions under which they were born. No, my friend, there is no danger of the children not at once accepting the new conditions under Socialism, and we have proved there will be so little loss through idlers, even in the first generation of old folks, that it will not be found worth bothering about. And as the old and infirm should of necessity be looked after with the best of everything from the very beginning, it will be found when the time comes that the thing to do will be to let everyone work and be sure that we have abundance of everything for all, and then let everybody help themselves, wherever they may be, to what we have on hand, as we do with what the public now owns. Indeed, they can be better trusted then than now, with all fear of the future banished forever.[36]

It is perhaps significant that this is the only one of Woodbey's pamphlets which ends without the second party convinced of the truth of the author's arguments and converted to socialism.

Probably Woodbey himself realized that he had tackled a difficult subject and that his presentation was too tentative to be effective in total conversion. At any rate, he ended his last letter:

> Hoping that I have been able to make it clear to you that under Socialism it will be possible to equitably distribute the products of industry and that you and your family will at once join the movement, I will close this somewhat lengthy correspondence by saying that I would be pleased to hear from you soon.
> Yours for the cause of the Revolution,
> G.W. Woodbey[37]

Reverend Woodbey's writings were largely addressed to winning new converts to the socialist cause. Within the Socialist Party itself, Woodbey actively participated in the most significant policy debates faced by the party. For example, he was a delegate to the Socialist Party conventions of 1904 and 1908; indeed, he was the sole representative of black people at these gatherings. At the 1904 convention Woodbey took the floor twice. On the first occasion, he expressed his opinion on the seating of A.T. Gridely of Indiana who was being challenged because he had accepted a position in the state government after passing a civil service examination. The question at issue was whether A.T. Gridely had violated the socialist principle of not accepting a position under a capitalist government. Woodbey spoke in favor of seating A.T. Gridely, arguing that in Germany the socialists boasted of the number of comrades in the army, noting that certainly such socialists were doing work for a capitalist government. "We all know," he continued, "that we work for capitalists when we work at all, and we would be pretty poor if we did not work for capitalists at all."[38] On the second occasion, he spoke up in favor of the Party National Secretary receiving a salary of $1,500 a year which he called "not a dollar too much."[39] But the failure of the convention to deal with the "Negro question" in the party platform, and of the delegates to discuss it once during the entire convention, aroused no comment from the only black delegate.

At the 1908 convention, Woodbey took the floor four times. On one occasion, in which the franchises held by private corporations were being discussed, Woodbey advanced the position—a very bold one for the Socialist Party—that the Socialists should declare themselves

> in favor as fast as they can get in possession in any locality, of taking everything without a cent, and forcing the issue as to whether there is to be compensation or not. (Applause.) I take the ground that you have already paid for these franchises—already paid more than they are worth, and we are simply proposing to take possession of what we have already paid for."[40]

On another occasion, Woodbey recommended that the National Committee elect its executive committee from its own members, and on still another, he opposed the imposition of a qualifying period before which a party member could be nominated for office on the Socialist ticket to ensure that he would not betray the movement. Woodbey argued that the danger of such persons "selling out" was just as great if they were members for years instead of months. "In my judgment, a man who understands its [the Party's] principles is not more liable to do it after he has been in the party six months than five years."[41]

The final occasion in which Woodbey spoke before the 1908 convention marked the only time during the two national gatherings that he commented on an issue related to the race question. That was when he took a firm stand, during the discussion of the immigration resolution, against Oriental exclusion and, indeed, exclusion of any immigrants. His speech, coming as it did from a California delegate, was a remarkable statement. While certainly not calculated to win friends among Socialists in his state, it was in keeping with the tradition of black Americans since the era of Reconstruction: in 1869, the Colored National Labor Union went on record against exclusion of Chinese immigration. Woodbey conceded that it was generally believed that all who lived on the Pacific Coast were as "a unit" in opposing Oriental immigration. Though a delegate from California, he did not share this view:

> I am in favor of throwing the entire world open to the inhabitants of the world. (Applause.) There are no foreigners, and cannot be unless some person comes down from Mars, or Jupiter, or some place. I stand on the declaration of Thomas Paine when he said "The world is my country." (Applause.) It would be a curious state of affairs for immigrants or descendants of immigrants from Europe themselves to get control of affairs in this country, and then say to the Oriental immigrants that they should not come here. So far as making this a mere matter of race, I disagree decidedly with the committee, that we need any kind of a committee to decide this matter from a scientific standpoint. We know what we think upon the question of race now as well as we would know two years from now or any other time.[42]

Woodbey scoffed at the idea that the entrance of Oriental immigrants would reduce the existing standard of living, arguing that immigrant labor was not the issue, for it was the "natural tendency of capitalism" to reduce the standard of living of the working class, and that if they could not get Oriental labor to do work more cheaply in the United States, they would export their production to the Oriental countries where goods could be produced more cheaply than in this country.[43] Woodbey's prediction that American capitalists would export production to cheap labor countries of the Orient was, as American workers today fully realize, to prove to be correct.

Continuing, Woodbey spoke eloquently of the contradiction between immigration restriction and the principles of international socialism. As he saw it, socialism was based "upon the Brotherhood of Man," and any stand in opposition to immigration would be "opposed to the very spirit of the Brotherhood of Man." Reminding the delegates that socialists were organized in China and Japan as well as in other countries, he asked:

> Are the Socialists of this country to say to the Socialists of Germany, or the Socialists of Sweden, Norway, Japan, China, or any other country, that they are not to go anywhere on the face of the earth? It seems to me absurd to take that position. Therefore, I hope and move that any sort of restriction of immigration will be stricken out of the committee's resolution. (Applause.)[44]

It is unfortunate that while he had the floor, Woodbey did not attack delegates like Ernest Untermann and Victor Berger for the anti-black character of their arguments in favor of Oriental exclusion. Nevertheless, Woodbey's speech on the immigration resolution ranks high in socialist literature even though it has been ignored by all students of the subject.[45]

Only once at either the 1904 or 1908 conventions did the delegates take notice of the fact that Woodbey was a black representative. That was when his name was placed in nomination as Debs's running mate in the presidential election of 1908. Delegate Ellis Jones of Ohio presented his name to the convention in a brief but moving speech. "Comrades... the nomination that I want to make for our Vice President... is a man who is well known in the movement for many years. The Socialist Party is a party that does not recognize race prejudice, and in order that we may attest this to the world, I offer the name of Comrade Woodbey of California."[46] But Woodbey received only one vote—that of Jones.[47] The nomination went to Ben Hanford who had been Debs's running mate in 1904. Had Debs, who did not attend the convention, wired the delegates that Woodbey's nomination would be a major contribution of American socialism to the struggle against racism, the vote would possibly have been different. But Debs did not believe that the party should do anything special on the "Negro question," and this view was shared by all at the convention except for the one delegate who nominated and voted for Woodbey. Since the fact that Woodbey was even placed in nomination has escaped the attention of every historian of the Socialist Party,[48] it is clear that the significance of the one vote he received has been generally overlooked.

Following the 1908 convention, Woodbey began a tour of Northern cities with fairly large black populations and delivered a series of soapbox speeches in favor of the Socialist ticket.[49] In addition, the national office of the Socialist Party circulated his four-page leaflet, *Why the Negro Should Vote the Socialist Ticket.* The author was described as a member of the State

Executive Committee, Socialist Party of California, and formerly Pastor of the African Church in Omaha, Nebraska. Typical of Woodbey's propaganda technique, the leaflet consisted mainly of a speech, supposedly delivered by a Reverend Mr. Johnson, Pastor of the African Baptist Church, who had called his congregation together to explain why he had decided "to vote the Socialist ticket at the coming election."

The socialist movement, he pointed out, sought to bring together all working people into a party of their own, so that through such a party "they may look after the interest of all who work regardless of race or color." Since Negroes were nearly all wage workers, it was clear that only such a party could really represent them. "All other parties have abandoned the negro, and if he wants an equal chance with everyone else, he can get it in no other way than by voting the Socialist ticket." No other party, including the Republicans, stood for eliminating poverty; further, just as once the elimination of slavery was crucial for the Negro, so today was the elimination of poverty. Socialism would create a society without poverty, a society in which the land, mines, factories, shops, railroads, etc., would be owned collectively, and the Negro, "being a part of the public, will have an equal ownership in all that the public owns, and this will entitle him to an equal part in all the good things produced by the nation." In this future society, moreover, he would not have to abandon his belief in religion. On the contrary, by providing all with sufficient food to eat and decent places in which to live, socialism would be fulfilling the fundamental ideas set down in the Bible.

Finally, Woodbey called for unity of white and black workers, urging them to "lay aside their prejudices and get together for their common good. We poor whites and blacks have fought each other long enough, and while we have fought, the capitalists have been taking everything from both of us." The socialist movement was the embodiment of this unifying principle, for it was

> part of a great world movement which includes all races and both sexes and has for its motto: "Workers of the world unite. You have nothing to lose but your chains; you have a world to win."[50]

Woodbey's first published appeal directly to his people on behalf of the Socialist Party is an excellent illustration of the black minister's great ability to take a complex subject and simplify it so that even a political illiterate could understand it.

Woodbey expanded on several points in his leaflet in articles early in 1909 in the Chicago *Daily Socialist.* In "The New Emancipation," he emphasized the common interests of black and white workers under capitalism, condemned black strikebreaking and the doctrine that Negroes should seek to solve their problems by the accumulation of wealth. Even if a few Negroes could become wealthy, the fact still remained that "their brothers are getting poorer every day." What then was the answer?

> Give the negro along with others the full product of his labor by wrenching the industries out of the hands of the capitalist and putting them into the hands of the workers and what is known as the race problem will be settled forever. Socialism is only another one of those great world movements which is coming to bless mankind. The Socialist Party is simply the instrument for bringing it about, and the negro and all other races regardless of former conditions, are invited into its fold.[51]

In another article, "Socialist Agitation," Woodbey called for the use of all forms of educational techniques to reach the black masses, "the press, the pulpit, the rostrum, and private conversation." Socialist agitators must understand that they would face imprisonment and other forms of maltreatment, but this was to be expected when one sought to overthrow an evil system. "For attempting to overthrow the slave system, Lincoln and Lovejoy were shot, John Brown was hung, while Garrison, Phillips, and Fred Douglass were mobbed." Naturally, Socialist agitators "are equally hated and despised," and they faced constant distortion of what they stood for.

> Because the Socialists recognize the existence of a class struggle they are sometimes accused of stirring up class hatred. But, instead, they simply recognize the fact that capitalism, by its unequal distribution of wealth, has forced on us a class struggle, which the Socialists are organizing to put down and bring on the long talked of period of universal brotherhood.[52]

When Woodbey advised Socialist agitators to expect to be persecuted, he spoke from personal experience. At the time he was a delegate to the 1908 Socialist convention, he was out on bail, having been arrested in San Francisco early in the year with 30 other Socialist speakers for defying a ban against street-corner meetings. This was in the midst of the economic crisis following the Panic of 1907, and the Socialists were holding meetings to demand relief for the unemployed.

Even before the spectacular free-speech fights of the Wobblies, Socialists had engaged in such battles and had used specific aspects of the strategy followed by the IWW.[53] In the case of the 1908 San Francisco free-speech fight, the Socialists deliberately violated a city ordinance forbidding street meetings without police permits for all organizations except religious groups. When a speaker was arrested for speaking without a permit, his place was speedily filled on the soapbox. Speaker after speaker, men and women, black and white, mounted the soapbox, were arrested, and dragged off to the jail. Woodbey was one of the first to be dragged off and jailed. Along with his comrades he was released on bail.[54]

"The police can't stop us," Woodbey told a reporter during the 1908 convention. "They can and do arrest us when we speak, but they can't stem the tide that has been started no more than they can the ocean. The more they ill treat us, the more Socialists there are." Despite police opposition, the Socialists were determined to obtain relief for "the hordes of honest working men [in San Francisco] who are starving because they can't get the work they so earnestly desire."[55]

With the aid of liberals and labor groups, the Socialists were able to force the City Council of San Francisco to repeal the objectionable ordinance, and charges against Woodbey were dropped.[56] He continued to participate in free-speech fights and in 1912 was a key figure in what was probably the most famous free-speech fight in American history—the free-speech fight in San Diego, California. San Diego was, of course, Woodbey's home town, and the place where he was the pastor of the Mt. Zion Church for several years—until, that is, he was removed because, as one who knew him wrote, he "loosened up his flock with the Bible, then finished his sermon with an oration on Socialism."[57]

On January 8, 1912, the San Diego City Council passed an ordinance creating a "restricted" district, 49 blocks in the center of town, in which street-corner meetings might not be held. Unlike ordinances in other cities banning street speaking, that in San Diego made no exception for religious utterances. All street speaking was banned in the so-called "congested district." The reason given was that the meetings blocked traffic, but it was clear that the real purpose was to suppress the IWW's effort "to educate the floating and out-of-work population to a true understanding of the interests of labor as a whole," as well as their determination to organize the workers in San Diego who were neglected by the A.F. of L. Among these neglected workers were the mill and lumber workers, laundry workers, streetcar conductors, and motormen. This determination had infuriated John D. Spreckels, the millionaire sugar capitalist and owner of the streetcar franchise, and he and other employers had applied pressure on the City Council to pass the ordinance. Certainly, San Diego had plenty of room for her traffic, and no one believed that this little town in Southern California would suffer a transportation crisis if street corner meetings continued.[58]

Two days before the ordinance was supposed to go into effect, the IWW and the Socialists held a meeting in the center of the restricted district at which Woodbey was a leading speaker. The police broke up the meeting but did not intimidate the fighters for free speech. On January 8, 1912, the *San Diego Union* carried the following on its front page:

SOCIALISTS PROPOSE FIGHT TO FINISH FOR FREE SPEECH

> Following a near-riot Saturday night during a clash between the police department, on the one hand, and Socialists, Industrial Workers of the World on the other, the Socialists and I.W.W. members held a running street meeting last night at Fifth and H streets, but the meeting was orderly, and there was not any semblance of trouble.

During the meeting members of the organizations policed the sidewalks and kept them clear, so that the city police would have no objection to make. Among the speakers were Mrs. Laura Emerson, Messrs. Hubbard and Gordon for the Industrial Workers of the World, and George Washington Woodbey, Kaspar Bauer, and Attorney E.F. Kirk for the Socialists.

The part played by the police in the affair of Saturday evening was denounced, but none of the speakers grew radical. It was announced that the fight for free speech will be waged with vigor, but in a dignified manner.

The police, aided by vigilantes, responded with more than vigor and in anything but a dignified manner. The brutality against the free-speech fighters in San Diego was so horrendous that after an investigation ordered by Governor Hiram Johnson, Colonel Harris Weinstock reported: "Your commissioner has visited Russia and while there, has heard many horrible tales of high-handed proceedings and outrageous treatment of innocent people at the hands of despotic and tyrannic Russian authorities. Your commissioner is frank to confess that when he became satisfied of the truth of the stories, as related by these unfortunate men (victims of police and vigilante brutality in San Diego), it was hard for him to believe that he was not still sojourning in Russia, conducting his investigation there, instead of in this alleged 'land of the free and home of the brave'."[59]

Woodbey was several times the victim of brutal police assaults as he insisted on exercising his right of free speech, and he filed charges of "Malicious and unofficial" conduct against the chief of police, captain of the detectives, and several policemen whom he accused of brutality.[60] As a leading figure in the Free Speech League, the organization which coordinated the free-speech fight, Woodbey was frequently threatened by vigilantes, and on one occasion, he barely escaped death. *The Citizen,* official organ of the Labor Unions of Southern California, reported in mid-April, 1912:

Rev. Woodbey, a negro preacher, has been threatened for his activity. A few nights ago he was taken to his home by a committee from the Free Speech League. As the party left the car at a corner near Woodbey's home an automobile was noticed in front of the house. Upon examination it was found to contain two armed men. Across the street another vigilante was stationed, and in the alley two more armed men were found. The strength of the committee with Woodbey probably saved his life, as members of the League challenged the vigilantes to do their dirty work. The preacher's house was patrolled by armed men from the League all night.[61]

The free-speech fight in "Barbarous San Diego" was still in full swing in late April, 1912, when Woodbey left to attend the Socialist Party national convention in Chicago as a delegate from California. By the time he returned home, the struggle was still continuing and he did what he could to help the cause, faced with defeat as a result of the power of the police, vigilantes, and the state government. Wobblies continued to be clubbed and arrested, and there was little that could be done to prevent the wholesale violation of their civil rights. "They have the courts, the mails, and funds," Laura Payne Emerson lamented.[62] It was not until 1914 that the right of the IWW to hold street meetings was established. Although the ordinance still remained on the statute books, the police no longer interfered when Wobblies spoke at street corners in the forbidden district. On the invitation of the IWW, Reverend Woodbey was one of the regular speakers at such meetings.[63]

Woodbey's associations with the IWW may not have pleased some California Socialists and his role in the free-speech fights probably disturbed members of his congregation. But he was candidate for state treasurer on the Socialist ticket in 1914 and was still listed as Pastor of Mt. Zion Church in San Diego and member of the state executive board of the Socialist Party in *The Christian Socialist* of February, 1915, which published two articles by the militant black Socialist minister. These, the last known writings of Reverend Woodbey on Socialism, were "What the Socialists Want" and "Why the Socialists Must Reach the Churches with Their Message." The first was in the form of a dialogue, a familiar Woodbey technique, between the minister (here called

Parker) and George Stephenson, a black mail carrier. Stephenson asks to be told "in short, and the simplest way possible, just what it is you Socialists are trying to get any way," and Woodbey proceeds to enlighten him, pointing out the features of the socialist society which he had presented in greater detail in his previous pamphlets. When the mail carrier leaves convinced that there was no way to answer the arguments in favor of socialism, his teacher shouts after him: "Hold on a minute, we would solve the race problem of this and all other countries, by establishing the brotherhood of man which Christ taught."

In the second piece, Woodbey insisted that the socialists would never succeed unless they won over "the millions of working people who belong to the various churches of the country," and proceeded to indicate how he did his part in this endeavor. His chief weapon was to play up the point that "the economic teaching of the Bible and of Socialism is the same, and that for that reason he (the church member) must accept Socialism in order to stand consistently by the teaching of his own religion." After having shown the church member that the Bible, "in every line of it," was "with the poor and against their oppressors," it was necessary to convince him that the solution for the ills of society was not charity, which was at best "only a temporary relief," but the collective ownership and operation of the industries. The last point had to be reached slowly and step by step, but if the socialist agitator keeps using the Bible as his authority, he will carry the church member along to that conclusion. The danger was that too many socialists antagonized church members by linking antireligion with socialism. Hence, he advised against using agitators "who do not understand the Christian people, to carry this message, for the reason that they are sure to say something that will spoil the whole thing."

We know nothing of Reverend Woodbey after 1915. But we leave him at this point in his career still as confirmed a socialist as ever. "I would not vote for my own wife on a platform which did not have the Socialist message in it," he told an audience in December, 1914.[64]

Just how many blacks Woodbey converted by the method he outlined in his last socialist writing is impossible to determine. But Hubert H. Harrison, a militant black Socialist in New York, said of Woodbey's work as a national party organizer: "He has been very effective."[65] At least one prominent black Socialist attributed his conversion to socialism to Reverend Woodbey. In the Chicago *Daily Socialist* of September 29, 1908, Reverend George W. Slater, Jr., Pastor of the Zion Tabernacle in the Windy City, wrote:

> For years I have felt that there was something wrong with our government. A few weeks ago I heard Comrade Woodbey, a colored national organizer of the Socialist Party, speaking on the streets in Chicago. He showed me plainly the trouble and the remedy. From that time on I have been an ardent supporter of the Socialist cause.[66]

PHILIP S. FONER

NOTES

With respect to the references below citing works by Woodbey, Slater, Holly and Ransom, the reader will find these works reprinted in the present volume. The page numbers given in the references are from the works as originally published.

1. The articles are Earl Ofari, "Marxism, Nationalism, and Black Liberation," *Monthly Review* 18 (March, 1971), pp. 18-33; Earl Ofari, "Black Activists and 19th Century Radicalism,"*Black Scholar* 5 (February, 1974), pp. 19-25; R. Lawrence Moore, "Flawed Fraternity— American Socialist Response to the Negro, 1901-1912," *Historian* 26 (November, 1969); pp. 1-14; Sally M. Miller, "The Socialist Party and the Negro, 1901-1920," *Journal of Negro History* 56 (July, 1971), pp. 220-39.
2. The only book dealing with this subject is Philip S. Foner, *American Socialism and Black Americans: From the Age of Jackson to World War II* (Westport Conn.: Greenwood Press, 1977).
3. Rev. George W. Slater, Jr., "The Cat's Out," *Chicago Daily Socialist*, (September 29, 1908).
4. Rev. George W. Slater, Jr., "Race Problem's Socialist Cure," ibid. (March 27, 1909).

5. Rev. George W. Woodbey, *What to Do and How to Do It or Socialism vs. Capitalism,* in *Wayland's Monthly* 40 (August, 1903), pp. 37-38.

6. *Ohio Socialist Bulletin* (February, 1909).

7. Foner, op. cit., p. 84.

8. *AME Church Review* 3 (October 1886), pp. 165-67.

9. Rev. James Theodore Holly, "Socialism from the Biblical Point of View," *AME Church Review* 9 (1892-93), pp. 244-58.

10. Rev. R.C. Ransom, "The Negro and Socialism," *AME Church Review* 3 (1896-97), pp. 192-200. In his study *Black Religion and Black Radicalism* (New York: 1972), pp. 187, 188, 220, Gayraud S. Wilmore mentions Reverend Ransom and lists him as a militant, but makes no mention of his advocacy of socialism. Apart from my own study, *American Socialism and Black Americans*, there is no discussion of the influence of Christian Socialism among blacks.

11. *AME Church Review* 13 (1896-97), p. 442.

12. *AME Church Review* 1 (January, 1895), p. 287.

13. *Chicago Daily Socialist* (May 11, 1908); John Mather, *Who's Who of the Colored Race,* (Chicago: 1921); A.W. Ricker in *Appeal to Reason* (October 31, 1903).

14. Woodbey, op. cit., p. 4; A.W. Ricker, op. cit. Correspondence with the Omaha Public Library, the University of Nebraska Library, the Nebraska State Historical Society, and the United Methodist Historical Society at Nebraska Wesleyan University has failed to turn up any information on Reverend Woodbey in their files and his role as a Populist and Socialist in Nebraska.

15. *Los Angeles Socialist,* (July 12, 1902).

16. *Los Angeles Socialist,* (May 2, 1903; December 17, 1904); *Common Sense,* (Los Angeles, August, 1905; October 8, 1904, October 27, 1906, March 7, April 11, 1908).

17. A.W. Ricker, *Appeal to Reason* (October 31, 1903). Robert Blatchford's *Merrie England,* published in London in 1894, was a book of 26 chapters and 210 pages in which the superiority of socialism over capitalism is brilliantly set forth in clear, plain language.

18. Woodbey, op. cit., p. 3.

19. *Chicago Daily Socialist* (May 11, 1908).

20. Woodbey, op. cit., pp. 5-7, 15-20.

21. Ibid., pp. 20-21.

22. Ibid., p. 24.

23. Ibid., pp. 37-38.

24. Ibid., p. 44.

25. Compare, for example, Woodbey's discussion of an international credit system under socialism (pp. 36-37) with Bellamy's discussion of the same system in Chapter 8 of *Looking Backward*.

26. In a letter to William Dean Howells a few months after the

publication of *Looking Backward*, Bellamy wrote that "the word socialist is one I could never well stomach. In the first place it is a foreign word in itself, and equally foreign in all its suggestions. . . .Whatever German and French reformers may choose to call themselves, socialist is not a good name for a party to succeed with in America. No such party can or ought to succeed which is not wholly and enthusiastically American and patriotic in spirit and suggestions." Quoted in Arthur E. Morgan, *Edward Bellamy*, Porcupine Press (New York: 1941) p. 374; (Philadelphia: 1974).

27. For a discussion of *The Iron Heel*, see Philip S. Foner, *Jack London: American Rebel*, Citadel Press (New York: 1964), p. 87-97; (Secaucus, N.J., 1969).

28. Woodbey, op. cit., p. 7.

29. G.W. Woodbey, *The Bible and Socialism: A Conversation Between Two Preachers*, (San Diego, 1904), Preface.

30. Ibid., p. 7.

31. Ibid., pp. 69, 83, 90.

32. Ibid., p. 69.

33. Ibid., p. 96.

34. G.W. Woodbey, *The Distribution of Wealth*, (San Diego, California, 1910), p. 7.

35. Ibid., pp. 41, 44-45.

36. Ibid., pp. 54-55.

37. Ibid., p. 68. Woodbey's fellow-California Socialist closed his letters, "Yours for the Revolution, Jack London."

38. *Proceedings of the National Convention of the Socialist Party, Held at Chicago, Illinois, May 1 to 6, 1904*, (Chicago, 1904), pp. 47-48.

39. Ibid., p. 182.

40. *Proceedings, National Convention of the Socialist Party, Held at Chicago, Illinois, May 10 to 17, 1908*, pp. 208-9.

41. Ibid., pp. 290-91.

42. Ibid., p. 106.

43. Ibid., pp. 106-07.

44. Ibid., pp. 107-08.

45. The most detailed discussion of the 1908 convention in relation to the immigration issue is Charles Leinenweber, "The American Socialist Party and 'New' Immigrants," *Science and Society*, XXXXII (Winter, 1968), pp. 6-12. It does not even mention Woodbey's speech in opposition to the resolution calling for a study of the necessity for immigration restriction.

46. *Proceedings, National Convention . . .*,1908, p. 163.

47. Ibid., p. 164.

48. Neither Ira Kipnis nor Ray Ginger mention Woodbey's nomination in their discussions of the 1908 Convention.

49. New York *Evening Call*, (November 2, 1908).

50. Reverend G.W. Woodbey, "Why the Negro Should Vote the

Socialist Ticket," four-page leaflet, undated, copy in Socialist Party Papers, Duke University Library.

51. G.W. Woodbey, "The New Emancipation," *Chicago Daily Socialist*, (January 18, 1909).

52. G.W. Woodbey, "Socialist Agitation," *Chicago Daily Socialist*, (January 4, 1909).

53. Philip S. Foner, *History of the Labor Movement in the United States*, Vol. IV, (New York: 1965), p. 173.

54. San Francisco *Call*, San Francisco *Chronicle*, (February 1-8, 1908).

55. *Chicago Daily Socialist* (May 11, 1908).

56. San Francisco *Call* (June 12, 1908).

57. In a letter to the author, Harland B. Adams of San Diego summarized a conversation he had with Dennis V. Allen, a black San Diegan who, in the years 1912-16, as a postal clerk, delivered mail to the home of Reverend Woodbey. According to Mr. Allen, Reverend Woodbey lived at 12 29th Street, San Diego. He described Woodbey as "a rather dark Negro, slender and about 5 feet 11 inches. Mrs. Woodbey was extremely stout, almost to the point that with her age and weight, it was difficult for her to get about. She was known by nearly everyone in the small Negro population of San Diego at that time as Mother Mary or Mother Woodbey. She was a devout Baptist Christian and regularly attended the Baptist Church at 29th and Clay, which still exists." The Woodbeys, Mr. Allen continued, owned the property where he lived, as well as the house next door which he rented to a Negro who was a veteran of the Civil War.

According to Mr. Allen, he was in a group that drafted Reverend Woodbey as the pastor for the Mt. Zion Baptist Church, and was also part of the group which had him removed. Although extremely popular, and though he drew large crowds to his sermons, his dismissal "was a direct result of mixing too much Socialism with his Bible, and this the members of his church resented."

Dennis V. Allen organized the San Diego Race Relations society in 1924, and held the post of president for 36 years.

58. Foner, op. cit., Vol. IV, pp. 194-95.

59. Ibid., pp. 199-200.

60. San Diego *Union* (February 22, 1912). The charges were ignored by the authorities.

61. *The Citizen* reprinted in *St. Louis Labor* (April 27, 1912). In her study, "The I.W.W. Free Speech Movement San Diego, 1912," *Journal of San Diego History*, (Winter, 1973), pp. 25-33, Rosalie Shank does not once mention Reverend Woodbey.

62. *Industrial Worker* (October 17, 1912).

63. *The Wooden Shoe* (Los Angeles, January 22, 1914).

64. *California Social Democrat* (December 12, 1914).

65. New York *Call* (December 16, 1911).

66. For the text of Reverend Slater's article, *see* p. 303 of this volume.

PART 1

Writings and Speeches of Reverend George Washington Woodbey

What to Do and How to Do It

or

Socialism vs. Capitalism

1903

Dedication

This little book is dedicated to that class of citizens who desire to know what the Socialists want to do and how they propose to do it. By one who was once a chattel slave freed by the proclamation of Lincoln and now wishes to be free from the slavery of capitalism.

Preface

Nothing original is claimed for this little book, the principal object of which has been to make the subjects treated as plain as possible to the reader. To the Socialist who may think it worth while to read it, the author would say that its object is to meet the demands of that large and increasing class of persons who have not yet accepted Socialism, but would do so if they could see any possible way of putting it into practice. No one knows better than he that any plans suggested may undergo various modifications; yet it would not be sensible to start to build a house without a plan.

The author has tried to describe the workings of the capitalistic system in a few brief words; and to make plain the impossibility of taking over the entire industrial plant except through the organization of the working class into a political party for that purpose. He has tried to show how the Socialist Party if in power might proceed to take over the industries; and also a possible plan by which the whole people might operate the land, factories, and means of transportation, as joint owners, for their own benefit.

The author's experience as a speaker has shown him that

many things said, while perfectly plain to the Socialist, go over the head of the hearer who has not studied the question; and so with much that is written in some otherwise excellent books on the subject.

If this book is found to have any merit it will be seen in its attempt to make the subject treated plain, so that "the wayfaring man though a fool may not err therein." People are often confronted by attempts at explanation which they cannot understand. As to whether this book is open to the same objection, the reader must decide.

As to the needs of simple explanation in making Socialists, the author speaks largely from his own experience in becoming a Socialist, and in trying to make others understand. He has been asked many times to embody some of the things he has said to the thousands who have listened to his talks, in a written form, and this is an attempt to answer that request.

G.W. WOODBEY

I

Introductory

It was at the breakfast table the first morning after my nearly seventeen years' absence from her that mother said to me: "I believe you look very much like you used to, but I never was so much astonished as when you wrote me you had gone off with the Socialists. Have you given up the Bible and the ministry and gone into politics?"

No, I replied, since studying Socialism I believe more firmly in every word of it if possible than I did before. Much of it I just now begin to understand. I know and respect your firm belief in the Bible, so let me remind you of a few things that perhaps you haven't thought of.

Well, the first thing the book tells us is that the earth was given to mankind as a home, and that he was to have dominion over it; not only over the earth, but the fish of the sea and the fowls of the air, and everything that lives on the face of the earth. (Gen. 1, 26-29.)

We are told that God overthrew the people of Egypt and delivered the Jews, because their masters had taken their labor for nothing. And the reason the Jews were told on leaving the country to go and borrow every one of his master, gold, silver and raiment, was because their labor had produced it all and they were entitled to it. (Read Ex. iii:7-9. Ex. xi:2.)

The first thing after their delivery from slavery and oppression was to give them a government in whose constitution there were ten articles known as commandments, which were read to both the men and the women for their acceptance. (Ex. xx Chap.) This government was administered by judges, appointed by the people, for five hundred years, until the people rejected God's plan, we are told in the book of Samuel, and set up a monarchy. (I Sam. viii.)

Under that government the jubilee law prevented the making of public debts. (Lev. xxv:8-17.) The land could not be deeded away forever. (Lev. xxv:23.) Interest and mortgages were unlawful. (Neh. v:1-13.) The prophets spent their time largely in preaching against the corrupt governments of the world, including the Jews, when they broke the law. And one of the principal charges was that they oppressed the poor by taking the products of their labor. "For ye have eaten up the vineyard, the spoils of the poor are in your houses. What mean ye that ye beat my people to pieces and grind the face of the poor? saith the Lord of Hosts." (Isaiah iii:14-15.) Some politics in that, isn't there mother? The prophet points out here the law of surplus value which is the spoils of the poor taken by the rich, creating the class struggle.

Christ drove the bankers and profit-mongers out of the temple, and called them thieves; and if their business was stealing it would have been as bad anywhere else as in the temple. (Matt. xxi:12-13.)

"But George," said my mother, "some of the men in your Socialist party don't believe in either God or the Bible, or that the world, or man, was created."

Yes, I said, and I found a still larger number of unbelievers in the Republican party before I left it some twenty years ago, and I understand that the other parties have their equal portion. While I believe in the Bible account of God, the origin of the earth and man, and that God gave the earth to man as a home, my Socialist comrade who does not accept that will agree with me that man is here, and the earth is here, and that it is the present home of the race, at least.

While I believe in the reality of life here and hereafter, I will not fail to agree with them about Socialism because we cannot agree about the hereafter. Whoever is willing to make things better here, which the Bible teaches is essential to the hereafter, I will join hands with as far as we can go. And as Socialism is a scheme for bettering things here first, and each skeptical comrade thinks he can hold his own peculiar views of God, creation, and the future and not find it necessary to give them up in order to become a good Socialist, neither am I required to give up my belief in all these things in order to be equally as good a Socialist.

Some may hold that only science teaches Socialism, but I am free to believe that both science and the Bible teach it. Some are Socialists only because they think it for their best interest here to favor it; others, like myself, are Socialists because they think that mankind is entitled to the best of everything in both this world and the next.

Some other time I will tell you more about what the Bible teaches on this subject. What you want to know at present is, what the Socialists want and how they expect to get it.

So under Socialism every person will be free to have their own religion or none, just as they please, so long as they do not interfere with others.

II

Capitalism

Before I try to make plain to you what the Socialists want, let us take a look at the present condition of things. If the present conditions are all right, then we do not need any change.

We all agree that the earth is the home of man; the Bible, science, and common sense all teach us that. From our very nature we must have land, air, and water in order to live. When I say we need land, I mean all the earth contains that which is necessary for our life and happiness, such as food, clothing, houses, etc. Now, you can see that if all the people allow a few of the people to in any way get possession of the earth—which is the home of all—then the majority will find themselves without a right to live on the earth unless they pay others for the privilege. You can see, mother, that is just the condition we are in at the present time. Since no man, or set of men, made the earth, no man, or set of men, have the right to attempt to divide the land among men by title deeds, or sell or rent to us the right to live on the earth. Who gave the first man the right to sell the land?

If a man has a right to any amount of land under deed, then he has a right to all he can get. If a limit is to be placed on it, where can we fix it so as to be sure not to injure future generations? The Creator said, "The land is mine and it shall not be sold forever," and philosophers like Marx,[1] Spencer,[2] and others, have recognized the truth of that principle, namely, that the land shall not be sold forever.

But I started to tell you why we call the system we are living under now capitalism. By capital, we mean the tools, buildings, machines, and all other things we use to work with. By capitalism, we mean the system which allows a number of the people to own the earth, the tools, buildings, machines, factories, railroads, and other means of travel, production, and transportation, and thus take from the worker what he produces.

With the land, machinery, and means of transportation privately owned, those who are not owners cannot live on the earth, work with machinery, transport anything, or travel, without paying rent for a home, giving nearly all their labor will produce to the owner of the machines and then with their wages buy back what they have produced in the shop or factory, or on the farm, with a large profit added.

If the laborer produces in a small way and undertakes to ship his produce, the owners of the railroads and steamships get it all; so it comes about that under capitalism we have rent, interest, and profits, which enables a few to live at the expense of the many.

I suppose I need not remind you that here again the Bible stands with the Socialists; when speaking of both the brother and the stranger it says: "Take thou no usury of him or increase—thou shalt not give him thy money upon usury, nor lend thy victuals, for increase." (Lev. xxv:36-37.) Mark you, all increase is here forbidden. The people doomed to destruction in the land of Canaan were the only ones the Jews might loan to on increase until Socialism is established, which will, as we proceed, be shown to be only the golden rule put into practice. Christ said: "Loan hoping to receive nothing." (Luke vi:35.)

The system under which we now live, where each man produces for himself and competes with his neighbor for a market, is sometimes called the competitive system, but as this is growing less and less so, as the trust organizes and gets the capital into the hands of the few, we prefer to call it the capitalistic system. This system of private ownership is lawful only because the capitalists, who are the owning class, make all the laws; and the things that are now owned by the people are managed by the capitalists so as to get as much out of them for this class as possible. The enormous price paid to the railroads for carrying the mail—some forty-three millions of dollars annually—shows what I mean.

Under capitalism the money of the people has been given to the capitalists, the public lands have been given to that class, valuable franchises granted, on one pretense or another, through laws of their own making.

Billions of national, state, and municipal debts have been created and held by the capitalistic class on which to draw interest out of the labor of the poor; for labor pays everything, on the universally admitted principle that all wealth is created by labor. Labor exists first and produces all capital; which is simply the tools, machines, and other things with which it works, as I have said before.

It follows, therefore, as a rule, that the capitalist, who is not a producer, furnishes nothing except as he takes it through rent, interest, and profits from the worker, by private ownership of capital, and places it in other enterprises. It is in the very nature of things impossible for all to become capitalists except through cooperative ownership of all capital.

In the past some have made their first start into capitalism by saving their earnings as wage workers; but single persons could succeed at saving only because the masses did not try the same thing; for the reason that had all, or even a majority, tried saving, the thing they were working at for wages would have stopped and thrown them out of employment; because there would, under the capitalist system, have been no market for the product of their labor. The laborers largely form the market for the sale of what they produce for the capitalist. Under the system of capitalism now in operation it is the man who spends his money who keeps things going, and not the man who saves it.

That capitalism has not been a blessing to the masses of mankind, the condition of extreme wealth on the one hand, and extreme poverty on the other, shows too plainly to need any argument. It cannot be denied, even by the opponents of Socialism, that whatever of misery, poverty, and dissatisfaction exists now, is the result of capitalism. The present system divides men into two classes, the capitalists who rule, and the poor, who, as I have said, produce the wealth. Thus men are divided into hostile, warring camps.

You may ask, if the Bible as well as science favors Socialism, why haven't we got it before now? Because the world is not yet ready for it; these teachings are to get us ready. According to the Bible we have had first the age of the patriarchs, which suited the conception of men at that time. Then followed the period of the law, which upon questions of economics, as we have shown, stood where the Socialist stands as to land and interest, and against the exploiting of the poor. "The law was our schoolmaster to bring us unto Christ." "The law made nothing perfect," but was the training school to bring men to those higher ideals found in Christ. (Gal iii:24.)

When we get to Christ we find in him and his teachings the perfect doctrine of social brotherhood. That some people who accept Christ in other things have not grown to a full understanding of his economic teachings is not strange, since he taught for all time to come. We cannot afford to denounce men who have not grown as fast as we have, but must continue to teach them, and at the same time go on learning ourselves.

Every Socialist will recollect that there was a time when these things, which now look so plain to him, were first brought to his notice, and that many of us who are now Socialists were equally as slow to accept the truth as those we are now dealing with both in and out of the church; so it is not common sense to denounce men for not seeing at once what it took us years to find out. The capitalists are not yet all united along the line of their class interest, as the many independent business concerns, not yet united by the trust, shows. The trusts are organizing the capitalists, and the Socialists are organizing the workers for the final contest at the ballot box.

III

Socialism

"I think I understand what you have said," mother replied. "I have to pay rent to one of the richest men in town for the right to set my house on the earth that God made. The thing I want to know now is, what you Socialists want to give us in the place of what we have? When I know that, I can begin to know what to expect when the Socialist party is elected to power."

Well, mother, the Socialist platforms, not only in the United States but in all countries where there is any, ask for the cooperative ownership of the means of production and distribution. To one who understands Socialism, that is all plain enough and easily understood, but to you, mother, it may need some explanation.

In a factory, or on a railroad, the workers all cooperate, or work together, like the wheels of a clock; but, as I have shown, the owners of the machines, or of the roads, get nearly all of the products of their labor, because the workers don't own the factories and the roads. A carpenter produces a house by means of his knowledge in using his tools on the raw material. By means of hand and brain, skilled in the use of tools, we produce wealth.

"How can we produce anything without money, George?"

Money never produces anything; it only represents things; it only entitles one to go into the markets and get so much wealth. What little money the laboring man gets is a check to the store for so much of the wealth his own labor has produced, and which the owners of the capital took from him and now sell back to him at a profit. The laborer gets thirty-two cents for producing a Stetson hat in a factory for which he would have to pay five dollars in order to buy it. If the people who do the work owned the factory, the worker would get the hat at cost, and so with all other things.

Just as old Mr. Jones and his sons who own the farm over there don't have to buy at a profit what they raise on the farm—they earned that by their labor—so if the whole nation works together like Mr. Jones and his boys and raise crops of all kinds, animals of all kinds, make furniture, build houses, run railroads, and steamboats, in fact do everything they now do, they owning the tools, and the land and roads, as the Jones' do their farm, they will not need to buy what their own labor produces.

"I have heard some Socialists talk, but when they get done I couldn't understand what they did want to do; but so far I can understand you all right," said mother.

What the Socialists want is simple enough for a child to understand. There are only four things they demand: First, they want all the people to have an equal interest in the land, like Jones and his boys in their farm, because the earth is our home and no one can live without it. It is the source from which we get everything. I have shown you how we would produce what we need by working together.

The second thing the Socialists want is to have the whole people own the tools they work with to produce wealth from

What to Do and How to Do It 49

the earth. Everything, from a spade to a large factory, is simply a tool which is used to work with. If the workers allow a few of the people to own all the tools they will still charge them nearly all they produce, for the use of the tools, just as they do now; yet all these tools are made by the workers and represent what they had to leave in the hands of the capitalists in order to get the work without which they would starve.

The third thing the Socialists want, is to have the workers, who are to own the earth and the tools, own also the means of taking both themselves and their goods wherever necessary or desirable. This means that the people should own all the railroads, ships, and other means for hauling their goods, or for travel. The fourth thing is the working class must have the right to make all the laws to govern the industries by direct vote.

"Then George," asked mother, "you wouldn't have anybody own anything, themselves?"

Yes, all these things when produced, and distributed to the people who produced them, would be their private property; but all the people who were capable of it would have to do their part of the work, or get nothing. No one could live, then, by charging them for the use of the land, tools, and means of hauling persons and goods.

"But," questioned mother anxiously, "I have worked awful hard for this little old shell of a house; would I have to give it up?"

I suppose you wouldn't mind having a better one, would you? With your share of the products of the nation you could have a good house, all fire-proof, with the latest modern improvements in it. That house with all its belongings would be yours— your children could have the same, and the other people as well. The people can make their own houses just as well as their own postage-stamps.

"You keep on talking about wealth, and means of production and distribution; what do you mean?" asked mother, rising and beginning to clear up the table.

By the means of production, we mean, as I have said, any tools, or process by which we produce wealth. By wealth we mean anything that is necessary for human comfort or pleasure, such as the necessary food, clothing, houses, and fuel.

As man is not altogether an animal, it is necessary for him to have knowledge through the means of books and other sources; and pleasure through travel and intercourse with his fellow men.

The earth with its various things, such as coal, iron, lead, copper, zinc, and other treasures too numerous to mention, together with the things growing out of it, and roaming over it, forms the principal source of wealth. We sometimes fail to distinguish between these sources of wealth, and actual wealth, which can only be produced by the skill of man in preparing them for his various uses.

Our mental necessities, which can only be supplied to us through means of books, travel, and intercourse with others, are largely dependent on our skill in the use of the sources of wealth, in their promotion; for we can have neither knowledge, pleasure, or intercourse, in their completeness, without the use of these resources of the earth, in a greater or lesser degree, as necessity may require.

Under the head of means of production, I repeat, would come the earth, and the various machinery now in use, or to be used in the production of the necessities of life. All these the socialists want the whole people to own, instead of a few individuals, as now.

By way of illustration, just as in a joint stock company consisting of one hundred men with one share each, who are equal owners of the whole concern, so the whole people, under the cooperative system, will be equal shareholders in all the wealth of the United States.

While the post office is not conducted on a basis of equality in compensation for the services rendered, as it would be under complete Socialism, the ownership is vested in the whole people, just where the Socialists would put everything else. In this way all would be interested, all being equal shareholders in the plants of industry. There would then be no class without property. And there would be no more danger of your losing your equal share in the cooperative commonwealth than there is now of your losing your share in the post office, the public road, or the public school.

IV
Agitation

The first step toward bringing about Socialism is agitation, which is the only means by which the public can be educated. It may be done through the press, the pulpit, the rostrum, and private conversation. Socialism is now passing through this period of agitation and thousands are anxiously listening to the glad tidings.

It has been well said that the cooperative commonwealth must first be builded in the minds of the people before it can be put into actual practice. This work of building the new commonwealth is now going on night and day in all parts of the world. Socialism when once intelligently understood is a fire in the bones of its converts, and must flash out; so when you have made one intelligent Socialist, he makes another one, and so on indefinitely.

The Socialist press throughout the world is now a great power amounting to many hundred publications, from monthly magazines to great dailies; and these in the languages of all the civilized nations. Vast book concerns are running night and day, sending out tons of literature. In all ages the agitators of new ideas, in religion, science, or government, have created a new literature adapted to their purpose, just as the Socialists are now doing.

The American Revolution was brought on by agitators. Moses and the prophets were agitators, who met with great opposition. Christ was an agitator and sent forth the twelve as such; in fact, all founders of new systems of religion, science, or politics, have, in the very nature of the case, been agitators. The delivering of speeches and the writing of books have always formed a necessary part of the work.

We are not contending that a thing is necessarily right because it has its agitators and its literature; the claims of a question at issue, to be right, rest upon a different ground.

"Then," said mother, "all that don't make the Socialists right, George."

No, of course not. All I was trying to show in this connection is, that the Socialists are proceeding in the usual way with the work before them. Among all the men of history, Paul was possibly the greatest agitator, both as speaker and writer. In the very nature of the case every true preacher is an agitator. In this country the Socialists are following in the footsteps of the abolitionists in agitating the question at issue, and in the use of press, literature, and speakers. Speakers, books, periodicals, and papers are increasing daily.

In the beginning of the movement many persons were imprisoned and otherwise maltreated, in all countries; but Socialism has steadily grown, until almost all legislative bodies of the world have their Socialist members and the question can no longer be ignored. While in some nations Socialism promises to become dominant at no distant day, the most significant thing in the Socialist movement is to be found in the substantial agreement of Socialists throughout the world.

The first thing the capitalist parties of this country have done is to ignore the movement. But that day has about passed, and when they have to meet the Socialist agitation, the growth of Socialism will be much more rapid.

The attention given Socialist speakers and the demand for literature is significant.

V

Organization

The next step is organization, which is in its infancy and comparatively incomplete in this country. Although some local propaganda organizations have existed here for many years, only recently, especially in the United States, has the matter entered the domain of politics, where it must be finally settled at the ballot box.

In other countries Socialism has longer been a factor in politics and has made great headway, notably in Germany; but from this time on the indications are that political organizations here will advance speedily. The rapid consolidation of the forces of labor in this country under the name of the Socialist Party is an indication of what is coming in the near future. The time is ripe and organization will now proceed with marked expedition.

Believing in direct legislation, all questions of importance are referred to the members of the party by the officers of the national, state, county, or city organization; or they originate in the local branches and are referred to the members of all the branches, each member having a vote. Thus, as far as is practicable, Socialists practice direct government already. This is an essential difference between the Socialist and other parties: if you are a member, no important step can be taken without your vote.

Curiously enough Socialists are only using a political party to get into power and transfer the entire power of government into the hands of the people, that they may directly originate and pass their own laws. When the Socialist party has done its work there will be no more political parties, either Socialist or otherwise; for like abolition, there will be no opposition to Socialism once it is put into operation. It is for this reason the cause is considered greater than the man, with the Socialist. The Socialist party looks at the office under our representative government, only as a means to an end; and that end is the establishment of the new government which is to be known as the cooperative commonwealth.

It is the attempt to organize the working class into a political party to take control of the powers of government, and set up the cooperative commonwealth, thus doing away with all classes.

Because the Socialists recognize the existence of a class struggle, they are sometimes accused of stirring up class hatred. But instead they simply recognize the fact that capitalism, by its unequal distribution of wealth, has forced on a class struggle which the Socialists are organizing to put down, and bring on the long talked of period of universal brotherhood.

VI

How to Get Control of the Government

"It seems to me you have a big job on your hands getting control of government," remarked mother, "how are you going to do it?"

By getting the majority of the votes, of course. The history of the movement, both in this and other countries, shows that, taken as a whole, it never loses ground. There is an irrepressible conflict between the worker and the capitalist, which cannot but redound to the advancement of Socialism, simply because there is no other possible solution of the difficulties which create it. All this the Socialist party is everywhere taking advantage of.

The party is most likely to win in some of our large cities first, and then in single states. When that happens, whatever can be will be done to take over local industries without conflict with the capitalistic authorities in charge of the general government; and Socialistic management of local industries would be far different from capitalist management of publicly owned industries. Capitalists operate public industries for their own benefit, while the Socialists would have the interests of the worker in view; and that would aid us in getting control of the rest of the machinery of general government.

After a while we will get some men in congress, as they have done in most other countries, and that will enable us to turn the searchlight of Socialism on the schemes of the capitalists at the national capital, which will hasten the day when we shall get entire control. Of course, in order to succeed the party must be firm and uncompromising in its principles, making no deals and taking advantage of every honest means to forward the cause.

The Socialist control of government will, as we said, come

by winning victories in the cities and the counties first, as we are already doing in different parts of the nation.

Next, as the state governments begin to wheel into line, we will through them march steadily on to control of the national government. Be the time long or short, the Socialists know they cannot get control by fusion with capitalist parties of any name or kind, in such a way as to benefit the laboring classes.

Let it not be forgotten that government ownership with capitalist party control is not Socialism. Nor would even the laboring classes if placed in control of government without a knowledge of their class interest set up Socialism.

VII
How to Get Control of the Industries

Having got control of the government, the next thing in order will be to get possession of the means of production and distribution by act of legislation. The earth was once public property, like the air and the water, but was legislated into the hands of private individuals. The machinery by which wealth is produced was all created by the workers, including everything we call capital, and was taken from them by the non-producing class by means of rent, interest and profits, under the protection of legislation passed and controlled by the capitalists.

The means of transportation, by which wealth is distributed, was built by the producer, for the non-producer, on franchises granted to corporations by legislation. All these things, which once belonged to the people as a whole, were legislated out of their hands to the private parties now in possession of the people's property, and they are protected in that possession by the police power of the state, the court, and, if need be, by the military of the nation.

The legal and moral right of this has been interpreted by majority rule, to which we must submit until such time as a majority come to believe in the Socialist ideal. And when those who believe in the cooperative commonwealth are placed in charge of government they will proceed to interpret matters along the line of the new majority, who will then rule, just as majorities in the past have done.

They will proceed by act of legislation to undo what has been done in the way of turning the people's property over to a few individuals, and will restore it again to the whole people, from whence it came. One set of legislators legislated large bodies of the public lands into the hands of syndicates and private individuals; and another set may place it back where it was. We have no laws that may not be repealed when we get ready.

A minority may protest at the time, as will be their right, just as minorities did against the granting of these rights to private individuals in the first place. If the act of the majority in placing the property back in the hands of the public is confiscation, and therefore robbing the private individual, then why was not the act of taking these things from the people for the benefit of private persons, confiscation, and robbing the public?

But the case of the public, or the people, is still stronger; for if the title of the people to common ownership was good in the first place, then it would only be giving back to the whole people what was always rightfully theirs.

It may be contended that if the title was vested in the people, they might rightfully dispose of it to private individuals, which is what they did; but men have no moral right to work injury to themselves nor to their posterity. Then, too, men may be endowed by their Creator with rights which they may not dispose of and be guiltless; such, for instance, as "life, liberty, and the pursuit of happiness."

But it is not proposed to divest individuals of private property in the means of production and distribution, without giving them something better, as the sequel will prove. Of course, as to the way in which this is to be brought about the majority must be left to decide, or there would be an end of all just government.

The possession of the means of production and distribution on the part of the people is essential to "life, liberty, and the pursuit of happiness." If "all just governments derive their power from the consent of the governed," then the system of private ownership of these things can continue only so long as the governed consent.

Socialism does not take away one's ownership, but simply changes it from private to cooperative: as, for instance, when private individuals form a joint stock company, each owns an interest in the concern as his property. If it be objected that such holdings cannot be disposed of, I reply: Men only dispose of their properties today because they deem them unsafe, or think to better their condition; and as no safer investment can be found than a joint ownership in all the property of the nation, no one would want to dispose of it.

"Suppose a man owned a farm which under Socialism becomes public property—what will he get?" asked mother.

Why, he will be given an equal share with all the rest, in all the lands, factories, and means of transportation, of the nation. All he could get out of the farm was what he could produce on it. Let us suppose that by his own efforts he could produce each year one thousand dollars. At ten per cent that would represent a capital of ten thousand dollars. Then, again let us suppose, that the nation, working collectively, does not produce any more than the reports show we are now doing on an average; which is about twenty-five hundred dollars to each worker. Thus the income of that farmer who once owned the farm would be twenty-five hundred dollars per year for his work, in place of one thousand, showing that on the same basis of ten per cent, he would exchange his capital of ten thousand dollars in the farm, for a capital of twenty-five thousand in the cooperative commonwealth.

"But," objected mother, "what about the fellow who didn't have anything to turn in—are you going to make him equal with the farmer?"

Why didn't the slave have wealth at the close of the war? He had worked hard.

"Because his master got it," mother replied.

The wage worker's master got what he produced, too.

"But wasn't he paid for his work?" asked mother.

Yes, about seventeen cents on every dollar's worth of wealth he created; so the man who turns over a large amount of capital created by labor which he did not do by his own hands, only turns over what he has taken from the man who has nothing to turn over. The very rich man ought therefore to be satisfied, since he and his children, who have done nothing but live off the labor of those who have nothing to turn over, are to be given an equal share of interest with those who have produced it all; so you see we Socialists are not such bad fellows as you thought. We propose to do good unto those who spitefully use us, and to those who curse us, by giving them an equal show with ourselves, provided that they will hereafter do their share of the useful work. It is amusing to hear the man with a little money talk about Socialism taking everything from him, when today he is exploited on all sides by the trusts, railroads and other combines.

"When the Socialists get control of congress and pass laws taking the land, factories, and means of transportation, won't it bring on war?" mother asked anxiously.

Do you mean to say that so long as the capitalists are in power, passing laws making everything private property, it is the duty of the Socialists to be good citizens and allow the majority to rule—and we Socialists think so, too—but when the majority become Socialists and elect the Socialist party to power thereby telling them to pass laws taking over the industries, then the capitalists, who will be in the minority as we now are, will not be under obligations to abide by the rule of the majority, but will rebel? I thought you were a republican, mother!

"Well, that doesn't look just right does it?" mother admitted.

The men who owned the slaves were willing to abide by majority rule, as long as the majority went their way; but when Lincoln was elected, although they knew he had the majority of the electoral vote, they did exactly what you ask now if the capitalists would do. But the capitalists in order to bring on a war must hire one set of poor men to fight the others.

There will never be any trouble until the Socialists have carried an election, and then the capitalists will confront a different situation from any which has ever been known before. The Socialists would call on the poor man to fight and take for his pay an equal share of the nation's wealth, while on the other hand the capitalists would call upon the poor man to fight, against his own interest, and would offer him in payment only a small part of his share of the nation's wealth. And, mark you, the majority would already have become convinced that Socialism would give them their full share, or the Socialists could not have carried the election which caused the war, so no war could last long with those advantages on our side.

The slaveholder did not dare to arm the Negro, on his side, without proclaiming emancipation, and to do that was to lose his cause; so with the capitalist, if he dares to offer all to the poor man who must fight his battles, he has lost his cause; and with this condition confronting the capitalist, there is no danger in taking over the entire industrial plant as soon as the Socialists can be elected and pass the necessary laws. And the Socialist party will go into power just as soon as the majority finds that the only way to secure to itself its entire product is to vote that ticket.

"Have the people a right to do all this?" said mother.

One of the main objects of government, according to the Declaration of Independence, is "life, liberty, and the pursuit of happiness." "That to secure these rights, governments are instituted among us, deriving their just powers from the consent of the governed; that when any form of government becomes destructive of these ends, it is the right of the people to alter or to abolish it and to institute a new government, laying its foundation on such principles, and organizing its powers in such form as to them shall seem most likely to effect their safety and happiness." On this Socialists stand. Lincoln said just what the Socialists now say.

"Any people anywhere being inclined and having the power have the right to rise up and shake off the existing government and form a new one that suits them better. This is a most valuable, a most sacred right—a right which we hope and believe is to liberate the world. Nor is this right confined to cases in which eople of an existing government may choose to exercise ... y portion of such people that can may revolutionize and make their own of so much territory as they inhabit. More than this, a majority of any portion of such people may revolutionize, putting down a minority, intermingled with or near about them, who may oppose their movement. Such minority was precisely the case of the Tories of our own revolution. It is a quality of revolutions not to go by old lines or old laws; but to break up both, and make new ones."

Speech of Abraham Lincoln in U.S. House of Representatives, January 12, 1848.

(See Abraham Lincoln's complete works comprising his speeches, letters, state papers, and miscellaneous writings. Edited by Nicolay & Hay. Vol. 1, p. 105. Century Co., N.Y.)

VIII

The Agricultural Department

The means of production and distribution, once in the hands of the people, there is no intention on the part of Socialists to let things go on in "confusion worse confounded," as is the case under competition; but on the contrary, they will proceed to carry on the industries on the most systematic basis possible. The food product being the first essential to physical life, Socialists would proceed to organize a real agricultural department instead of the one we have now, which is one only in name.

This department could be made responsible for the production of all the food necessary to feed the nation. All the lands of the people would be operated by this branch of the cooperative commonwealth on a gigantic scale. This would require a secretary of agriculture with a corps of under-secretaries in the different sections of the country. The statistics of population and consumption being before them, they would know just how much to produce; and, having the choice of all the lands of the nation, they would know where things could be best produced. With men educated and trained in scientific agriculture, we could have a corps of chemical experts experimenting all the time and making the needed improvements in the soils.

The very best of labor saving machinery could be used, which would reduce the hours of labor and make farming a pleasure instead of the drudgery which it is today, and the only cost of this machinery would be the labor which it took to produce it, as the profit system would be abolished. At present on the farm everything is done under the profit system, and in the most expensive manner.

The vast steam plows and harvesters used on some of the bonanza farms, are only an inkling of what could be done by the whole people, with all the resources of the nation at their command. It is said that wheat has been produced in the sack for three and a half cents per bushel on some of the large farms, which is doubtless comparatively true.

Hundreds of millions of dollars worth of wasted labor might be saved in the single item of fencing alone, to say nothing of the unnecessary waste of competition, which would be eliminated by cooperation. All farmers could then work in the agricultural department of the nation, as the mail carriers work for the post office department. I think the farmer would be glad to exchange his hard toil of from ten to twelve hours a day, for a three or four hour day. A vast department like this would doubtless be divided into a number of subdivisions for the convenience of operation.

On these lands operated by the department of agriculture could be raised all the livestock of the nation. The farmer and his family would not be isolated in some dreary, out-of-the-way place, shut off from all the enjoyment of polite society, unless he so desired; for all the faculties of rapid transit to and from work would be at his command; with short hours of service, giving plenty of time for study, pleasure and recreation.

The department could soon have an irrigation system so complete that there never need to be a failure of crops, and the farmer would not have to suffer from low prices, as he would have an equal share of interest in all the other industries, and would therefore have his proportionate share of everything the nation could produce.

Nor would a large portion of the produce rot—rot because the people could not buy it—as is often the case now; because each worker, being also an owner, would get his equal share of the products. The men who are now farmers could run this department for the nation.

IX

The Department of Manufactory

As the people cannot live on food alone, but must have clothes, shoes, houses, furniture and a thousand and one other things, we must have one vast manufacturing department, with many subdivisions, to make all these things for the use of the people.

This is another place in which labor saving machinery would lessen the hours and benefit the worker. Years ago, when the tools of production were more simple, the worker was not at such a disadvantage, because he was then his own employer. But since, for example, the last, the pegging awl, and the shoe hammer, have passed into the great shoe factory, the worker has lost control of the tools of production, and the owner of the machine takes all but a small pittance of the worker's product, because he owns the tools by which it is manufactured.

Cooperative ownership would again give the worker possession of the tools of production, and its manufacturing department would undertake in a systematic way, not only to produce all the goods, but also all the implements and other things along the line of manufacturing; being governed only by the needs of the whole people.

All mechanics of every grade and description could find employment in some of the branches of this department. The best scientific schools, conveniently located, for training those who desired to pursue their chosen branches of the trades, would be established.

The object being to save men rather than to make profits, the factories could be turned into palaces, in place of the unsanitary death traps men, women and children are working in today. Here again the department would be governed solely by the demands of the people. And the demands of the people would be governed by their needs; as they could not dispose of a surplus for the very good reason that all would be equally well provided for. This, of course, would not prevent the accumulation of a temporary surplus in the national depositories, to guard against possible failure.

This work of manufacturing is now being done by the same class of workers who would do it under the cooperative commonwealth; and they work at present collectively, for the great trusts who own the factories and keep the products made by the workers. The difference is that under Socialism the men who do the work would be the owners of the factories, and the farms, and the means of transportation, which they have helped to run, as I have told you.

"Do you think they would know how to do the work, if it was turned over to them?" asked mother.

Why, the workers are the only ones who do know how to run a factory. The stockholders who own the concern know nothing about doing the work. If the girl who weaves in the factory should be told that Socialism is now established, and that henceforth she is to have shorter hours of labor, a beautiful sanitary place to work in, and an equal share of all the wealth of the nation, to be taken in any kind of thing she wants, do you think she would forget how to work? And if, on the other hand, all she produces is to go to the girl who does nothing but own the stocks, then she can work right along? Seems to me you might see the absurdity of that, mother.

"I believe I do see, now," she said, after a moment's hesitation.

Then apply that illustration about the girls, to all the workers, and you will get my meaning.

X
The Department of Transportation

While the agricultural department, and that of manufacturing, might produce all the people need along their given lines, the fact remains that the produce must be transferred and stored at points convenient for the use of the people. This would necessitate a transportation department in which could be placed all the means of transportation, such, for example, as railroads, steamboats, steamships and all other possible means of public carriage.

The business of this department would be to receive all goods from the producing departments before mentioned and to deliver them to any stores of the nation where they might be needed for the use of the people; just as the post office delivers letters to any part of our vast domain, or to foreign nations.

The men who worked in these departments would be working in concerns in which each would be an equal shareholder, as I have said before, instead of working for the benefit of a company consisting of a few private individuals, and would naturally take a deeper interest in their own interest. Each worker on the road would accordingly be respected by other workers, as the stockholders of privately owned roads are now.

This department could be held responsible to the whole people for all sorts of transportation. Competing lines, jealousy and rivalry would disappear. The unnecessary men, if any, could at once go to other productive branches of labor in other departments. The more we produce, the more each one's share would be, until we reached the limits of necessity.

If the Socialists were in power, and had passed a law turning the lines of transportation over to the whole people, the railroad men and sailors would turn out just as usual without a hitch; but with the understanding that the property belonged to the public, and that they were a part of the public; that the hours of labor were shortened, with the compensation equal to that of any other person's in the nation, provided they did their part in serving the public; that they each had an equal say in all that was going on; and that the majority would decide all important questions as to managers and management.

Then the sailors and railroad men would be the real gentlemen—not a few stockholders merely. Managers, captains and mates could not compel the sailors and railroad men, who had elected them to their positions and could recall them, to take off their hats and do them homage; and they would get no more compensation than other workers because of having been chosen to manage affairs. And every possible device to make the work desirable, safe, sanitary and easy, could then be put into operation by the men who had the work to do.

XI

The Department of Distribution

Goods delivered by the transportation department would be received at the stores of the nation by the department of distribution, whose business it would be to deliver them to the residences of the workers, on their order. It would be the business of the storekeepers of the nation—just as it now is of the postmasters, to get what is required for distribution through the post office—to send to the departments of production and have delivered by the department of transportation, a necessary supply of all the produce of the nation. This would include food, furniture, books, and all other things which the workers might need for their own use. Once in the workers' hands it would cease to be public property; and as his private property he could do what he liked with it.

But remember that speculation in anything then would be impossible, from the very nature of the case, just as it is now in postage stamps; as the departments would furnish all the workers whatever they needed of anything, at cost.

As the object of the workers would be to furnish themselves with just what they might want, some might prefer to lodge in public hotels. The keepers putting in their short hours working in these hotels would be earning their living by serving the public, and would get the same compensation as other workers. And when off duty they might in their turn be served in the same hotels, if they wished. Such a service would be mutual and would have no more of the menial attached to it than when we occasionally serve our guests of equal standing with ourselves financially, under the present system.

It is not serving others that makes one despised—it is the want of equal compensation; the menial dependency upon those who are served. Jesus Christ said: "If any man will be great among you, let him be your servant." The true measure of greatness lies in the value of one's service to humanity; and in this, Christ is our example; so, under the new order of things, only the worker for the common good of humanity would be respected, and not, as today, the parasite and exploiter of it.

The department of distribution would not only deliver the mail, but everything else which the worker wanted, as well. In fact the one institution would do what a dozen stores, express companies, telegraph companies, dairies and other private concerns do, in every little town now. This work of distribution would not be something entirely new, since it is being done today by many small concerns in an unsystematic way, but under the new order of things it would be done by the public, and reduced to a science.

XII

The Department of Intelligence

This department should have charge of the telegraph, telephones, newspapers, magazines and periodicals of all kinds. It should have charge of the publication department of the nation, as our public printers now do, in a limited way.

Having plenty of leisure, any one in any department of the industries of the nation, who was capable, might write a book, or contribute to periodicals, for which society might reward him with the same pay as any other worker. That could be done by reducing his hours of service in his department, in proportion

What to Do and How to Do It 67

to the demands for the book, up to the point where the writer might be liberated from any demand for service and still draw his equal share of wealth from the nation's resources; having paid for his income from the public, by his writings.

Nor need there be any one in authority to decide beforehand on the probable merit or demerit of a book or the demand for its circulation; since, if when published no one wanted it, the author would be fully able to stand the expense of the first issue himself, and could then stop its publication.

"But what would he pay with?" asked mother.

He could pay for it out of his labor, of course, just as he would for anything else; and the work of publishing would be done at cost.

Instruction in way of public lectures might be given in the same manner, provided they were on topics that concerned the whole people. Those who aspired to this work and for any reason failed, could still remain in the department they had formerly worked in. The time would doubtless soon come, under Socialism, when, being provided with all the comforts of life, writers and speakers would be only too glad to give their leisure hours to this work, without further remuneration than the praise and distinction it would give them.

That class of persons who are apt at gathering news for the information of the public, could still be thus employed. Editors of papers and other periodicals, like other workers, would hold their positions because of their ability to serve the public in that capacity. And then you could rely upon the news, as the editor under the same pay as other workers, could gain nothing by falsehood; nor would he lose his position by telling the truth. Newspapers would not be filled with lying advertisements caused by a heartless struggle for existence.

Public libraries would then mean something as we would have time to read; and the trashy book written only to sell would disappear. All sources of intelligence being open alike to every person, the average level of knowledge would be largely increased, thus giving each one a chance to improve his or her natural faculties, to their fullest extent.

We will only have to sufficiently enlarge and extend our public printing plant, throughout the country, under the management of the whole people, in order to accomplish this work. The gathering of current news is now left almost entirely to private enterprise, and colored to suit the notion of capitalist speculators. The Associated Press gives us an idea of how the department can operate, running a series of papers and periodicals; for it would have absolute control of all lines of communication. Much wasted labor might be saved by ceasing to duplicate daily papers of the same kind in one locality.

XIII

The Department of Education

The department of education would then be national instead of local. The terms and instruction would be uniform, and would have a special view to training for usefulness in the various departments of industry. The very highest branches of learning would be open to all alike and universities and colleges would be established in every convenient location. The higher branches of education would then pass out of the hands of private individuals into those of the people.

"What about religious schools?" enquired mother.

Let the church hire the building department of the nation to build them the necessary buildings, the membership paying for them on their own account. A few men would not then be allowed to exploit hundreds of millions of dollars from the workers with which to build a few colleges which the children of the workers who paid for them by their labor could not attend; and even if they could, would only be taught a false theory of economics, so as to make them better tools for the capitalist. You can train persons under the present system to be masters of any trade, but with the tools of production in the hands of the capitalist they are at his mercy, because in case of a contest the capitalist can live longer than the worker.

The first advocates of free schools were thought to be crazy and were everywhere denounced; and so with almost every attempt to improve the school system; yet today it stands out as one of our greatest public institutions needing only extension and improvement.

A valuable improvement already spreading is the free textbook system. Under the complete Socialism of all industries this would be extended to free board, clothes and housing; and then orphans would be just as well provided for as those whose parents were living, so far as wealth was concerned.

This would not take the children who had parents from their home and care, any more than is now done by the free schools. But it would set apart from the common stock a sufficiency to care for the children in every respect—such as providing homes for the homeless until they were educated and ready to go into service in some one of the national departments, where they could make a return for what had been done for them by helping to do the same for others.

This would entitle parents, over and above their own income, to draw a sufficient amount for the board, clothes and housing of each child. Mark you, this is only an extension of what we are doing now, so far as free schoolhouses, teachers, textbooks, etc., are concerned, and the same arguments support the one as the other.

The parents of children are performing the highest duty to the state; without which it could not exist. The effect of all this would be to cause people to desire children, because they would then see how they could care for them; and that nothing could hinder them from stepping out of school into useful and lucrative employment.

Behind the great American sin of the destruction of child life, stands the gaunt specter of poverty with all its immediate or prospective wretchedness. The poor wage-slave knows that he cannot care for his children; and even the rich man—knowing the uncertainty of riches, that they may take to themselves wings and fly away, leaving his children unprovided for—fears for the future.

Socialism would provide for the children's future as certainly as the common school insures them the opportunity for an education. Our cities would not then be full of homeless waifs, torn from the bosoms of their parents by the relentless hand of greed, which is as ruthless as the hand which separated the chattel-slave mother from her child. If anything at all is done for homeless children today it is to send them away among strangers; and millions of half starved little ones from five years old upwards, which under the cooperative commonwealth would be in school, are now in the mines and factories of this country grinding out profits for the capitalists.

Under Socialism the children who had no parents would be provided with as beautiful homes and as good care, as those who had; nor could they be robbed of what was furnished them since those workers whose duty it would be to care for them, would get the same pay as other workers in the various departments of the nation; and there would be no way of disposing of anything stolen, as all would have everything they needed, and to offer a thing for sale would be to admit theft.

XIV
The Department of Health

"How about doctors?" said mother.

We could have a department of health then to whom all that could be left.

Then only the very best of remedies would be used, and the vile decorations gotten up by quacks that kill more people than they cure, would disappear at once because they were only sold for the money there is in them. There is possibly more lying advertisements under this capitalist system, along the line of cure-all remedies, than almost anything else. I think all this will be seen and freely admitted when the cooperative commonwealth is set up.

It would be the duty of the department of public health rather to try to prevent rather than cure diseases.

There would then be no lack of anything necessary to the profession either along the line of education or apparatus.

Specialists will be placed in charge of the work they are best adapted to. Nor will any one be compelled to go without the best attention such a department of health can give, for want of means to pay with, for the reason that each man or woman engaged as a doctor in the nation would have the same pay from the resources of the country as any other workers.

In time the education of the people along the line of hygiene, would doubtless be such that medical aid would rarely be called in, except in difficult cases. That the danger of epidemics can be lessened by sanitary regulations is evident from what has been done at New Orleans and Havana, Cuba, as to yellow fever.

People under the new conditions would naturally seek the more healthy localities for residence, away from the stench of decaying vegetation, and all the filth being removed from the streets of cities, with houses on the most sanitary plan that science could suggest, disease would be greatly modified. In the shacks of poverty, where the poor workers are huddled together, like hogs in a pen, originate most of the epidemics that spread to the more sanitary parts of the cities.

Overwork and the eating of vile decaying food, filched out of the swill barrels of the rich, or bought from necessity because it is cheap, by the worker as the only thing his wages will afford, is one of the prolific sources of disease which Socialism will at once remove.

All sanitariums, health resorts and hospitals, etc., would be in charge of this department. Nor will a few rich idlers be able then to get all the benefits of such things, while the workers perish for want of them. All will then be workers and treated alike.

The profit system will not be on hand to rob the sick as the keepers of these resorts will, like the doctors and nurses, be paid from the resources of the state.

The organizations of doctors may still hold their annual

meetings, but under more favorable conditions, and discuss the interest of their department.

You know that we furnish hospitals and medical attendance, such as it is, for the soldiers who serve the capitalists by fighting their battles in exploiting the workers of the world.

A sort of medical assistance and hospital accommodation is given to some of the wornout workers, in the cities, counties and states throughout the nation, in insane asylums and poor houses. This will be extended to the furnishing ungrudgingly the best the nation can afford to all the sick and unfortunate.

Like other workers, the doctors and nurses could have their regular hours, on and off duty, their times of vacation and travel, etc.

A few physicians would not be worked to death, while others equally as good were idle. On the first establishment of Socialism all the capable doctors, both men and women, would at once find their places in the nation's department of health.

All the details and government of such a vast department with its subdivisions, should be left to the workers therein.

The best of schools and every facility for doing the work would be furnished by the nation.

XV

Churches and Local Societies

"What will become of the church?" asked mother, "and the other societies under your new commonwealth?"

There will be no use for societies whose only object is insurance; because the new industrial system, from its very nature, insures every man, woman and child the best of everything, for a small amount of labor. But those societies that have other objects in view can continue as long as their supporters think them necessary.

As far as the church is concerned, which Christ established to keep alive his doctrines and teachings, Socialism, which is only another name for the golden rule, will unfetter and release her from the load of capitalism which hinders her progress as did chattel slavery in its day.

Any denominational or society papers, periodicals or books can be published by the publishing department of the nation; the church or society paying for the work by their own labor account, so that those who do not believe in it will not have to support it.

As the hours of labor will be hardly more than enough to give health to the workers, the preacher can do the amount of work required and preach too, thus being entirely independent of the church he preaches to. However, if it suited him and his people, he could arrange to have the workers of his church divide the time he owed to the department, between them doing the work themselves and having it placed to his credit. The same plan would apply to the teachers in religious schools, as a method of paying them for their services.

"But," remarked mother. "you see we would have to have church buildings the same then as now, George."

Yes, of course. Let the denomination or society have just the kind of one they want, put up by the nation's building department, and pay for it out of their own labor.

"What do you mean by paying for it in their labor?" mother asked.

Why, as each worker belonging to a church or society would be at work in some one of the nation's industrial departments, and would have an income from the nation, in whatever he had a mind to take of the nation's products, let him take as much of it in the cost of the church or society building as he and his people can agree on.

As everyone's income from the nation would be ample, there need be no lack of buildings to accommodate churches or societies at any time. Missionaries could be supported on the same general principles outlined above, as you can readily see; that is, by the workers who may wish to support them, providing for them by their own work.

XVI

The Ample Resources of Wealth

"But," asked mother, "where is so much wealth coming from, George?"

Do you think we cannot produce wealth enough to meet the needs and supply the common luxuries of all the people? Under the cooperative commonwealth all waste will be eliminated from the work of production and distribution, and the drones will have to go to work making honey in the hives of industry; thus millions now idle will be employed. Only a small number of the workers are now engaged doing anything that produces wealth; all would then do something useful.

The hundreds of millions of dollars of wasted labor now used by the present system in advertising goods, will be turned into producing wealth. The great host of servants now looking after the rich will then be producers. Every appliance that it is possible for the skill of man to produce for the production of wealth, will, as I have said, be put to use.

Our heavenly Father has placed an ample supply of the resources for food, clothing and houses as readily at our command as the air and water, and if we work cooperatively there need be no more lack of them. A system of government which would enable us all to do as we wish to be done by would give us all the luxuries of life.

The United States census bulletin, number 150, which is issued under the Republican administration and so will not be suspected of leaning towards Socialism, says the average wealth production for each laborer is $2,451 per year. These figures are sufficient to show, without going into particulars, what is now being done, even under capitalism. Under Socialism the worker would get the $2,451 in place of the $437 which the same report shows that he is now getting as wages.

Suppose a hundred families get water out of a bubbling spring which affords more than all can use—who cares how much the others get? So with the sources of production; when the genius of man is cooperatively applied, more than all can consume will be produced, until at last, as with the inexhaustible spring, no one will care what another gets so long as each does his part of the work as best he can. That is the ultimate condition bound to prevail.

It has been asserted, and is doubtless true, that the land we possess between the two oceans if put under the highest state of scientific cultivation, would support all the inhabitants of the globe. The resources of the earth for wealth production are practically limitless, and for that reason the overpopulation theory is simply nonsense. It is capitalism which is starving people to death; under Socialism more wealth can be produced than could be consumed or made use of.

XVII
How the Workers Would be Paid

"But how are the workers to be paid for their work?" mother enquired.

Suppose you worked in one of the departments of industry: the workers in that department, including yourself, would each have a vote as to which of you should be your timekeeper—a thing you have nothing to do with now—and he would have the place only so long as the majority of those he kept time for wanted him to, and would do just what the majority said. His pay would be the same as those he kept time for; and he could not profit by any false entries as to time.

The produce created by the different departments would of course be put into the stores and warehouses of the nation there to wait the order of the workers, who would take from the stock anything they wanted, as pay for their work.

"How are you going to get at the cost of things?" was mother's next question.

The cost of a thing could be estimated by the time it took to produce it, all above that being profit. If a worker wanted a house he would decide just what kind he wanted to pay for out of his labor, and it would cost him the number of hours it took the building department to put it up. This house he could hold as long as he needed it, and other working members of his family would have a like opportunity.

But if any of the worker's children preferred the use of his house in the place of a new one built on the same plan, he or she could have it, as such houses when they reverted to the people collectively could be disposed of to others who wanted them, and could be remodeled; or they could be torn down, according to time and conditions.

Under Socialism the worker would want food, clothes, furniture, books, pictures, and in fact everything he wants and produces now, but often cannot get under the present system. The books of each department would show the name of each worker and each would be credited with the time put in; and as the workers drew their pay from time to time each account would be properly balanced. If workers wished to keep their own accounts, check books similar to those now in use in our dealings with banks could be used.

There could be no motive for those who would do the timekeeping part of the work for society to cheat, as bankers now sometimes do, since they would only get the same pay for their work as the other workers, in any event.

"How about money?" mother enquired.

It would not be impossible to use money in which each worker could be paid, representing the number of hours put in, and good for anything at the public stores. I called attention to the check system as more convenient than money because private persons could make no more at buying and selling the things furnished them by the nation, than can now be made out of postage stamps; but of course the majority of the workers would adopt the method which suited them best.

It is likely that all articles would be marked with the number of hours and minutes it took to produce them, and that the workers would pay for them in the hours and minutes of their own labor; so all persons—those in active service, persons on the retired list, orphans, mothers raising families, children in schools, and the mentally and physically dependent—would have their appropriate claims against the entire product of the nation, and could be supplied, in the way before outlined.

For remember while we have private ownership of the industries at present, and use money now, we can only get a living from the produce furnished by the workers, just as the Socialists propose, the difference being that under private ownership the worker gets but a bare existence while the idler gets the lion's share, whereas under Socialism all who were fit for service would do their part, and all would fare alike.

XVIII

Travel and Vacation

"It seems as if one would never get to go anywhere," mother said.

How much do you get to travel now? Not much I think. If you wanted to travel you would do it through means of the transportation department, which would include the publicly owned and operated railroads, steamships, etc. As you understand, the workers in the transportation department would be getting their pay, like all other workers from the common funds.

You could go where you pleased, as the roads would belong as much to you as to any one else in the nation. All the ships plying the great waters would belong to the whole people instead of only the war vessels as now; and as they would be operated in the same way as the land transportation, all sailors being paid directly from the resources of the nation as are those now employed on the war vessels, they would simply take you where you wished to go.

But you want to know about travel and intercourse with foreign countries. The agents of our commonwealth would of course be authorized to exchange products with other countries so as to get what we do not produce and place it in store for the whole people. And you see in traveling in any other country your credits against the American commonwealth would be as good in exchange as the bonds of the nation now are, as the entire resources of the nation would be behind them, making good their payment.

"But," objected mother, "suppose they were still using money in the countries you wished to travel in."

That is not at all probable, as Socialism is an international movement, and will very likely come about the same time in most of the great nations; but if it was gold and silver they wanted, then the traveler could get all of it he needed to take with him, as pay for his work, from the departments of the nation, and weigh it out to the foreigner as we do now; for as you know, mother, the metals out of which we make money go by weights when we use them in other countries, even now.

As to vacations, that would all be arranged for by the workers, as they would be the sole owners and managers of the departments of industry, as the stockholders are now. The matter would be settled by the vote of the majority, and as all would want some time for leisure and travel, ample vacations would be the natural result.

"Yes," mother assented, "I fear it would all be vacation."

But think a moment; in that case who would run the system of transportation, and from what would the incomes be derived, as nothing can be produced without work?

"I reckon that's so," mother replied.

All travel would then be first class, by land or sea, simply because all would want the best of everything, and would have an equal right to it.

"But," mother questioned, "suppose you wanted to go and stay?"

Well, you could go, and could take as much of your earnings with you as you had paid for by your labor. But when Socialism is adopted in all countries as a system of industry, in place of the present one of capitalism, aside from natural conditions, such as climate, etc., one country will be about as pleasant to live in as another. Say you had a year's credit with the department of industry in this country; it would be honored in the exchange of goods between the two countries, and would enable you to draw to the extent of your credit there as well as if you were here.

XIX
The Women

"Like all other women," said mother, "I want to know where we are to come in."

The women are doing their part in all the fields of useful labor, both mental and physical, under the present system, and under Socialism the single women and those who were not bringing up families would no doubt still follow some useful occupation in the departments of industry. But the women who were rearing families would be doing the most useful work and would have no further duties thrust upon them.

Each woman would, like each man, have her own equal independent income. As she would be an equal shareholder in the industries of the nation she would not need to sell herself through a so-called marriage to some one she did not love, in order to get a living. Where there is no love there can be no real marriage.

Under Socialism the idle parasite of a woman would have to reform and do something useful, or have no income from the nation. If a woman's friends should choose to use their own incomes to keep her in idleness I presume no one would object, but there would be no way, as now, to compel any one to support her. As she would have no credit at the departments of the nation she would not have the same opportunities as the women who did their part of the work; and those who divided their incomes with her would thus be lessening their own incomes; so instead of being looked up to, as under the present system, her idleness would cause her to meet with the disapprobation of all those around her, and the idea of what constitutes a real lady will be changed from the idle parasite to the working woman.

Under Socialism, as equal shareholders in the nation's industries, and like women stockholders in private concerns today, women would stand on a par with men when it comes to voting on anything, and would be just as eligible to any position.

A political freedom which did not make women economically

free could only result in leaving the mass of women where most of the men are today—if not despised to be at least treated as fools. "We demand the absolute equality of the sexes before the law, and the repeal of all law that in any way discriminates against women," says the Socialist platform.

It is to the interest of the women, more than the men, if possible, to be Socialists because they suffer more from capitalism than anyone else.

It has been well said by some one, the working man is a slave and his wife is the slave of a slave.

XX
Transfers

"What about a person moving from one part of the country to another?" was mother's next question.

When there was an opening for work in the public service in some place where a worker wished to move, he could go and it would not cost him a fortune to travel, as I have explained before; so the opportunities for moving would be much better then than now, and with the absolute certainty of lucrative employment.

All vacant houses would be in the hands of the building department, from which they could be obtained. When a house which a worker had left was taken by some one else from the public agent who had been given charge of it, the worker could of course be given credit for it on his new home, or in the departments.

"But," asked mother, "suppose the house was never taken, what then?"

Well, suppose a house is not sold when a fellow moves under the present system, what then? When you answer one question, you answer the other. No one would take a house at any more than cost, as he could have a new one put up for that; so there could be no speculation then, as there is now.

Of course those not in active service would need no transfers to move from place to place; for just as postage stamps are the same price anywhere beneath our flag, so a man's income would be the same, and could be as easily drawn at one point as another.

XXI
The Retired List

"I would like to know what one would do when they get old if they failed to lay up something," said mother, as she busied herself with the work.

You would be put on the retired list, where you ought to have been twenty years ago. It is possible to put one on this list in the prime of life, on full pay. This, as I have shown, could be easily done through the use of modern machinery in the rapid creation of wealth.

The reason why this seems impossible now is because we do not consider the vast fortunes accumulating in the hands of the idle rich, at the expense of the poor, which they cannot use themselves and will not let others use.

You see if you had as good a living as any one else assured you and your children for life, the idea of "laying up for yourselves treasures on earth where moth and rust doth corrupt and thieves break through and steal" would disappear forever.

"It seems to me," mother remarked, "your whole retired list would simply be a burden upon society."

On the contrary, those on the retired list would be only getting back the help they had given to others while they were at work supporting the children in school, and those who were on the retired list when they were among the workers.

Indeed, this is only a little further extension of what we are already doing on a large scale now. The millions of children are supported and educated by the workers—so are all the non-producers, including those who live from rents, interest and profits, the tramps, those out of work, the old and poor in state and national institutions of charity, however rich or poor may be their fare.

The old soldiers are another class on the retired list. True, they may not get all they should, but when we quit having a large number out of work, and so many others working at something which does not produce anything, as I have said before, and cease to give the idle rich—for them to waste—the wealth produced by the workers, there will be plenty for all. When poverty is abolished, and we cease, as the Saviour commanded, to worry about what we shall eat, drink or wear, then life will be worth living.

Now it seems to me if we can afford to put men on the retired list for killing people in time of war, and destroying the wealth of the country, we certainly can afford to put them on the retired list for saving human life and creating wealth.

Capitalists place themselves on the retired list with large incomes at the expense of the workers, who have it to pay.

XXII

Socialist Government

"How are you going to govern your new commonwealth? And will not your representatives sell you out?" mother questioned.

When Socialism is established the representative system of government will be at an end.

"But," urged mother, "how are you going to get along without someone to make the laws? Won't you always be voting?"

No; when the land, factories, and means of transportation all belong to the people collectively, we will need but few laws. We make a large number of laws now, trying to regulate and govern all kinds of things in private hands. All that will then be done away with. We make many criminals laws now, because men are led into all kinds of wickedness in order to make a living.

The present system of privately owned industries keeps us in a state of strife with one another, even forcing the unfortunate to steal or rob in order to live. The capitalist class makes laws legalizing their methods of exploiting the people; and thus protect themselves in so doing, and the poor are imprisoned if they violate them.

Under Socialist government any general law affecting the people could be drawn up by any citizen, and when petitioned for by the requisite number of voters—for example, five per cent, as in some countries where this is already in effect as a means of making laws—a vote could be taken and if carried by a majority would become a law.

All rules and laws regulating departments, or which only related to particular departments and did not affect the interests of the general public, could be left to the workers of such departments, because they alone would best understand them. These rules of the several departments could be submitted to a vote of the workers in each department by the same method used in submitting the general laws to the whole people.

As each worker would be an equal shareholder, not only the department in which he was a worker, but also in all the other industries of the country, no bosses would be needed in any place where the workers understood their work; as we would need no boss to keep us at our own work we would have less bosses and more workers.

Thus you see that under Socialism the people would make all their own laws by voting for or against them, instead of voting for a few men to make laws by which they must abide whether they liked them or not. So the majority of the people would make the laws by which the officials would be governed, in place of the officials making the laws to govern the whole people, and the majority of the people would therefore constitute the head of the government; and the officers, who would be merely occupying clerical and executive positions instead of being lawmakers, would do what the people said, or the voters who elected them would drop them back into the ranks and put others in their places.

Under Socialism criminals would soon disappear, because the conditions which breed crime—those embraced by our present industrial system—would be gone. Men would, as now, have to abide by the laws made by the majority, or suffer whatever penalty was prescribed by the law. So long as tribunals for the enforcement of the law were needed, they would be provided by the people, and no longer. There would be no private interests to defeat the ends of justice, such as big corporation suits, wills, deeds, and so on.

A general law establishing an equal distribution of the products of industry would be inevitable, because when it came to a vote on distribution the workers—each of whom would be an equal shareholder with every other—would agree to nothing less, and if there were any who did not like it they would have to abide by it; as the majority would decide what it thought was just and right.

Under Socialism the free schools of the nation would be fitting men and women for their positions in the public industries; and with equal opportunities much of the apparent differences among individuals would disappear. The unequal distribution of wealth is an outgrowth of capitalism. The few who privately own the capital decide how the wealth of the nation shall be distributed; but under Socialism the worker would own the capital, and would decide as to the distribution of wealth by a majority vote.

The justice of economic equality can be seen in the fact that all the different workers are equally essential to the mechanism of production as are its different parts of machinery to a watch.

The people could by vote fix by law the number of hours all must work, as is often done now, except that the people do not get a vote on it. These hours could be changed with the advancement of machinery. If any would not abide by the laws passed by the majority of the workers, they would have to go without a living, as there would be no private employment, all the industries being owned and operated by the whole people.

The statistics of each department would of course be published that the workers might know just what had been produced for their use. Taxation would then be a thing of the past, as that which was formerly taxed as private property would then have become public property.

It is quite probable that under Socialism the largest number of persons would live in towns for the sake of association, but as municipal ownership would then be completely established, the government of towns and cities would doubtless be left to the direct vote of the people, just as the larger industries would be governed. It is as true of city government that few laws would be needed under Socialism, as of the government of the industries, when everything is owned and operated by the entire people.

The Socialists are doubtless now in their government through the locals gradually developing the form of government that will control the cooperative commonwealth in place of our representative form of law making.

XXIII

Conclusion

It is sometimes said that it is useless to attempt to outline any possible plan of procedure for cooperative industry, and that all must be left to the future. But it has always seemed to me that certain great principles of industrial management cannot be avoided under the new commonwealth.

For instance, most of the departments which I have mentioned are already operated by the workers collectively, and must still be operated in that manner when taken over by the working class, so far as labor is concerned, the difference being one of ownership and government.

Then again, the opposition to what is known as government ownership on the part of the scientific Socialists is based on the fact that under our representative form of government large salaries would be voted by the irresponsible representatives to themselves, while a comparatively small wage would be given to the real wealth producers. This abuse being inherent in the nature of our representative form of government it would be asking too much to insist upon leaving the same power in the hands of any set of men; it should be given to the whole people to whom it rightly belongs. Hence what I have said as to a new form of government here, is as pertinent as though we were living under a monarchy. Unless the possibility of this fraud is taken away, everything would have to depend upon the continued honesty of our class conscious representatives after Socialism was established.

"I think I have heard Socialists themselves say that it was not possible to say beforehand just how things could be managed," observed mother.

What we have said is only to show that it is possible to do the things that must be done and [this plan] will not be followed out if anything better can be done. But when, as a speaker, men have questioned me as to how things could be carried out I have found it not at all convincing to tell them I could see no way and we must wait till the time came before offering a possible plan.

As things are going now everything will be organized to our hand and all we will have to do is to take the industries and go on with the work.

"Well, you have convinced me that I am about as much of a slave now as I was in the south, and I am ready to accept any way out of this drudgery," mother remarked as the conversation turned on other subjects.

Wayland's Monthly, August, 1903

The Bible and Socialism

A Conversation
Between Two Preachers

1904

Dedication

This work is dedicated to the Preachers and Members of the Churches, and all others who are interested in knowing what the Bible teaches on the question at issue between the Socialists and the Capitalists, by one who began preaching twenty-nine years ago, and still continues.

Preface

One, among the many reasons that induced the author to undertake the preparation of this book, was because there exists no work, so far as he was aware, in our Socialist literature exactly covering the ground here set forth. He asks only that you read and study this book first and criticize afterwards.

There may, however, be some work covering the same ground that he has not seen, but those that he has seen touching the subject do not treat the matter in a manner the author thinks likely to convince the firm believer in the Bible.

The work has been written by one who believes in all the Bible teaches and who, as a preacher, still holds fast his allegiance to the church and the ministry.

He believes that no book, expressing doubt as to the truth of the Bible, is calculated to reach the great mass of the working class who belong to the different churches and believe in the Scriptures.

There are considerable more than twenty millions of people belonging to the churches of this country, and to set up the Cooperative Commonwealth the Socialists must have their part of them.

It is intended to set forth only what the Bible teaches on economics, leaving other matters alone.

Those who would like to know more fully how it is possible to put Socialism into practice are recommended to read our book: *What to Do And How to Do It.*

The class struggle is made prominent in the present work.
The reader will find the style plain and simple.

The language, in referring to the rich exploiter of the poor, may, at times, appear to be a little harsh, but a moment's reflection will show that it is not more so than that of the Bible.

The object in quoting so extensively from the Bible is to let it speak for itself.

There may, also, appear to be some repetitions in it, but they are made purposely in order to keep the one great subject before the reader, and that is Socialism. There is no attempt at either learning or literary excellence.

Those who believe in the Bible, as well as those who do not, must know from the very nature of its subject matter, that there is much said on the subject at dispute between the rich and the poor, and as many people, besides the author, regard its teaching as infallible authority, it is necessary to know what it does say.

The greatest difficulty the author found in writing the book was the fact that so large a portion of the Bible is made up of economic teachings. He has tried, however, to pass in review all those passages having the greatest bearing on the subject.

If the work will only contribute toward removing the prevalent belief that Socialism is a foe to the Bible and Christianity, the author will be satisfied.

San Diego, California
January 21, 1904

I

Introductory

Some months after our last conversation, regarding Socialism, mother said, on returning from church, on Sunday: "I thought you promised to tell me more about what the Bible says concerning Socialism?"

"So we did," we replied.

"Well," she continued, "I give one of your new books to our Pastor, the Rev. Mr. M_____, and he says 'there is no Socialism in the Bible.' So, now, I would like to have this thing straightened out. How are we members to know, when you preachers differ among yourselves? But, very well, there he comes now. I told him to come over, as I wanted you both together. Come in and be seated, Pastor," said my mother, giving him a chair.

"Now, I have you two preachers together. If the Bible teaches Socialism, I want to know it, and if it don't, I want to know it."

After some general conversation, we said by way of introducing the subject at hand, which the pastor seemed somewhat backward in approaching: "So, mother give you one of my little books?"

"Yes," was the reply. "And, of course, as Socialism, and the Socialist party, has to do with politics, very naturally, I told her that the Bible had nothing to do with such matters."

"What is politics? Suppose you define it, Pastor."

"Of course, primarily, a politician is a statesman. Thus making politics the science of statesmanship. But you know we are a long ways from that now, everything has grown so corrupt," he answered.

"That don't prove that politics and politicians are not good things, no more than corruption proves that preaching and preachers are not good things.

"The fact that we have rascals in public life, today, does not prove that like conditions did not exist in Bible times.

"I accept what the Bible teaches, on all other subjects, but let us confine ourselves, wholly, to what it says on economics. The Jews, on coming out of Egypt, formed a state, and, of course, had their statesmen, not to make, but to enforce the laws, as they had no legislature."

"You say the Bible is not authority on questions of politics, but does it not contain the Five Books of the Law, which governed that state?"

"But," said the Pastor, "recollect, the Law of Moses was given of God."

"So much the better, then, for our contention, as the politicians and politics has the sanction of God. You know that the first verse of the twentieth chapter of Exodus says: 'And God spake all these words,' and then follows the whole law. So God is there represented as giving the Jews a regular system of government, touching every phase of human life, too numerous to mention. Indeed, I know of no relation of one man to another that is not touched upon in the Law of Moses, which you are reading in your churches and Sunday schools every Sunday throughout the land. And, yet, you say there is no politics in the Bible, because some politicians have proven corrupt. You had as well teach that there was no true prophets in the Bible, because there were false ones; no true apostles, because there were false ones, and, last of all, no true Christ, because there are impostors. The same argument would rule the God we worship out of the Book. The Jewish Rulers and Kings were as shrewd politicians as any we have today, and often violated the law given of God to govern the Jewish state, and became equally as corrupt as the politicians of our own country."

"Well, at least, they did not have the kind of politics in the Bible we have now," remarked the Pastor.

"Then, why is it said of one king, 'Now, it came to pass that he did evil in the sight of the Lord,' and, of another, 'He did good?' Was it not because one enforced the law better than the other did? But in order to find whether there is any Socialism taught in the Bible, let me call your attention to the definition of Socialism, given in our little book, *What to Do and How to Do It.*

"There are only four things that they demand: First, they (the Socialists) want all the people to have an equal interest in the land, like Jones and his boys in their farm, because the earth is our home and no one can live without it. It is the source from which we get everything. The second thing the Socialists want, is to have the whole people own the tools which is used to work with; to produce wealth from the earth, everything, from a spade to a large factory, is simply a tool which is used to work with. The third thing the Socialists want is, to have the workers, who are to own the earth and the tools, own also, the means of taking both themselves and their goods wherever necessary or desirable. This means that the people should own all the railroads, ships, and other means for hauling their goods, or of travel. The fourth thing is, the working class must have the right to make all the laws to govern the industries by direct vote."

We can show that the Bible is in harmony with the principles here laid down, which the world is just beginning to understand.

"What do the Socialists expect to accomplish by these extraordinary demands?" the Pastor asked.

The Socialists, which consist of the conscious working class, make these demands to cut off rent, interest, and profits, the three means by which they are exploited of what they produce, by the capitalist class.

Christ, in speaking of the Old Testament to the Jews, told them to read it and said: "They are they which testify of me." (John v:39.) The four Gospels claims to be a record of what Christ taught, and the Epistles a record of what was taught by his apostles. Now from these books, which comprises the Bible, we can find what Moses, the prophets, Christ and the apostles, taught on the question of Socialism.

"It seems to me," remarked the Pastor. "I have heard even Socialists say that none of these could have taught Socialism, because it was too early and economic development had not yet prepared the world for it, and that it was left for Karl Marx to discover."

Perhaps you did, but that would prove too much, if true. For it would show that Marx could not have discovered Socialism, himself, because the world is not yet ready for it. That wonderful man lived, wrote, and died without the sight of the new commonwealth, which his writings has done so much to bring about. Most great discoveries have largely been based upon what had gone before, from time immemorial; for instance, letters, mathematics, astronomy, medicine, architecture, etc.

It will be remembered that Marx, the greatest philosopher of modern times, belonged to the same wonderful Hebrew race that gave to the world Moses, the Lawgiver, the Kings and prophets, and Christ the Son of the Highest, with his apostles, who, together, gave us the Bible that, we claim, teaches Socialism. Doubtless Marx, like other young Hebrews, was made acquainted with the economic teachings of Moses, and all the rest of the Old Testament sages and prophets, whatever we find him believing in after life.[3]

If we are able to show that the Bible opposes both rent, interest and profits, and the exploiting of the poor, then it stands just where the Socialists do.

"Does not Scientific Socialists teach that men are usually moved only by what they deem their class interests, and don't you teach the same?" said the Pastor.

I plead guilty, Pastor; but while I hold that as true, I also know that men may shut their eyes, wilfully, when the light comes, and fail to recognize what is for their highest interests. That I find often in the laboring men who refuse to accept Socialism and vote with the capitalist, many of them thinking that to be to their best interest.

Capitalism is not the best thing even for the Capitalist, as he will find after it has passed away. Socialism, then, is for the best interest of all. We must not expect, however, those who are blinded by capitalism, as a class, to put it down.

So we hold that when a man hears and understands these truths, whether taught in the Bible or by the Socialist, he is morally responsible. It cannot be successfully shown that what a man thinks is for his best interest, is always so. Nor can you separate morals and religion from economics.

If so, it would follow that so long as the laboring man thinks it to his interest to vote with the capitalist, he is right. We recognize that there is a class struggle, and want to put it down by adopting Socialism, because it is not to the interest of either side to be divided and struggling against each other for an existence.

Capitalism is the private ownership of the source of wealth, and the tools for producing wealth, so as to take from the laborer all he produces except enough to keep him in shape to produce more.

"My notion is, if you will get the people saved through conversion, all these things will care for themselves," remarked the Pastor.

Saved from what?

"From sin, of course."

John says, "Sin is the transgression of the law." (I John iii:4.) "Thou shalt love thy neighbor as thyself," is one of these laws which, under capitalism, we are violating continually. And, again, in the same book, at the eighth verse of the same chapter, we read: "For this purpose was Jesus Christ manifested that he might destroy the works of the devil." I presume you will admit that all wrong is the work of the devil? When a few men owned the Negroes as a chattel slave and took what they produced, all but enough to keep them in working order, that you will admit, Pastor, was sin and the work of the devil.

Now when a few men own all the capital, such as land, factories, and means of transportation, and take the larger portion of what the poor produce, why is not that, also, the works of the devil, which Christ was manifested to destroy?

As it was not necessary to wait for all to be converted or saved in order to overthrow chattel slavery, neither is it necessary to wait till all are saved to overthrow the wages system.

As God used men who were not Christians, as instruments to destroy chattel slavery and other works of the devil, in the past, he will do the same again in this case.

Open your Bible, Pastor; at Isaiah, fifty-fifth chapter and fifth verse, and there read: "Let the wicked forsake his way, and the uprighteous man his thoughts; and he will have mercy upon him; and turn to our God, for he will abundantly pardon." Let men forsake capitalism, and then turn to God for mercy and pardon. When the Socialists have forced them to forsake their way that will make it possible for you to go on with your church work.

You don't have to preach against slavery since it has been destroyed, and so it would be with these other great sins you are trying to save men from. First remove the cause, which is capitalism (another name for sin), and then you can cure the disease.

If the capitalist system, which the Socialists are opposing, is not the works of the devil, please, Pastor, tell me what are the works he is doing?

While the great mass of mankind have, as Marx demonstrated, usually been affected by their material conditions, yet some have, in all ages, been able to rise above the surrounding economic conditions, and thus point the struggling masses to a higher and better life in the future, such was Moses, the prophets, Christ and the apostles, and Marx himself.

"But Marx, the great apostle of Socialism, was not a Christian," said the Pastor.

Of course not. But according to the Bible, now in consideration, God used Nebuchadnezzar, Pharaoh, and many others, who were not his followers, to carry out his purposes. Christians recognize the hand of God in the overthrow of slavery, although few of the leaders in the war were professed Christians. Economic development, by which God brings about results, is only another name for law or rule of action.

The Socialist party, as such, has nothing to do with man's religion, whether Jewish, Christian, or any other of the religions of the world, only so far as the change from capitalism to Socialism will effect them. Socialists propose to leave the religions of the world to fight their own battles, intellectually, and stand or fall on their own merits, when Socialism is adopted; is not that all that we as Christians ask?

We, therefore, extend the hand of welcome, as a party, to men of all religions, or none, just as the case may be, who can agree with us in the setting up of the Cooperative Commonwealth. All we are trying here to get at is where the Bible touches upon the questions at issue between the Socialist and the capitalist, on whose side does it stand?

As millions are ready to accept the Bible as authority, and knowing it to be on the side of Socialism, we propose to take advantage of its teachings on that point.

One man accepts the teaching of Socialism as infallible authority, and another man accepts the Bible as infallible authority, and we intend to show that on questions of economics they agree.

"You admit that Socialism was not in practice at that early age, then how could the prophets, Christ and apostles be

Socialists? said the Pastor.

Marx and his associates were Socialists only in theory, as they could not conquer the powers of government so as to put it into practice in their day. The Socialists of Europe and America, although amounting to millions, can no more practice Socialism than did the prophets, Christ, and the apostles. Of course, in all ages, there has been some things that were Socialistic in practice, and the believers in Socialism have taken advantage of it.

The word "Socialism," as applied to the economic conditions of mankind, has only been used in the last half century. It is another name for the same thing taught by the writers of the Bible. And when Socialism is established, it will be the carrying out of what they taught on economic questions. . . .

II

Rent, Based Upon Private Ownership of Land

"You said that the Socialists wanted the people to own the land, factories, and means of transportation, to cut off rent, interest and profit," observed the Pastor. "Now, by what process of reasoning are you going to prove that the Bible is opposed to rent, for instance?"

That is easy, it seems to me. Let us examine this matter of rent. It is the price paid to the man who privately owns the land or the buildings thereon, for their use by the man who is not an owner, and who must have the use of them in order to live. Without the private ownership of the land and what it contains there could be no such thing as rent.

The first thing we are told in the Bible is, that "God created the heavens and the earth." (Gen. i:1.) Next, all the living creatures was placed on the earth, and, last of all, man, the crowning act of creation. When Adam, the father of the human race, was created, we are told that God said: "Let us make man in our image, after our likeness, and let them (mankind) have dominion over the fish of the sea, and over the fowl of the air, and over the cattle, and over all the earth, and over every creeping thing that creepeth upon the earth. So God created man in his own image, in the image of God created he him, male and female created he them. And God blessed them, and God said unto them: Be faithful, and multiply, and replenish the earth and subdue it and have dominion over the fish of the sea, and over the fowl of the air, and over every living thing that moveth upon the earth. And God said, behold I have given you every herb bearing seed, which is upon the face of all the earth, and every tree in which is the fruit of a tree yielding seed, to you it shall be for meat." (Genesis i:26-29.) Here we learn that the earth was given to the whole human race, as a home, and not to a few individuals of the race as we find it today. The dominion over the sea, with its fish, the herbs, the beasts and fowls was given to man collectively. God gave the earth to mankind as a home, with all that is necessary to happiness but we have turned it over to the few, while the masses suffer in poverty.

Now this common right to the resources of the earth is in strict accord with what the Socialists are contending for, namely, the co-operative ownership and operation of the land, and all it contains, by the whole people.

This violation of the rights of the masses of mankind, through the few cunningly getting into possession of the earth, which is the source of wealth, is what the Bible calls a sin, or the violation of the law of common ownership, laid down by the Creator at the beginning.

This violation of law lays at the foundation of the class struggle over the products which the capitalist is able to take from the worker, because of his private ownership of the earth.

"Did not Christ come to restore to us what we lost through Adam? Is not that what all us preachers teach?"

Are not the views of most of us preachers too narrow, when we talk only about getting to heaven through Christ? Forgetting that he said: "Blessed are the meek, for they shall inherit the earth." (Matt. v:5.) Did the angels not tell the shepherds, who were among the poor of ancient Judea, that the mission of Christ was to bring peace on earth, and good will to man. (See Luke xi:14.) The system of private ownership of the sources of wealth, which, according to the Bible and the Socialist, should be the common possession of all, lies at the bottom of this struggle among men.

And whatever may be said of the future life, which we both believe in, one of the missions of Christ was to restore to man the earth, which he had lost through exploitation, and it can only be done, Pastor, through a class conscious movement, such as the Socialists are now heading.

The Socialists are simply one of the instruments through which this work is to be done. And the church, or preacher, that fights Socialism, fights, also, Christ and the Bible.

"Why, your Socialists, many of them, don't recognize the existence of God, much less believe the Bible," said the Pastor.

These men are largely what this system of exploitation has made them. It is my belief that a large number of them are what they are because the churches and theologians have persisted in telling the people that, according to the Bible, we are not to expect any great change in our condition, in this life, but we must endure oppression without making any special effort to better our condition by the ballot; and all will be righted in heaven.

I have no doubt about all being right in the hereafter, providing all things be made right here first. Hear what the prophet said to the Jews about conditions on earth.

"Ye who turn judgment to wormwood (bitterness) and leave off righteousness in the earth." (Amos v:7.) So our courts, like those of the Jews in the Prophet's day, are simply made instruments of bitter torture, in place of justice; and, still, many churches and preachers say, wait till the hereafter in place of doing right here.

We Socialists stand with the prophet, in this case, and say that on earth is the place to begin doing right and that the courts have been turning the judgment of the poor into the bitterness of wormwood long enough.

Please open the Bible, you hold in your hand, and read: "The land shall not be sold forever, for the land is mine." (Lev. xxv:23.) Now, is not one of your deacons a real estate man, who sells the earth to men and to their heirs forever, and don't he come to the church and pray to the same God, whose Word he mocks? And when you preach, do you condemn the practice?

If you do not, why do you wonder at those who are enlightened enough to see this inconsistency, losing faith in the church?

But we will be charitable; it may be that many of the church members, deacons and preachers, are where some of the Socialists were a few years ago, they have not yet learned these things.

While the Jewish law was, in some respects, only a stepping stone to something higher and better, as taught by Christ, yet under it there could be no such a thing as a land monopoly on which to base rent, as it was restored at the year of jubilee. Read again, before you put the book down, Isaiah v:8. "Woe unto them that join house to house, that lay field to field, till there be no place, that they may be placed alone in the midst of the earth." What are the people on the outside to think when they see, not only church members, but whole denominations engaged in the mad scramble to add "field to field," etc. Many denominations own millions of dollars' worth of property, outside of their preaching places, through which they exploit the poor and this thing can only be stopped, as the Socialists contend, by removing the cause, which we call capitalism.

The exploiters in the days of Isaiah, as today, violated the law by seizing everything around them so that there was no room, in order that they might be alone in the earth, separate from the common herd. This is noticeable in every country on earth today. The poor and rich are separated from economic reasons.

The difference is: that the prophets preached against it, while you defend it and profit by it. Mark you: We are not trying to show that men did not violate the law then, but what was the law. In fact, whether practiced or not, Socialism has always been the relation that should exist between man and man.

"Let me refer you to some other teachings of the Bible that, it seems to me, do not harmonize with your views of

Socialism," said the Pastor. "Did not the wages system exist under the law of Moses, and all throughout the Old Testament scriptures?"

Why, certainly. Allow me to read from my little book: *What to Do and How to Do It.*

"You ask: if the Bible, as well as science, teaches Socialism, why haven't we got it before now? Because the world is not yet ready for it. These teachings are to get us ready. According to the Bible, we have had, first, the age of the patriarchs—which suited the conception of men at that time; then followed the period of the law, which, upon questions of economics, as we have shown, stood where the Socialists stand, as to land and interest, and against the exploitations of the poor."

Paul said: "The law was our schoolmaster to bring us unto Christ. The law made nothing perfect." (Gal. iii:26.)

It was the training school to bring men to those higher ideals found in Christ.

The teaching of the Bible is, that man started at an early period of his existence into disobedience of these economic laws laid down by his Creator.

The Bible is, in a measure, a history of the class struggle going on between the rich and the poor. We shall see as we proceed.

Of course, men have tried, in every way, to avoid this law of justice between man and man.

The Bible makes mention of adultery, theft, murder, and every crime known to mankind, not because they are sanctioned, for they are all forbidden in the most plain and unmistakable terms.

The law governing the ownership of the land, and other things yet to be referred to, was not given because the people was ready to receive it, but to get them ready, by gradually bringing them up to that standard, through long ages of training, accompanied by economic development.

Of course, in all ages, there were some living who were willing and ready to accept these conditions we are contending for, but they were in the minority. Those who were willing to accept the truth, as it came to them, the Bible commended, while those who would not stood condemned.

"I thought you Socialists taught that it was the advancement of modern machinery that makes Socialism possible, which was not possible in any other age," said the Pastor.

There is no difference of opinion among well-informed Socialists about what Socialism is, or the steps leading up to it. The mission of modern machinery is that of helping the workers more rapidly to see the necessity, of that which the Bible has taught in all ages. The history of the past proves that teaching must go hand in hand with economic development. However, as we started in to find out what the Bible taught on this subject, we will have to pass this matter by with this slight reference, at present and stick to our text, as we preachers say.

That some persons may be in advance of others, one has but to read The Communist Manifesto which was written by Marx and Engels[4] before the people were ready to receive it, and well it should be, for how else would the world ever be brought to it?

"What about this passage in the twentieth chapter of Matthew, the first sixteen verses?" was the Pastor's next inquiry.

In that chapter we have a land owner who claimed to be a good man, hiring others under the wages system, at the third, sixth and eleventh hours of the day, and then, beginning at the last man hired, he paid them all equally, a penny a day. The object Christ had in view in telling the incident about the man is plain when we read the sixteenth verse, which explains the whole purpose.

"So the last shall be first, and the first last, for many be called but few chosen."

Some of the people Christ addressed were like those we talk to, anxious to know what they are to get out of the thing.

This you will find by reading the last four verses of the nineteenth chapter of Matthew. There you find his followers wanted to know who would be rewarded first. And Christ replied: "The last shall be first and the first last," and gave them the story of the householder, to bring out his meaning. Of course, this man was doing even better than some did, under the wages system, by paying all equal.

Socialists do business under the wages system, and will be

compelled to or give up business, until they can get the people to accept the higher law of Socialism, which we contend is laid down in the Bible, as well as by Marx. So what Christ said is no more of a sanction of the wages system than when a Socialist says the same thing to the people now, in relating some everyday incident.

The fact that men are condemned, in the Bible, for keeping back the hirelings' wages, is no sanction of the wages system. The iron law of wages allows a man simply to exist and to keep that back, as has been often done, is to starve the worker to death, which is still worse.

James condemned this attempt to starve labor when he said: "Behold the hire of the laborers, who have reaped down your fields, which is of you kept back by fraud, crieth: and the cries of them which have reaped are entered into the ears of the Lord of Sabbath." (James v:4.)

"But did not the Jew in Palestine hold the land in private possession, so that he might sell it subject to redemption, at any time; or have it return to him at the year of jubilee?" said the Pastor.

All of that is true. Understand, I am not contending that the law established Socialism among the Jews, but that the whole teaching of the Bible was, primarily, intended to bring about that result in time.

The law which every seventh year released all debts and the Jubilee which prevented land monopoly, also prevented the accumulation of millions of dollars of debts for parasites to live upon from age to age, as they do today. For a debt could not go beyond the seventh year. No generation of men are under any moral obligation to pay a past generation's debts, according to the Bible.

The government of the Jews, as given in the Bible, was temporary, designed for the transition period, until Christ came and laid the foundation of the Cooperative Commonwealth. Solon is represented as saying of the laws he gave to the people of Athens: "I have given them the best that they were able to bear." So it may be said, God gave the Jews the best they were able at the time to bear. It is under the dispensation of Christ that we now live and not the Old Jewish Law, that we are to get Socialism, and so far as conditions in the world are concerned; that is one of the supreme objects his Gospel was intended to bring about.

Private ownership of the land, then, enables the holder to rent to others the rights to live on the earth, which, according to the Bible, ought to be the right of all persons without asking any one else for the privilege.

So, to follow the Bible on the land question is to become a Socialist and do away with rent forever.

The declaration: "Moreover, the profit of the earth is for all" (Ecc. v:9.) together with: "The earth hath he given to the children of men" (Psalms cxv:16.) shows the same idea of common ownership and enjoyment of the earth and the produce of labor the Socialists are contending for. Under the Cooperative Commonwealth, the earth, and its products, would go to the benefit of all.

III

The Jewish Law Opposed to Interest

Don't you know that the Bible you preach from is opposed to all kinds of interest?

"The Bible, as I understand it, simply opposes usury! that is, more than the law allows," said the Pastor.

Let us see what the law does say on that subject. You will remember that the Socialists want to overthrow interest, through the public ownership and operation of all capital, to prevent the worker from being exploited of his product by having it to pay.

Both Moses and the Socialist could have but one reason for the abolition of interest, and that is to prevent one set of persons from having to keep another thereby. There is much more said about interest in the Bible than about either rents or profits. For the very good reason that the term rent, interest, and profits, is only three names for the same thing, and the overthrow of the principle of interest means the setting aside of the other two.

The man who sells goods, runs a railroad, or rents lands or houses, does so to get an interest on what he terms his investment.

Recollect, the Jews had just been relieved from a condition in which others had been profiting at the expense of their labor in Egypt, so one of the first things in the law given them at Mount Sinai was a statute forbidding usury or interest.

Please open your Bible at the twenty-second chapter of Exodus and read the verses 25-27.

"If thou lend money to any of my people, that is poor by thee, thou shalt not be to him as an usurer, neither shalt thou lay upon him usury. If thou at all take thy neighbor's raiment to pledge, thou shalt deliver it unto him by that the sun goeth down; for that is his covering only, it is his raiment for his skin. Wherein shall he sleep? And it shall come to pass when he crieth unto me, that I will hear; for I am gracious, saith the Lord."

As there was no statute known to the law of Moses allowing any sort of interest, then the word as used in the Scriptures must mean charging something for the use of a thing. Three hundred years ago the word "usury" was used everywhere among English-speaking people in the exact sense which we now use the word "interest."

But, if you are not satisfied about the use of the term "usury," I think, as we advance to other texts, the law will make plain its own meaning. In the meantime, let us glance at the pledge system mentioned in the text. It was, in some respects, similar to our chattel mortgage system. It was a security for the loan, which, it appears, must be returned by sundown, whether the debt was paid or not. If the practice of taking all sorts of things for pledges, as we do at present, prevailed, it is not found, so far as we are aware, in the law of Moses. If the Lord would hear when the poor Jew cried to him, against the man who held his raiment in pawn, why will he not hear the poor woman or man in our "sweat shops" or mines, who has been compelled to do the same thing?

The Bible, as you will see, held it to be desperately wicked to treat the poor in that way then, and yet you have these same pledge-takers in your church now.

The poor wealth-producers then, just as it has always been, was the borrower; and, at the end, had all the interest to pay. And even if the rich idlers borrows the money, he gets everything from the worker.

Notwithstanding all the theoretical teachings, then or since prevailing, we will always have the poor to whom a loan without interest will be a temporary relief until Socialism is established, which will abolish poverty. Here, in this passage, is the semblance of the class struggle between the poor and the rich, whether they were conscious of it or not.

When the members of the churches become conscious of this struggle between the rich and the poor, for the possession of the products of labor, as they will eventually, it will split the churches; but they will be reunited when Socialism is established.

"I think, if you will search the Scriptures, you will find that poverty will always prevail," the Pastor remarked.

The idea is based on a misunderstanding of certain scriptures, as we will show when we come to consider what the Bible has to say about the poor and their treatment by the rich.

In the mean time, let us go on to settle this question of the law on interest.

Read, if you please, Lev. xxv:35-37.

"And if thy brother be waxen poor and fallen in decay with thee, then thou shalt relieve him; yea, though he be a stranger or a sojourner, that he may live with thee. Take thou no usury of him, or increase, but fear thy God; that thy brother may live with thee; thou shalt not give him thy money upon usury, nor lend him thy victuals on increase."

The first thing here taught is the principle of universal brotherhood, everywhere recognized by International Socialism. As the ultimate end, which is Socialism, was yet in the distant future, temporary relief for the brother or stranger fallen into decay is taught. But the Bible, no more than the Socialists, holds out charity as a solution of economic difficulties, as we shall see as we proceed.

Does not the system we are living under now, and that you seem to think ought not to be abolished, bring about poverty and decay, as it has done in all the ages of the past? Your church members, who are money lenders and bankers, fleece the poor, just as others do, and will continue so to do, till the system we are living under is destroyed. In place of relieving the poor, we make him pay more for what little he is able to buy than the rich, who can buy in larger amounts. According to the Bible, the stranger is our brother, and should be treated as such, while today even church members stand for taking all sorts of advantage of the stranger.

"Take thou no usury of him or increase." Note that word "increase." No increase or interest, either on a loan of money or victuals was allowed. So that settles the matter whether a man has a right to live off the interest of his money, which is only a way of living off what the workers produce.

Don't you see that the church is tied hand and foot by the shackles of capitalism, and must be untied by Socialism taking the place of the present industrial system?

As the terms rent, interest and profits are names all expressing the same thing, when increase is forbidden, all three fall to the ground.

"But was it not the poor, who had fallen into decay, that were to be exempt from interest, while the rich and well-to-do might pay it?" asked the Pastor.

No, the rich owner of capital, who is not a producer, only pays interest out of what he gets from the labor of the man, who, for that very reason, has fallen into decay. As labor produces all wealth, it logically follows that it must, in the very nature of the case, pay all interest.

For, recollect, that money, in which interest is paid, only represents wealth.

Around us are millions of our brothers, that are fallen into decay through the system under which we are living; and the Socialists want to relieve them by giving them all the wealth they can produce through owning all the capital or tools with which to produce.

Now what is the outside world to think of the rich church member who helps his brother to decay by taking, under mortgage, what little his brother has left?

Are not the Socialists right when they say, "Come, let us stop this poverty and decay?"

"But here is a passage," remarked the Rev. Mr. M____, in the XXIII chapter of Deuteronomy and the 19th and 20th verses.

"Thou shalt not lend upon usury to thy brother, usury of money, usury of victuals, usury of anything that is lent upon usury, that the Lord thy God may bless thee in all that thou settest thine hand to in the land whither thou goest to possess it." Again, it is said to the Jews: "Thou shalt lend unto many nations, but thou shalt not borrow." (Deut. xv:6.) How does that harmonize with your idea that the Bible is opposed to all interest?

You will recall that the law, as laid down in Leviticus referring to the stranger who had become poor, said: "Thou shalt relieve him." And the Jews were commanded to love the stranger as themselves. The Ammonites and Moabites, together with the different tribes or nation of Canaan, are expressly excepted from this rule. The first, because they tried to prevent the Jews from going into the promised land and establishing a nation, whose teaching was destined to lead, ultimately, to the setting up of the Cooperative Commonwealth; and the other because of their wickedness. This truth is still marching on and the same will come to any other nation that stands in the pathway of progress today. (See Deut. xxiii:3-6.)

"Thou shalt not abhor (hate) an Edomite, for he is thy brother; thou shalt not abhor an Egyptian, because thou wast a stranger in his land." (Deut. xxiii:7.)

This entitles them to different treatment to those doomed nations.

"Had not the Egyptians oppressed the Jews?" asked the Pastor.

They did. And, as we are told, were terribly punished for it.

It would seem, therefore, that the term: "Unto a stranger thou mayest lend upon usury, that the Lord thy God may bless thee in all that thou settest thine hand to, in the land whither thou goest to possess it," refers only to those nations which the Jews were to dispossess.

These people of Canaan, according to the history of the times, as recorded in the twentieth chapter of Leviticus, was guilty of every gross immorality known to mankind.

The Bible historians are not alone in recording the cruelties, oppressions, and abominations of the nations of the past, such as Chaldea, Assyria, Persia, Greece, Rome, Egypt, and others, all of which went to destruction through war and conquest, just as Canaan did. This state of things will continue so long as the private ownership of the earth and its resources are recognized. The New Testament recognizes no such thing as strangers and foreigners. (Eph. 11:19.)

It is the belief of the Socialists that the modern nations would go just as Canaan and other ancient nations did, were it not for the on-coming of Socialism.

"I have heard some of your Socialists complain bitterly about the order to destroy the infants of Canaan," said the Pastor.

Perhaps you did, but they will admit that war has always led to the suffering of the innocent. As Socialism could not then be established among all nations, these children were better off dead, than many are in the hell of poverty and vice maintained by the present system.

And I need not say to those who believe in the heaven beyond, where Socialism is already the prevailing law, that those infants who ceased life here, and began it there, are the gainers thereby.

Of course, the older ones, both men and women, simply reaped the evil they had sown, which must always be the case, till we change the conditions, and cease sowing that kind of seed.

These people of Canaan had been pursuing the same economic course we are now pursuing, and harvest time came at last, just as it will with us, unless prevented.

Nations have been destroyed by all sorts of calamities, such as earthquakes, epidemics, etc.

To those of us who see the hand of God in the destruction of nations, there is no more wrong in having one nation destroyed by another, than having it done in any other way. Indeed, it would not be just if the heedless exploiters of the working people did not, ultimately, reap the fruit of their doings.

"But you cannot make some of your Socialists see the justice of God's commands to destroy these people," said the Pastor.

I cannot compel any body to receive any sort of truth, and God won't compel them.

These Socialists, you keep speaking of, are like some of you church people, we cannot make accept the principles of Socialism, although laid down in the Bible you profess to believe in.

Whatever some may believe about the destruction of these people of Canaan, they will be compelled to admit that the Jews, who superceded them, had a law forbidding interest in all its forms.

The Socialist who aims to do the same thing carries out what the Bible teaches, whether he recognizes it or not.

This whole transaction in Canaan is but a part of the economic history of the world.

It appears it was the custom at that early age to have not only money on interest, but victuals and other things; all of which the Bible forbids, and it is this that lays at the foundation of the present method of producing and distributing wealth.

So far, you must admit, Pastor, the Bible agrees with the Socialist.

"But if you cannot compel men to accept these truths, you cannot get Socialism," said the Pastor.

Like other great truths, the majority will be compelled by their material conditions, and the others will accept as soon as Socialism is established and they see the benefit of it.

IV

Interest Under the Jewish Kings

All kings and rulers, in every age, have lived by exploiting their fellowmen, and the Jewish kings was no exception to the rule.

"We have no king in this country," said the Pastor.

No, we elect our monarch every four years, and place more power in his hand than the king of England. And then it costs us more, as workers, to keep our untitled nobility than all the crown heads of Europe. As an exploiter of the worker the rulers of the Old World are not to be compared to our Standard Oil king, who alone gets more than all these crown heads.

The teachings of the law of Moses was, as we have seen, opposed to interest of all kinds. But as forced obedience is no part of the divine plan it has required a series of ages to bring mankind in sight of the ultimate goal, which is Socialism. For that reason Paul spoke of the law as "Our schoolmaster to bring us unto Christ, that we might be justified by faith." (Gal. iii:24.) No one, tolerably acquainted with the Jewish religion, will attempt to deny that it has to do almost wholly with this life, in its attempt to bring about economic justice as fast as the people could be educated up to an understanding and acceptance of it.

"If you are correct, why was the Jews so often punished for what they were not sufficiently advanced to receive" said the Pastor.

Because ignorance of the law never prevents the effect of its violation.

We are suffering now all sorts of poverty and inconvenience, in the world, because of our ignorance of Socialism, which is only another name for justice, between man and man. And our ignorance of Socialism no more prevents our suffering than our ignorance of electricity prevents our dying if we take hold of a live wire.

It was the business of this law, as a schoolmaster, to educate the people in the primary and pass them on to the final graduation into social justice, as fast as economic conditions would permit.

"We were, by the law, to be brought to Christ, and not to Socialism," said the Pastor.

To bring one to Christ, certainly means to bring one to a belief and acceptance of his teachings, and that, necessarily, must include what he taught on Socialism, as well as anything else he taught, and, as a Socialist, all I want to know here is, what he said on that subject.

In coming to Christ, we must accept the brotherhood of man, which he taught.

It seems to me that the notion that the teaching of Christ was aimed almost wholly at the future world, and not intended to change conditions here, is a very common mistake that must be laid aside.

Read what Paul said in Hebrews vii:19:

"For the law made nothing perfect, but the bringing in of a better hope did; by which we draw high unto God."

"The whole thing is an unwarranted twisting of the great and wholesome doctrine of justification by faith," remarked the Pastor, warmly.

Let us see. In short, to justify means to vindicate. That is to say, faith in Christ's teachings will be our vindication. How then can professed Christians be justified or vindicated without accepting Christ's economic teachings as well as the rest?

And why do you leave off one and teach the other?

What is faith? Let the same author answer:

"Now faith is the substance of things hoped for, the evidence of things not seen." (Heb. xi:1.)

When Paul said the "law made nothing perfect," but gave the people a hope for better things, he said what was true as to the overthrow of interest, in all its forms, through the coming in of socialism. We are asked here to have faith in things to come, only on what, to us, is found to be sufficient evidence. The coming of Socialism is based upon faith, or the evidence of things hoped for.

So I am not asked to have faith in a thing without evidence.

What is taught in the Bible on Socialism is not true because found in the Bible; but was put there because it was true; and the Socialists have shown it to be based on scientific evidence as well.

We Socialists have hope of bettering the conditions for mankind and think there is sufficient evidence that it is near at hand.

"You have not made good your assertion that the Jewish kings were exploiters of the people," said the Pastor.

Before proving that, let us notice what is meant by drawing near to God. Is it not then by doing what he teaches? How can you church members draw near to God by simply putting on a sanctimonious face and going on to skin the people through interest, which he forbids?

Now for your question about the Jewish kings.

The Jewish government did not provide for a legislative body, or any one else to make new laws, or amend old ones, but left the statutes as first given to be enforced by the people, just as the Socialists want to do. (Deut. xvii:18.) In the time of the judges, which lasted several hundred years, Samuel and his sons lived. We are told that his sons "walked not in his ways, but turned aside after lucre, and took bribes, and perverted judgment." (1 Sam.iii.) These judges were like some we have today. For, remember, it paid then to give and take bribes, and will continue so until Socialism makes it impossible. The people complained of this condition of things, and justly; but, like us, they adopted the wrong remedy.

The people, then, did not live up to the teachings of the Bible, nor do we.

"Thou shalt not covet thy neighbor's house, thou shalt not covet thy neighbor's wife, nor his man servant, nor his maid servant, nor his ox, nor his ass, nor anything that is thy neighbor's." (Ex. xx:17.)

"Thou shalt love thy neighbor as thyself." (Lev. xix: 18.)

"But the stranger that dwelleth with you shall be unto you as one borned among you, and thou shalt love him as thyself." (Lev. xix:34.)

Now I want to leave it to you, Pastor, if covetousness does not lay at the foundation of our present industrial system? It was what actuated those judges. It is what made men rob their neighbors of the proceeds of their labor and take their houses, then, as now, under mortgage. To love our neighbors as ourselves is to want them to have everything that we have, and it cannot be done except under Socialism, which would place men on an economic equality.

In the treatment of the stranger the doctrine of universal brotherhood is taught, for which, as we said, the Socialists everywhere stand.

This teaching, which is the very essence of Socialism, is what the Jews ought to have been guided by. But, instead, when they cried out: "Make us a king to judge us like all the nations," they only done as we often do, choose themselves a worse master. (1 Sam. viii:5.)

When the Jews chose a king, the Lord said to Samuel: "They have not rejected thee, but they have rejected me." (1 Sam. viii:7.)

When they rejected God's plan of righteous economic government they rejected him.

Now, Pastor, if you will please read from the eleventh to the eighteenth verse of the eighth chapter of First Samuel you will see that God said the Jewish kings would be oppressors of the people.

"This will be the manner of the king that shall reign over you; he will take your sons and appoint them for himself, for his chariot and to be his horsemen; and some shall run before his chariots. And he will appoint him captains over thousands, and captains over fifties; and will set them to till his ground and to reap his harvest, and make his instruments of war, and instruments of chariots. And he will make your daughters to be confectionaries, and to be cooks, and to be bakers. And he will take your fields and your vineyards and your olive yards, even the best of them, and give them to his servants. And he will take the tenth of your seed, and of your vineyards, and of your olive yards, and give them to his officers and to his servants. And he will take your men servants, and your maid servants, and your goodliest young men, and your asses, and put them to his work. He will take the tenth of your sheep; and ye shall be his servants. And ye shall cry out in that day because of your king, which ye shall have chosen you; and the Lord will not hear you in that day."

The history of the kings show that they did just as was here foretold.

These kings took the working people, lands, vineyards, houses, and produce for themselves and their officers, just as they do now. And what difference does it make to the worker, who has everything to produce by his labor, whether the man who robs him wears a crown and is called a king, or whether he is a trust magnate? His produce is gone, just the same.

The poor men were drafted into the armies then, as now, to fight the battles of the rich. All that divided men into classes and kept up a continual struggle between them.

If God made it the duties of his ministers, then, to warn the people against these parasites who live on the backs of the people, as Samuel warned them, how can you be a true minister of the same God and not do it now?

You know, Pastor, that the rich parasites spent fifty million dollars of the money taken out of the hard toil of the workers on Queen Victoria's jubilee, while millions of her subjects perished of hunger in India, and your churches raised money and corn to send to the famine sufferers, and loudly praised the Queen as a Christian when she died.

Last year we paid eighty-eight millions of dollars to John Rockefeller and the Standard Oil Company,[5] while hundreds and thousands of working men and their wives and children, who produce all this, are in extreme poverty, wretchedness and hunger.

Remember, if you, as a shepherd, warn not the people, the Bible says their "blood will I require at thine hand." (Ezek. iii:18.)

"You do not mean to say that I have not preached the gospel in its fullness?" said the Pastor, rising and walking the floor.

"If you have ever said anything against such things, I never heard it," said mother. "And did not I hear you say that both the Queen and Rockefeller were good Christians, in one of your sermons?" she continued.

That the Jewish people, surrounded as they were, on every hand, by nations ruled by despots, would eventually demand a king, in place of the plan laid down in the law of Moses, is set forth in Deut. xvii:14.

Of course, with a lot of kings and nobles living as usurers

on the back of the people, which they must do so long as we have that class; the Jewish law could only be indifferently enforced, which kept the nation in trouble all the time.

They, of necessity, ignored the law against interest, in its different forms, just as they did the law which said to the king: "Neither shall he multiply wives to him." (Deut. xvii:17.)

The law was not enforced against the rich class, then, for the same reason that they are not enforced against that class now; that is, because the power to execute the law, under the kings, was in the hands of the rich, and they would no more punish themselves than the same persons do it now.

"Where does any of the Jewish rulers say anything about interest?" said the Pastor, resuming his seat.

If you will read the fifteenth Psalm you will find David asking two questions:

"Lord, who shall abide in thy tabernacle, who shall dwell in thy holy hill?"

And, among other things, giving the following answer:

"He that putteth not out his money to usury."

If a man who took interest then was not right before God, how can the church members and the preachers, who do the same thing, be alright now?

"But what can be done about it?" asked the Pastor.

Why, tell your people to vote the Socialistic ticket, and take away the cause of all this, which is the private ownership of capital, and turn the same over to the public to own and operate collectively for the benefit of the worker.

As great an exploiter of the people as Solomon was, he uttered a great truth when he said:

"He that by usury (interest) and unjust gain increaseth his substance, he shall gather it for him that will pity the poor. He that turneth away his ear from hearing the law, even his prayer shall be an abomination." (Prov. xxviii:8, 9.)

Here interest is classed as unjust gain; when did it get to be just? And if the man's prayer who took interest then was an abomination to the Lord, how can it be alright now? That the

Bible called Solomon's administration oppressive, we will show when we come to consider the rich and their oppressions.

V
The Position of the Jewish Prophets On Interest

A few evenings after the above conversation, the Rev. Mr. M____, being now thoroughly interested, true to his promise, called again and the investigation was resumed.

Suppose we look up what some of the Jewish prophets said on this question of interest on money, we remarked.

We presume you will agree with us that these prophets were the preachers of the old dispensation, as the preachers of today are of the gospel dispensation.

Let us find how their attitude on interests will compare with the attitude of the preachers of today; for they are given as examples for us to follow.

In the twenty-fourth chapter of Isaiah, the first three verses, the prophet declared the Lord would turn the earth upside down, and scatter abroad the inhabitants. All kinds of people, the priest, master, servant, maid, mistress, buyer and seller, together with the silver and taker of usury, was to be involved in the general destruction. So usury, of some kind, has destroyed all the nations of the past, bringing calamity upon the innocent along with the guilty, as we showed.

Are we to understand that these people reaped the fruits of their doings, and we can sow the same seed and get a different crop?

It seems to me, Pastor, what we need is a few more Isaiahs in our modern pulpits.

Continuing, the prophet said:

"The earth, also, is defiled under the inhabitants thereof, because they have transgressed the law, changed the ordinance, broken the everlasting covenant." (Isa. xxiv:5.)

One of the ordinances which they had changed was that against interest, and this helped to defile the earth.

Is not the earth still defiled today, and that, too, by the aid of church members, through the violation of the same underlying principle, which disgrace can only be removed by Socialism, which will make interest impossible?

"What is to keep the ordinances from being violated again if Socialism is established, just as they were at this time?" asked the Pastor.

Socialism, or opposition to usury, has always been the relation that should be between man and man; but government has always been left to the rich, who profited through usury at the expense of the poor producer of wealth. Socialists propose to give the power of government into the hands of the producer, so he can get all he produces in place of giving it all for interest of different kinds. That will force all to be producers, and once in possession of the power to keep his product, self interest will cause him to cling to it. Of course, the producer has the power to take over the industries now, but has yet to be convinced of it.

During a period of great national corruption, after speaking in the most unmistakable terms about the judgments of God upon the exploiters of the people, Jeremiah exclaimed:

"Woe is me my mother that thou hast borne me a man of strife and a man of contention to the whole earth. I have neither lent on usury, nor has man lent me on usury, yet every one of them doth curse me." (Jer. xv:10.)

Here, according to the prophet, the worst thing that could be said of a man was to call him a usurer. Everybody cursed them. How is it today? The church not only receives, but blesses them, and set on to the Socialists, who feel about it as the prophet did.

Here, the Socialist party, which makes no pretension to be a religious organization, agrees with the prophet in opposing usury, while many church organizations, which claim to believe in the teachings of the prophets, join in heaping curses on the Socialists, in place of the usurer. But all the church members are not to blame. The churches are full of the best men and women in the world, as well as some of the worst. It is all because they have not studied cause and effect, as those who are Socialists have.

It is our duty, as preachers, to place the teaching of the Book we profess to follow, before the churches in such a light as to remove this stigma. Every true believer in the economic teaching of the Bible must, necessarily, be a Socialist as soon as he understands it.

The eighteenth chapter of Ezekiel is still more severe on the usurer, if possible, than what we have just noticed. After classing the interest taker along with the adulterer, the idolater, the murderer, and other oppressors of the poor, the prophet says:

"He hath given forth on usury, and hath taken increase; shall he then live? He shall not live, he hath done all these abominations; he shall surely die, his blood shall be upon him." (Ezek. xviii:13.)

Here the Lord is harder on the exploiting class of usurers than the Socialists, for, in the general overthrow of the nations, he held that they were worthy of death and should "surely die."

Now, the majority of preachers tell these robbers of the poor that they are not only worthy to live here, but hereafter, and claim to be followers of the same God.

Of the son of this same usurer who had forfeited his life, the prophet says, among other things:

"He neither hath oppressed any, hath not withholden the pledge (goods mortgaged), neither hath spoiled by violence, but hath given his bread to the hungry, and hath covered the naked with a garment, that hath taken off his hand from the poor, that hath not received usury nor increase, hath executed my judgments, hath walked in my statutes; he shall not die for the iniquity of his father, he shall surely live. (Ezek. xviii:16, 17.)

This last man, here described, is the kind of a man Socialism would make of every man. We would have the usurer take his hand from off the poor, and cease to spoil by violence, and our system would give bread to the hungry and clothe the naked with the best garments their skill could produce.

Don't you see that whatever opposes Socialism is standing in the way of carrying out what the prophets contended for? In the twenty-second chapter the same prophet charges the Jew with almost every crime known to mankind, and ends by saying:

"Thou hast taken usury and increase, and thou hast greedily

gained of thy neighbor by extortion, and hath forgotten me saith the Lord God." (Ezek. xxii:12.)

Here, again, the interest taker is classed with the worst men on earth, while we hold them among the best. What are our wealthy men of today doing but greedily gaining of their neighbors, the workers, by usury and extortion, and if the men who did that then had forgotten God, so have they now. But, today, the greatest usurers in the world are leaders in the churches, and all but a few of the preachers who occupy the place of the prophets of old, are like dumbdogs.

But the time is at hand, Pastor, when these men who misrepresent God and Christianity, will be held up before the world in their true light, as the prophet did the pretenders who robbed the people in his day.

VI

Nehemiah on Mortgages

Ancient history, as recorded in the Bible, and discovered in the ruins of the past, tells us that the Jews were carried into captivity by Nebuchadnezzar, some five hundred years before Christ; and after the overthrow of the Chaldean empire by Cyrus and Darius, they were permitted to return, and that under the Persian king, Artaxerxes, the prophet Nehemiah was appointed governor and judge of the Jewish province, which was still held subject to a foreign power. Now, Pastor, if you will open your Bible at the fifth chapter of Nehemiah, we will find how he dealt with that class of men, who took what the workers produced through mortgages. This chapter contains the history of a case brought before Nehemiah as a judge.

The Jews, under the Persian administration, was compelled to pay a revenue for the support of a foreign government, and, outside of that, was left to enforce their own laws. Here is the same evils of private ownership that the world is suffering from now. Nations now, including our own, are seizing other countries and laying them under tribute. Who got the benefit of the revenues collected from the Jewish laborers? A few idle rich in the Persian empire, just like a few idle rich benefit at the expense of the people of the Philippine Islands and India. But suppose you read the first five verses, which is a history of the indictment brought into court before Nehemiah:

"And there was a great cry of the people and of their wives, against their brethren the Jews. For there were that said: 'We, our sons and our daughters are many, therefore we take up corn for them that we may eat and live.' Some also there were that said: 'We have mortgaged our lands, vineyards and houses, that we might buy corn, because of the dearth.' There were those also that said: 'We have borrowed money for the king's tribute, and that upon our lands and vineyards, yet now our flesh is as the flesh of our brethren, our children as their children, and lo! we bring into bondage our sons and our daughters, to be servants, and some of our daughters are brought into bondage already, neither is it in our power to redeem them, for other men have our lands and vineyards.'" (Neh. v:1-5.)

This case came up under the law of Moses, and not under the law of Persia, as the Jews were left free to enforce their own laws, so long as they paid their tribute to the king of Persia.

Let us glance at some of the particulars in this indictment! It was one set of brethren that was robbing the other; then, as now. Again, it was the few rich robbing the many poor, as usual. There had been a failure of crops among the farmers and, being compelled to buy corn, the money lenders had taken advantage (just as they do now) to invest their money on good real estate securities. All of which was in open violation of the law, which says:

"If thy brother be fallen into decay with thee, then thou shalt relieve him; thou shalt not be unto him as a usurer, thou shalt not lay upon him usury or increase."

They had to borrow money to pay tax for the king's tribute and buy corn, and gave mortgages, just as our western farmers do today. The difference is that the money lenders of today do their robbing under protection of laws made by themselves, as they are now in control of the government; but these men in

Nehemiah's day did their robbing without the warrant of law.

In the fifth verse the poor claim that they and their children were as good as the rich and their children, which is true today. These poor people claimed that the mortgage indebtedness was bringing their sons and daughters into bondage, to be servants of the rich. "For other men have our lands and our vineyards," said they; that is, they had been taken from them under mortgage. And from that condition of bondage to the rich they were unable to redeem those near and dear to them. This amounts to the same claim made by the Socialists that mortgage indebtedness and wage servitude is nothing but a species of slavery. Today this country, and all others, is simply covered over with a blanket mortgage, and the sons and daughters of the poor are driven out from home to become servants, under bondage to the rich. And many of these mortgage holders, who drive our daughters into bondage, are professed believers in Christ and the Bible, and, unlike the ancient people who here agree with the Socialist in complaining against this condition, we, of today, call it freedom.

Special stress is laid by this people on the fact that some of their daughters had already been brought into bondage. How about our daughters, today, who are driven to become the servant of the rich, in mansion, store and factory, subject to all sort of abuse and temptations, and often driven from that into dens of infamy, worse than death, where it is said more than three hundred thousand of them are today.

"Why wasn't your Socialist teaching of that day better enforced?" asked the Pastor.

That only proves the truth of the Socialist contention that the economic conditions were not ripe, nor was there then enough people sufficiently enlightened to take in the whole truth. There was those then, in advance of others, as now. Here, again, is your class struggle over the product of labor. The materialistic basis of history, which Marx taught. Let it not be forgotten that our ability to enlighten the people depends largely on moral convictions.

"That is the thing I exceedingly dislike in your Socialist

philosophy," said the Pastor. "Because it ignores all moral basis for history."

Oh, no; just to the contrary. This dispute among the Jews brought before Nehemiah was, in your judgment, a question of right and wrong, was it not, Pastor.

"Well, yes."

Was not the land and the products of labor the material basis of this whole contention? Coveting my neighbor's goods or anything that is his, which is forbidden in the ten commandments, is a moral question, yet the material things of my neighbor is the basis of the covetousness.

Recollect, Nehemiah was a minister of god, as well as a governor and judge, and what he did, and the stand he took is an example for every minister today, so far as his influence will reach. What effect had this complaint about mortgages and oppression, upon this minister? He says:

"And I was very angry when I heard their cry, and these words." (Neh. v:6.)

Here is a minister and judge filled with righteous indignation against men for taking mortgages on the land; while, today, we find ministers and judges indignant against the Socialists, who stand where the prophet did and oppose the system built upon robbery of the poor through mortgages. Who, according to the prophet, was to blame for this violation of the Jewish law opposed to mortgages and oppression?

"Then I consulted with myself, and I rebuked the nobles and the rulers and said unto them; ye exact usury, every one of his brother. And I sat a great assembly against them." (Neh. v:7.)

Pastor, we Socialists think you preachers had better do like this one did, consult yourselves and rebuke the nobles and rulers, who are loaded with mortgages on the people.

Here, in Nehemiah's day, the usurers are at work skinning the workers, but the prophet places himself on the side of the oppressed. And he takes the Socialist position and arrays, on his side, the masses against the classes, for he says: "I set a great assembly against them." Left it to the people. When the oppressed and oppressor confronted each other in the assembly, the judge:

"Said unto them: 'We, after our ability, have redeemed our brethren, the Jews, which were sold unto the heathen, and will ye even sell your brethren? Or shall they be sold unto us?' Then held they their peace, and found nothing to answer." (Neh. v:8.)

The Jewish mortgage holders claimed like professed Christian mortgage holders, that they had more light and knowledge than the heathen around them, and yet did as bad as any of them.

So we claim a higher civilization than the heathen around us, but where is the nation of natives, in the wilds of "Darkest Africa," a part of whose people live from mortgages on the others? Mark you, the judge in his address to the contending parties, held that these mortgages literally meant the selling of one man into the hands of another, and the same cause produces the like effect today.

"Then they held they their peace and found nothing to answer." Just as the position of the Socialists of today is unanswerable.

Seeing the advantage he had the judge continued in his withering address and said:

"It is not good that you do, ought ye not to walk in the fear of our God, because of the reproach of the heathen, our enemies?" (Neh. v:9.)

What was not good then is no better now; and those mortgage sharks brought the cause of God into reproach, just as the same class in the church has made Christianity a laughing stock among unbelievers today.

Today it is not an uncommon thing for preachers and judges to have their pockets full of mortgages. But here is a judge who said:

"I, likewise, and my brethren and my servants (officers) might exact of them money and corn; I pray you, let us leave off this usury!" (Neh. v:10.)

And here comes the court decision:

"Restore, I pray you, to them, even this day, their lands, their houses, also the hundredth part of the money, and of the corn, the wine, and the oil, that ye exact of them." (Neh. v:10.)

All at once. This decision is more far-reaching than what the Socialists are asking for. We are asking only that the system be so changed as to restore to the people the possession of the land, factories, and means of transportation, and we do not ask for the money, which will be of no further use under the new condition.

"Then why did Nehemiah make the demand?" asked the Pastor.

Because the new commonwealth was not yet set up, being taught, only, in prospect.

When these robbers of the poor saw that the great assembly of the people, and the judge, was against them, they said:

"We will restore them and will require nothing of them; so will we do as thou sayest. Then (said Nehemiah) I called the priest and took an oath of them, that they should do according to their promise." (Neh. v:12.)

It was the duty of the priest, it appears, to see that the judgment of the court was duly executed.

The session of the court is here closed with the following significant and solemn declaration:

"So God shake out every man from his house, and from his labor, that performeth not this promise, even be he shaken out and emptied. And all the congregation said, Amen, praise the Lord! And the people did according to this promise." (Neh. v:19.)

Unless this system of exploitation is stopped there will be a great shaking out and emptying of the modern nations, as it was with the ancients.

Go preach this wholesome doctrine to your congregation, Pastor, and see if they will say, "Amen, praise the Lord!"

Like Nehemiah, the Socialists believe that the masses of the people will do to rely upon to perform their promises, when they understand the economic conditions.

"In my talks with Scientific Socialists, when I offered the golden Rule as a solution for these difficulties, they laughed at me as Utopian," said the Pastor.

Sir Thomas More's *Utopia*,[6] written in 1516, has become another name for "visionary." That man has love, is as much a scientific fact, as that he has reason. And it is no more true that his love will be governed by his material interests than that his reason will. History will prove that men have had their scientific reasonings warped as much by their material interest as their love.

How, then, can any position be scientific that ignores any of the attributes of man? The only way any science of economics can escape being denounced as utopian or visionary by its opponents, is by being put into practice. Until put in operation Socialism will continue to be denounced as utopian. That man, only, is a Scientific Socialist who ignores none of the characteristics of man bearing on this movement. With the understanding that all of them may be affected, in a greater or less degree, by what we deem our material interest. The Bible, in dealing with man, uses not only the Golden Rule, but says, also: "Come, let us reason together!" (Isa. i:18.) Thus appealing to both love and reason.

Indeed, this case, before Nehemiah, is one in which the class struggle is very apparent, and the material interest is uppermost on both sides.

To say Socialism is a science is simply to say that it is based upon truth.

Whenever a thing is proven not to be true, it is shown not to be scientific.

We bring this subject to the Bible, because we Christians hold the Bible to be based upon truth. These plain teachings of the Bible ought to settle the question of Socialism with you and me.

VII

What Christ Said on Usury

"We are not living under the Jewish law now. Christ came to bring a new condition of things," said the Pastor.

Suppose we find out just what he did say regarding interest on money. He said to the Jews:

"Search the scriptures—and they are they which testify of me." (John v:39.)

Christ and his followers based their arguments upon the books of the old Bible as infallible authority. So it is safe to say that what these books teach, Christ believed.

Your church, I see, is wanting to borrow money to help out on your new building. There are professed Christian men who are money lenders; go tell them you want a loan on the conditions Christ prescribed and see how much you will get. If they want to know what you mean, tell them that Christ said: "Lend, hoping for nothing again, and your reward shall be great." (Luke vi:35.)

He didn't say five percent, six percent, or any other rate, but he stood upon the Jewish law opposed to robbing the workers through interest.

"But a man could not live and loan money that way," said the Pastor.

All that is admitted. But we do not need to maintain any such a system, in order that a few men may thrive at the expense of the many.

It is evident that what Christ meant was, that so long as this system lasts we ought to loan to our brother in need, as the Jewish law required, without trying to add to his burden by charging him interest. And the man who would borrow to re-loan, simply aims to rob his brother, and divide the steal with the man he borrowed from.

"But what will you Socialist preachers make out of this scripture?" said the Pastor, taking up his Bible and reading:

"For the kingdom of heaven is as a man traveling into a far country, who called his own servants and delivered unto them his goods. And unto one he gave five talents; to another two; and to another, one; to every man according to his several ability, and straightway took his journey. Then he that had received the five talents went and traded with the same and made them other five talents. And likewise he that had received two, he, also, gained other two. But he that had received one went and digged in the earth and hid his Lord's money. After a long time the Lord of those servants cometh and reckoneth with them. And so he that had received five talents came and brought other five talents, saying: 'Lord, thou deliverest unto me five talents; behold, I have gained besides them five talents more.' His Lord said unto him: 'Well done, thou good and faithful servant, thou hast been faithful over a few things, I will make thee ruler over many things; enter thou into the joy of thy lord.' He, also, that had received two talents came and said: 'Lord, thou deliverest unto me two talents: behold, I have gained another two talents besides them.' His lord said unto him: 'Well done, good and faithful servant; thou hast been faithful over a few things, I will make thee ruler over many things; enter thou into the joy of thy lord.' Then he which had received the one talent came and said: 'Lord, I knew thee that thou art a hard man, reaping where thou hast not sown and gathering where thou hast not strewed, and I was afraid and went and hid thy talent in the earth; lo, there! thou hast that is thine.' His lord answered and said unto him: 'Thou wicked and slothful servant, thou knewest that I reaped where I sewed not, and gathered where I had not strewed; thou oughtest, therefore, to have put my money to the exchangers, and then, at my coming, I should have received mine own with usury. Take, therefore, the talent from him and give it unto him which hath ten talents. For unto every one that hath shall be given, and he shall have abundance; but from him that hath not shall be taken away even that which he hath. And cast ye the unprofitable servant into outer darkness; there shall be weeping and gnashing of teeth." (Matt. xxv:14-19.)

This is the story of a rich man who had money to loan, and let it out to the three men here mentioned. It was customary among the nations around the Jews to loan money on interest. And it was lawful so to do. But the Jews could not do it without violating their law, as we have seen. It does not necessarily follow, therefore, that Christ had in view a Jew, when he used the parable. This money lender, who took his journey into a far country, was like the same class today who journey at others' expense. Two of the borrowers went into business and soon doubled their money, which could, of course, only be done through some one of the forms of usury or interest, which the Bible forbids.

When the money loaner returned and settled accounts with the two first men he was very much pleased with their wonderful business ability and invited them to rejoice with him. It is altogether likely they had a big feast as it was customary then as now.

"But what of the third man?" said the Pastor.

The third man, we are told, hid the money and, at the end, returned the principal without interest, giving as a reason that he knew the money loaner to be a hard man, reaping where he had not sown and gathering where he had not strewed.

That is exactly what Socialists say today: the capitalist reaps where he has not sown; that is, he takes the wealth created by the worker, without giving him an equivalent.

And where is there anything that so hardens a man as this sordid and heartless accumulation of wealth he did not produce, without regard to the suffering of the producer?

The usurer, himself, inadvertently admits that the man's complaint was well founded, when he said: "Thou knewest that I was a hard man, reaping where I had not strewn," etc.

"But why does the Lord Jesus commend the first two and condemn the last?" said the Pastor.

I see you fall into the usual error of the average preacher, and forget that all the way through this narrative the lord here mentioned is the money loaner and not Christ. Who else would the money lender be expected to commend but the fellow who had successfully fleeced the people. Just as that class does now, and condemn those who think that the usurers are hard men.

You hold, yourself, that the members of your church who have squeezed most out of the people are a success, while condemning the man as a failure who is too honest or conscientious to do the same.

So, as usual, the money was taken away from the man who had failed to fleece the people and given to the man who had showed his ability to do so. While the man who had failed, as was then the custom, was cast into a dungeon or outer darkness, which simply alludes to the ancient methods of imprisonment for debt.

The two men who had been faithful over a few things, were made rulers over many; or, in other words, promoted to better things, as all faithful servants of the capitalist class are today.

The money changers, mentioned in this connection, is only another name for bankers. And the man who hid the one talent was told that, in place of hiding it, he should have banked it, which would have brought enough to pay the interest along with the principal.

Keep it in mind that Christ is telling us of an every day incident to illustrate a point, just as a Socialist of today might do without commending the act.

"Well, in your judgment, what did he intend us to understand by it, if he did not mean to sanction interest?" said the Pastor.

It is plain, from what follows in the rest of the chapter, that he meant simply that, in the end of the world, he would be just as strict in settling accounts with men as the usurer. To make him sanction all there is in every incident he related would be to simply make him ridiculous.

But, in due time, we will prove from his own statements that he did not mean to sanction interest.

The only sense in which the money lender represented Christ was in the strictness of his dealing with the men he had loaned to.

A homely story will serve to illustrate the folly of holding a speaker to account for all the inferences that might be drawn from what he says. To show how a person may be found on first one side, and then on the other of the same question, we have often told the story of the Master who sent his slave to take another man a fine pig as a present, and the slave stopping at a drinking place on the way, laid down the sack containing the pig and went into drink, and while in the house some one took out the pig and put in a pup. When he reached his destination the man refused to receive the pup and started the slave back. But on his way the slave stopped again at the same place, and the parties took out the pup and put in the pig again. When he reached home again and found he had the pig again, as a solution of the mystery he declared the thing could be first pig and then pup.

Now, suppose some one was to construe us as favoring both slavery and drunkenness, as both appear in the story, uncondemned, and you have the way in which some insist on misunderstanding Christ.

Luke relates another parable of the Master's, very similar to the one given by Matthew, only, in this case, the money lender went off to receive a kingdom and loaned his money to ten persons on interest. And when he returned, the first and second man had doubled their money and was commended by him, while a third returned only the principal and was condemned. It is significant that in this case, as the one in Matthew, the usurer is accused of being bad and admitted it. Here the class of men called money changers in Matthew are called bankers by Luke. This incident may be found in Luke xix:9-26.

"But you promised to show that Christ was opposed to interest," said the Pastor.

Well, we are told that Christ rode into the city of Jerusalem, and went into the temple at the time of the great feast. What he did there is recorded by more than one of the apostles, but what Matthew says is enough:

"And Jesus went into the temple of God and cast out all them that sold and bought in the temple, and overthrew the tables of the money changers (bankers), and the seats of them that sold doves. And said unto them, it is written: 'My house shall be called a house of prayer,' but ye have made it a den of thieves." (Matt. xxi:12,13.)

Now, here is the same money loaning and exploiting class, mentioned in the two parables, and in place of giving them sanction Christ drove them out, declaring them a set of thieves.

"Oh, that was only because they brought their business into the house of God!" remarked the Pastor.

So they used to tell us in Sunday school, but we learned better than that before we became Socialist. It came to us that if that was all the trouble, stealing would be all right so long as it was not done in the house of God. For, mark you! these bankers were violating God's law against interest, and Christ condemned the thing as stealing. The difference is, that Christ drove these bankers, which he called thieves, out of God's house, and you take them in.

The church buildings are dedicated to God, as was the temple, why don't you do like your Master, drive these thieves out of the church of God? That is, turn them out! out of the church.

"It seems to me that you are taking a great deal on yourself, to call the many good Christian men among bankers thieves," said the Pastor.

Don't condemn me! I am calling them just what the Master calls them. If Christ came into the church today and found these men running things, would he not cast them out now as he did then?

These men, according to history, were doing just as our bankers do today. They loaned money to the people who came to the great feast from distant lands and exchanged for them the foreign coin for that of the realm for a rate of interest that Christ called stealing.

"Perhaps they were only making their rates too high," remarked the Pastor.

Did we not show you that the law under which they lived forbid any increase, or in other words, there was no law allowing interest on the Jewish statute books? It is evident, then, that Christ meant that taking any interest was stealing.

Go, follow the Master's example, and drive these thieves out of your churches. And to do this, it is not necessary for the church to wait to establish Socialism. Wherever a church does this, its individual members will be prepared to vote the Socialist ticket, by getting the beam of capitalism out of the eye of the church, so as to see clearly to drive it out of the state.

When the bankers met recently in their annual convention in the city of San Francisco, they were not only made welcome by professed Christians, but different city pastors opened the convention with prayer, asking the same Christ who drove them out as thieves to bless and prosper them in their robbery of the people. We have just seen how Christ treated the bankers' annual convention in Jerusalem two thousand years ago. At the same time we were holding meetings among the working class, which the bankers are fleecing, on the street corners of the same city, but the reverend gentlemen never came to our meetings once.

Such men simply misrepresent Christ and the Bible. The great mass of the church members belong to the proletariat, and when they rightly understand the Bible will be with us.

"What would you have us do under such circumstances?" says the Pastor.

Follow your Master, and denounce the bankers, and vote for Socialism.

"What do you think of Christ's doctrine of non-resistance, where he says: 'But I say unto you, that you resist not evil,' Matthew v:39?" said the Pastor.

Christ's own life, afterwards, shows what he meant by it. It will be admitted that he set the example, as we shall have occasion to show, of denouncing the cruel practices of men in the most severe manner, just as he drove them out of the temple. The Jews were then living under the Roman law, and Christ took the same position that every good Socialist takes, and that is, abide by the laws of the land until they can be changed. We tell the people that the capitalist majority, now in control, must not be resisted by physical force until we get the majority. In the meantime we go on, as Christ did, getting the people ready for the coming change.

"And if any man shall sue thee at the law and take away thy coat, let him take thy cloak also. And whosoever shall compel thee to go a mile, go with him twain" (two). (Matt. v:40,41.)

This was a Roman custom, compelling persons to act as government couriers; for we have shown that under Jewish law you could not take a man's coat or cloak for debt, or compel him to go a mile. These customs, according to Christ, were evil, but he would have the disciples show a readiness to obey while they lasted. And he then spent his entire ministry in teaching a doctrine that would overthrow these evils. Do not Socialists obey the laws, however bad, and go on teaching the evil of them, with the expectation that you who oppose Socialism will obey when the laws are changed, as you expect us to do now?

"I think that I have heard some Socialists remark that Christ's doctrine of loving our enemies and those which spitefully use us, is going a little too far," said the Pastor.

But ask that same Socialist what he wants to do with the capitalist, who has been starving and freezing him and his children, shooting laboring men down, cursing them, etc., and he will tell you that Socialism means the brotherhood of man, and that he wants to put this same enemy on an equal economic footing with himself. And is not that the only true way to show love to an enemy? The laboring man gets plenty of that so-called love, that comes only from the lips, now. But that don't better his condition.

"Don't you Socialists justify men in taking advantage of this condition, which you call 'skinning your fellow-men,' while it lasts? You certainly know that Christ did not, but taught that it was better to suffer wrong than to do wrong," said the Pastor.

All Socialists are not Christians. But some are. Therefore, they may hold different opinions as to whether it is better to skin or be skinned, under this capitalist system. But the economic conditions are such that we must do one or the other. Upon this all Socialists are agreed. But as most Socialists consist of the poor wealth producers, very few of them are so situated as to do anything but be skinned, in place of skinning. For my part, I agree with the Master, whether others do or not. He also said:

"Render, therefore, unto Caesar the things that are Caesar's." (Matt. xii:21.)

That is, pay your tax to the Roman government. No one who has read the discourses of Christ can suppose he sanctioned the tyranny of the Roman government, but like us Socialists, he meant, pay your tax and wait for better things, to be brought about through teaching the people.

To have taught the people to use physical resistance against oppression before the majority could be made to understand their economic conditions, would have been to bring destruction by force of arms, and a retarding of the movement, just as it would be now.

VIII

Christ and the Profit System

We have shown that rent, interest and profits all mean the same thing in principle, the only difference being that the profit taker can rob the people of so much more than rent or interest, so-called. You will recollect that Christ not only drove the bankers out of the temple, but, along with them, those that sold and bought oxen and doves as well. The history of the time shows that numbers of people from all parts of the land of Judea, as well as foreign countries, came every year to Jerusalem to the great feast. It is said by Josephus that some times an innumerable multitude came to the great feast to worship. If you will read in the Old Testament of the thousands of oxen, doves and sheep that was roasted on the altars as sacrifice, and eaten as sacred meat by the people, you will get some idea of the enormous business done during the feast each year. Then you recollect that the people from a distance had largely to buy the animals which they offered on the altars.

We have an idea that these men that bought and sold in the temple had organized what we now call a meat trust, and was getting rich out of the profits.

They are not accused of charging too much profit, but they are called thieves regardless of the amount charged.

"But how can we live and sell things without a profit?" asked the Pastor.

As we said before, we don't need to maintain the profit system. It is necessary, first, to know what we mean by profits. The merchant who makes profit must do it by charging something over and above all expenses, including the price he pays for the goods, the shipping price, rents, clerking and the expense of himself and family. And if he runs a factory or railroad the wear and tear of the machinery must be considered. When he has come out even on all these items of expense, he has not made any profit yet.

When Deacon Rockefeller and his oil company demand a dividend of eighty-eight millions of dollars in one year they meant over and above all expenses. So, then, if men were satisfied with a living they could do business without a profit, providing all were agreed. The same way about loaning having to receive nothing, if a man has not got anything he can't do it.

"But who so hath of this world's goods, and sees his brother have need, and shutteth up his bowels of compassion from him, how dwelleth the love of God in him?" (1 John v:17.)

After awhile we may have further use for this passage; but allow me to say, while passing, that before Socialism is established, the man who can ought to help the needy without robbing them first and then giving them a small pittance back, as we pointed out.

When the Cooperative Commonwealth is organized, and the people put men in the stores of the nations to distribute the goods among the workers, of course, the persons doing the distributing will receive their pay out of the same resources of the nation; which, as just stated, would be getting a living without selling goods at a profit.

So the Jewish law could have been fulfilled, if men had been willing to live on the best that their skill could produce, without laying up for themselves treasures. "Where moth and rust doth corrupt, and thieves break through and steal." But it requires both economic conditions and teaching to bring us to it.

The driving of these dealers out of the temple was a deliberate attack on the profit system, notwithstanding they went right on with the same thing the next day. But it put Christ and the new religion on record, before the people of all the distant lands there represented, as opposed to the whole profit system, whether they so understood at the time or not.

It is hardly necessary that we should dwell upon the meanness of the profit system, which aims to sell a thing, not for what it is worth, but for all that the purchaser can be compelled to pay.

Sometimes a thing is sold for a hundred times what it actually cost. A price that only covers the expense of handling an article, and allows no profit, is really only a part of the cost of production.

"If the Bible is opposed to profits, why don't it say so in so many words?" asked the Pastor.

Let me refer you to what it says in the Proverbs:

"He that by usury and unjust gain increases his substance, he shall gather it for him that pitieth the poor." (Prov. xxviii:8.)

"Thou hast taken usury and increase, and greedily gained of thy neighbor by extortion." (Ezek. xxii:12.)

I think language could hardly be plainer.

Profit is the greatest way of gaining of our neighbors by extortion, known to the exploiters of mankind.

"How do you make profit extortion? I thought that extortion was generally considered wrong by everybody, but you seem to be of the opinion that it may be legalized as well," said the Pastor.

Any institution, possessed of the power to compel us to buy at a profit of it, or go without, is an extortionist. Paul told the church not to keep company with an extortioner. (1 Cor. v:ii.) That is, not allow him to be a member. But many churches are glad of the company of Mr. Rockefeller and his class today—the greatest extortionist living.

Before you go, allow me to call your attention to the fact that the natural resources of the earth is sometimes called a profit.

Speaking of this fact, the Bible says:

"Moreover, the profit of the earth is for all." (Eccl. v:9.)

That is exactly what the Socialists are contending for throughout the world. The profits or produce of the earth, under the present system, goes to the few rich in place of to all.

When you come again, Pastor, suppose at our next setting we consider what the Bible says of the poor and their oppressors. All right! Good night.

IX

The Poor and Their Oppressors

When we met again, after some evening, to resume our research, the Pastor said:

"I dislike, exceedingly, the class hatred the Socialists are keeping up."

You misunderstand us, sir. We simply recognize the struggle the unequal division of wealth has forced upon us, and are determined to put it down by bringing about an equal division of the

The Bible and Socialism   137

products of labor among the producers. What is said of the poor and their oppressors in the Bible is but a history of the class struggle. And the Bible stands with the Socialist party in the defense of the poor.

Suppose we consider, first, the law of Moses on that subject.

In talking over the question of interest, we had occasion to point to the twenty-second chapter of Exodus, and the twenty-fifth verse, about loaning to the poor and taking their raiment to pledge; you remember that the law, which forbid interest and destroyed the mortgage system, was enacted for the benefit of the poor, which the rich was robbing then, as now.

We find, on looking through the Bible, so much said on this subject that we will have to confine our evening's conversation to a review of the most pointed passages, and that without quoting too extensively, leaving you to look them up at your leisure.

Suppose, while you have the book in hand, Pastor, you read from the sixth to the eighth verse of the twenty-third chapter of Exodus:

"Thou shalt not wrest the judgment of thy poor in his cause. Keep thee far from a false matter; and the innocent and righteous slay thou not, for I will not justify the wicked. Thou shall take no gift, for the gift blindeth the wise and perverteth the word of the righteous."

This was an instruction to those who had the law to enforce, not to decide in favor of the rich, as against the poor, as is generally done today. It is notoriously admitted that the poor stand but little show in a contest with the rich in the courts.

"But wasn't that true then, as now?" said the Pastor.

We are not trying to show that the Jews always kept the law, but, rather, that the law looked forward in the future to just what we Socialists do; and the nation went to pieces because they did not keep it.

The men who favor the present system are not keeping "away from false matters," but are, to the extent of their influence, responsible for the slaying of the innocents in mine and factory, by overwork, insufficient food and clothes, and at the hand of the military; and these victims are both men, women and little children.

"Gifts, which blind the eyes of the wise and pervert judgment," which the law here opposes, can only be prevented by Socialism taking away the opportunity to profit through gifts, by abolishing poverty.

The ninth verse of the chapter just referred to is careful to forbid the oppression of the stranger, in any way, the very thing that capitalism, everywhere, insists on doing. While the tenth and eleventh verses say:

"Six years thou shalt sow thy land, and shall gather in the fruits thereof, but the seventh year thou shalt let it rest and lie still, that the poor of my people may eat and what they leave the beasts of the field shall eat. In a like manner shalt thou deal with thy vineyards, and with thy olive yards."

There, every seventh year, the entire natural product of this wonderfully fruitful country was left to the poor. Think of the value of the olive oil, grapes, and fruits of the land, and you get some idea. And the owners were not allowed to take anything.

Perhaps the best way to understand this is to think what it would mean were the poor of the United States to be allowed the entire natural crop of the nation, all the fruit of our fine orchards, vineyards and nuts every seven years. And then, again, recollect the farmer was told during the six years:

"When ye reap the harvest of your land, thou shalt not wholly reap the corners of thy fields, neither shalt thou gather the gleanings of thy harvest.

"And thou shalt not glean thy vineyards, neither shalt thou gather every grape of thy vineyards; thou shalt leave them for the poor and the stranger." (Lev. xix:9,10.)

So the poor was not to be permitted to suffer during the six years, besides getting all the crop every seventh year. Now all this was not Socialism, but, as we said, it was to prepare.

"I admit it is decidedly a new view of the thing," remarked the Pastor.

If it is true, why not preach it to your people, and show them that Socialism is a part of what the Bible has been leading up to all this time, and that we are now about to make the final and last step in to the Cooperative Commonwealth. Under this law no one had to tramp the country, hungry, and be arrested and jailed by those who preach the brotherhood of man. But he was free to go into any man's vineyard, orchard, or grain field, and help himself if hungry. You will understand that Christ and his apostles were in harmony with the law when they were plucking the ears of corn on the Sabbath day. You recollect the Jews made no complaint about the corn, but pretended that it was a violation of the Sabbath. (Mark ii:23,28.)

"You say that this condition, under the law, was not complete Socialism. What is the difference?" asked the Pastor.

Under Socialism all industries, as we have explained, will be carried on by people working together collectively, and each one having his proportionate share of the products as his individual property. There would, then, be no one person poorer than another in the community, and poverty will be no more. That the law was intended to be temporary, and lead to better things, is seen in the declaration that a lawgiver should not depart from Judea till Shiloh come, which was Christ. (Gen. xlix:10.)

We pointed, before, to the temporary nature of the law in one of our previous conversations. Under the jubilee law a poor man or his friends might redeem the land, which his poverty had compelled him to sell, at any time, and if they were not able, it all returned to him or his family at the year of jubilee. The seventh or Sabbatical year cancelled all debts.

Thus establishing the idea, as Socialists now contend, that one generation of people are under no obligation to pay the debts of another. Socialism proposes to follow the Bible, you preach from, and release all the land by setting up the Cooperative Commonwealth, and canceling forever all the billions of debt in the civilized world. (Lev. xxv:25-34, Ex. xxiii:10,11.)

International Socialism is making ready to sound the trumpet of the jubilee around the world, proclaiming liberty to all mankind from the bondage of capitalism.

"This doctrine of the repudiation of all indebtedness, is another one of the obnoxious features of Socialism, which I cannot accept," said the Pastor.

By that, you mean to say that you do not accept the teaching of the Book you preach from, as does the Socialist party that makes no pretensions to be a Christian organization, but manifests its willingness to accept the truth, whether in or out of the Bible.

There is no doctrine more plainly taught in the Bible than this release from debt.

"But we are not living under the law of Moses, now," said the Pastor.

All the obligations of one man to another is not only binding on us yet, but were put into the law because they were binding. What is the use for us preachers to condemn infidelity, which is simply a want of faith in the Bible, and then deny some of its most wholesome teachings ourselves?

As things are now, debts accumulate mountain high and are like millstones around the neck of unborn generations. Socialism would not only set these debts aside, but the possibility of making more.

"But is not this a direct sanction of the wages system, as I said the other evening?" remarked the Pastor.

"Thou shalt not defraud thy neighbor; neither rob him; the wages of him that is hired shall not abide with thee all night until the morning," (Lev. xix:13.) quote the Pastor.

The man who, through law, places himself in possession of all capital, and defrauds his neighbor out of his product, violates the first part of the passage. The Socialists say that men ought to let the worker have the wages promised without keeping it back for months. Yet he does not therefore sanction the wages system. Nor does the law here say that the man who does the hiring produces the wages, but, only that he should not keep them back, as is done now.

All loans were to be released every seven years. This law did not extend to outside nations, but, only, to the stranger that dwelt among the Jews. So the benefits of Socialism could only extend to those who adopted it, but when adopted by the principal nations, it would soon become world-wide.

But, regardless of this law of release, they were required to loan the poor, ungrudgingly, all he needed, except at times when there was no poor in the land.

"Where do you find that?" said the Pastor, opening his Bible to Deut. xv:1-11. "The eleventh verse, here, corroborates what I said in one of our previous conversations. We are always to have the poor with us. I will read it," said the Pastor: "'For the poor shall never cease out of the land.' And Jesus said: 'The poor ye have always with you.' Now, putting these two quotations together, your talk about Socialism abolishing poverty falls to the ground, so far as the Bible is concerned."

The land referred to was the country of the Jews to whom the law was given. Knowing their disposition to violate the command: "Thou shalt love thy neighbor as thyself," God said: "The poor shall never cease out of the land." Had they kept the commandments the poor would have ceased.

All we claimed for the law is, that its ultimate end was Socialism. Christ said to Judas, when he complained that the valuable ointment the woman poured on his head might have been sold and the proceeds given to the poor: "The poor ye have always with you." Not the poor ye shall have always with you. Did not the disciples have the poor always with them? Now take the golden rule, do unto all men as you would they should do unto you, and see how poverty could continue with that enforced!

In your desire to have the poor always with you you misconstrue Christ's language into a declaration that poverty should always prevail, in place of a statement of conditions prevailing at the time and which will continue, only, till conditions are changed.

When I see the rich class so anxious to always have the poor with them, I suspect that, like Judas, they care not for the poor, but, as Christ said of him: they are thieves. Oh, I know that sounds a little harsh, but why not take in all of what Christ said in that connection, while we are at it? See Matt. XXXVI:6-13, John VII:1-8.

The incident, related by Nathan the prophet, of the rich man with "exceedingly many flocks and herds," taking the poor man's single ewe lamb, and the consequent indignation of David, showed a state of things contrary to the law then, which we have legalized now. You know that the man with exceeding many flocks and herds, houses and lands, takes what little the poor has left now; but do you condemn it as this man did? No; you stand with the rich, who takes the poor man's lamb. (2 Sam. xii:1-6.)

This condition went on till, finally, these robbers of the poor reaped what they had sown, as we find recorded in the twenty-fifth chapter of 2 Kings.

When Nebuchadnezzar destroyed Jerusalem and carried away and burned up what they had stolen from the poor, it is a sample of just what we will some day have here, unless we get Socialism. This was only, as usual, a war among exploiters in which the poor killed each other for their oppressors.

So Nebuchadnezzar, we are told, "left of the poor of the land to be vinedressers and husbandmen." That was to create wealth for their new masters, just as the capitalists do in conquered countries today. These things are recorded in the Bible, but the ministry fail to present them to the people in their true light.

"But does not Jeremiah say that Nebuchadnezzar 'left of the poor, which had nothing in the land of Judea, and gave them vineyards and fields,' at the same time?" said the Pastor.

That but brings out the Socialists' contention about the poor being robbed by the rich, as these people had nothing to show for their work. From these vineyards and fields the people had to work out the annual tribute, to be paid to the king of Babylon, as they continued to do in the days of Nehemiah, under the Persian administration.

The references to this struggle, between the rich and the poor, is so abundant in the book of Job that we will, in most cases, only refer you to it, Pastor, and let you read it in your own study.

One of Job's friends, as though reflecting on him, declared: "The triumphing of the wicked is short," and goes on to say, "His children shall seek to please the poor, and his hands shall restore their goods." (Job xx:1-10.)

So we say: Restore the capital of the country, which is a part of the goods taken from the poor producer, and only cooperative ownership will do that.

You will remember that Job lived in Arabia, before the law of Moses was given. But here is a passage so strikingly in harmony with the Socialist idea of the class struggle that I cannot refrain from reading it as a whole:

"Why, seeing times are not hidden from the Almighty, do they that know him not see his days? Some remove the land marks, they violently take away the flocks and feed thereof. They drive away the asses of the fatherless, they take the widow's ox for a pledge. They turn the needy out of the way, the poor of the earth hide themselves together. Behold as the wild ass in the desert go they forth to their work, rising betimes for a prey, the wilderness yieldeth food for them and for their children. They reap every one his corn in the field, they gather the vintage of the wicked. They cause the naked to lodge without clothing, that they have no covering in the cold. They are wet with showers of the mountains and embrace the rock for want of a shelter. They pluck the fatherless from the breast and take a pledge of the poor. They cause him to go naked without clothing, and take away the sheaf from the hungry; which make oil within their walls and tread their wine press and suffer thirst. Men groan out of the city, and the soul of the wounded crieth out. Yet God layeth not folly to them. They are of those that rebel against the light, they know not the ways thereof, nor abide in the paths thereof. The murderer rising with the light killeth the poor and the needy, and in the night is as a thief." (Job xxiv:1-14.)

None of these things, we are told, is hid from the Almighty. We see, here, the effect of trying to divide the earth among individuals, which led to the removing of land marks. The flocks and herds of the poor was taken from them. The widows and the poor had to give pledges, or mortgages, on their little all. Others were driven to live out on the commons, like the wild ass, and they and their children had to live on the wild fruits of the wilderness, exposed to the showers, and make their homes in the shadow of the rocks. While they reaped the fields and gathered the vintage of the wealthy they, themselves, were naked for clothing. And while they made oil for others, they often had the sheaf of raw again, which their pinching hunger made them glad to eat, taken from them, The groans of the poor workers, being murdered in the cities, had become terrible, then, as now.

There is not a thing in this description of the poor and their oppressors that is not paralleled in the conditions of today. That sort of thing destroyed the nations of the past, and would do the same thing for the modern nations, were it not for the oncoming of Socialism, which is God's plan of putting an end to this struggle of the ages. Compare this scripture with what you see recorded in your daily papers about the desperation of the poor, in mine, field and factory, and the babes, taken from their mother's breast, working therein.

Elihu, one of Job's friends, in his discourse, speaking of God, says:

"He delivereth the poor in his affliction, and openeth their ears in oppression." (Job xxxvi:15.)

God delivered the Negro from his oppression by using other men as instruments.

Now, here is an opportunity to let yourself be used in the work of delivering the poor from their oppressions, and they are about you on every hand, even attending your services.

"Your scheme of Socialism is visionary and impracticable," said the Pastor.

Then, so is the Bible we preach from, when it says:

"The needy shall not always be forgotten; the expectation of the poor shall not perish forever." (Psalms ix:18.)

Will you go before the people and tell them that passage is impracticable? And here is some more of the same thing you call impracticable prophecy:

"For the oppression of the poor, for the sighing of the needy, now will I arise, saith the Lord; I will set him in safety from him that pulleth at him." (Psalms xii:5.)

And here we find men, claiming to represent this God, who say that he can't do what he has promised.

We Socialists say it can be done, and we are the instruments he will use to do it with. Say, Pastor, let me give you a text for next Sunday. It is this:

"Lord, who is like unto thee, which delivereth the poor from him that is too strong for him; yea, the poor and the needy, from him that spoileth him." (Psalms xxxv:10.)

The poor is now being spoiled by the strong and crying for deliverance. If you do not like that text, may be this would suit you better:

"The wicked have drawn out the sword, and have bent the bow, to cast down the poor and the needy, and to slay such as be of upright conversation." (Psalms xxxvii:14.)

War always bears hardest on the "poor and needy," who have the fighting to do, for the benefit of the rich, but preachers laud war today as a blessing.

"But did not the Jews carry on war, and that at the command of God?" asked the Pastor.

Yes, war has been the means by which all the great robber empires of the past have been overthrown; and the Jews themselves, were told at the time that they would go the same way, unless they did the right thing, and they did. The Socialists are opposed to war, but they recognize that it is an outgrowth of economic conditions and can never be removed until we change capitalism for Socialism, or private ownership of capital for cooperative ownership. I think this was written for the encouragement of the class-conscious Socialists.

"Blessed is he that considereth the poor." (Psalms xlii:1.)

And then, if possible, we like this one better:

"He shall judge the poor of the people, he shall save the children of the needy, and shall break in pieces the oppressor." (Psalms lxxii:4.)

Go preach the first part of that text to the needy children of the poor in the factories, and apply the latter part to their oppressors or get out of the pulpit and make way for some one who will do it. And, in the meantime, the twelfth verse might help you out as a context:

"For he shall deliver the needy when he crieth, the poor, also, and him that hath no helper."

Don't you hear the cry of the needy for help?

This is what the Socialist party, throughout the world, has been organized for, to "Defend the poor and fatherless; do justice to the afflicted and needy; rid them out of the hand of the wicked." (Psalms xxxii:3, 4.)

Do you believe this, Pastor?

"I know that the Lord will maintain the cause of the afflicted and the rights of the poor?"

"Certainly, I do! Why do you ask?"

Go and do likewise, then. Although Solomon's administration was very oppressive, as we shall see when we come to consider the rich men of the Bible; among many things, he said some that harmonizes with the Socialist's views. For instance, when he said:

"The destruction of the poor is their poverty." (Prov. x:15.)

Poverty, which we want to abolish, has destroyed whole nations. Again:

"Much food is in the tillage of the poor." (Prov. xiii:29.)

That is, simply, a recognition of the principle that wealth is only created by the labor of the poor.

Here is the same thing that Socialists complain of:

"The poor is hated even of his own neighbors, but the rich hath many friends." (Prov. xiv:20.)

The same indictment we bring, that the life of the poor worker is considered of less worth than the product he produces. He is robbed by his rich neighbor, through interests and profits, and then despised because he is not rich, while everybody is the friend of the man who got rich at his expense.

"He that hath mercy on the poor, happy is he." (Prov. xiv:21.)

There can be no greater mercy on the poor than to give him what he produces.

"He that oppresseth the poor reproacheth his Maker, but he that honoreth him hath mercy on the poor." (Prov. xiv:31.)

And yet, under capitalism, we have the greatest oppressors of the poor in the churches, pretending to honor their Maker. Of the same import is the following:

"Who so mocketh the poor reproacheth his Maker." (Prov. xvii:5.)

Here is your classes, again:

"The poor useth entreaties, but the rich answereth roughly." (Prov. xviii:23.)

Showing the servility of the poor and the arrogance of the rich, which will continue until conditions are changed. That the unequal division of wealth separate the people, read this:

"Wealth maketh many friends, but the poor is separated from his neighbor." (Prov. xix:4.) That is, inequality of wealth divide men into classes.

This is a good one for the preachers whose ears are stopped

with dollars, in the shape of a salary:

"Who so stoppeth his ears at the cry of the poor, he, also, shall cry himself, but shall not be heard." (Prov. xxi:13.)

"The rich ruleth over the poor, and the borrower is servant of the lender." (Prov. xxii:7.)

Here, in these few words, we see the whole Socialist contention of the class rule of the rich over the poor, and how the rich loan back to them what they took from them, through keeping the larger portion of what they produced and thus, through billions of dollars of indebtedness, keep them forever their servants.

The Bible calls this condition the same thing we do, when it says, following after what we just read:

"Rob not the poor, because he is poor." (Prov. xxii:22.)

I think that the intelligent poor can fully appreciate the significance of this passage, as they have had enough of it:

"As a roaring lion and raging bear, so is a wicked ruler over the poor people." (Prov. xxviii:15.)

As a fair sample of what the rich have been to the poor, in all ages, hear this:

"The rich man is wise in his own conceit, but the poor that hath understanding searcheth him out." (Prov. xxviii:11.)

This was never truer than today. The rich man, who has robbed the poor producer of a fortune, is wise in his own conceit and looks with contempt upon the poor Socialist agitator, but understanding the economic situation enables him to search the true solution of the trouble.

Open thy mouth, judge righteously and plead the cause of the poor and needy." (Prov. xxxi:9.)

When the poor and needy, for which we stand, can get their cause rightly judged by the majority of the voters they will win, because justice is on their side. What you need, Pastor, is to get your mouth open in behalf of the needy.

"Well, there always has been poor people in the world," he answered.

True! But things are not going according to the Bible, as you see, from what we have read. The Creator fit the world up with an abundance of everything necessary for comfortable, human existence, and if the intention was that anybody should be poor, why array himself on the side of the poor as against the rich? Socialism is a movement of the poor against their rich oppressors.

"Well, I am much interested in the subject of the poor and their oppressors," said the Pastor, as he rose to take leave, as the hour was getting late; "and when I come tomorrow evening I would like to have the same subject continued."

X

The Poor and Their Oppressors (Continued)

You will remember, in our last conversation on the subject of "The Poor and Their Oppressors," we ended with the Book of Proverbs, we remarked, as we were seated around the table on the next evening, with Bibles in hand.

"Yes, I recollect that! What next?" said the Pastor.

Suppose we begin with Isaiah 1:10-17.

"Hear the word of the Lord, ye rulers of Sodom; give ear unto the law of our God, ye people of Gomorrah! To what purpose is the multitude of your sacrifices unto me? saith the Lord. I am full of the burnt offerings of rams, and fat of fed beasts, and I delight not in the blood of bullocks, of lambs or he goats. When ye come to appear before me, who hath required this at your hand to tread my courts? Bring me no more vain oblations, incense is an abomination unto me; the new moons and Sabbaths, the calling of assemblies, I cannot away with it, is iniquity, even the solemn meeting. Your new moons and your appointed feasts my soul hateth, they are a trouble unto me, I am weary to bear them. And when you spread forth your hands, I will hide mine eyes from you; yea, when you make many prayers I will not hear; your hands are full of blood. Wash you, make you clean, put away the evil of your doings from before mine eyes; cease to do evil, learn to do well; seek judgment (justice), relieve the oppressed, judge the fatherless, plead for the widow."

Every Jew knew when the prophet referred to Sodom and Gomorrah, in his discourse, that they were overthrown for their wickedness, among which was the oppression of the poor. And are we to gain nothing from past history?

The Jew, like some professed Christians, thought to go on with his oppression of the poor; and satisfy God with his sacrifices, offerings, keeping the Sabbath, solemn assemblies, and prayer meetings. But God declared he would not hear them, and gave as his reason for the refusal that they oppressed the poor, the widow and the fatherless. And the reference here to judgment shows that the courts was one of the principal means of oppression.

We, in our churches, profess to worship the same God that spake all these words, and, at the same time, have in our solemn assemblies and prayer meetings men whose hands are as full of blood as those of the Jews.

The blood of the men shot down by detectives, and the militia, in strikes for more bread; together with those who die of hunger, cold and neglect in mine, sweatshop and factory is on the hands of many professed Christians.

Indeed, all who do not vote opposite to capitalism are guilty of shedding innocent blood.

Our courts, like those of the Jews, are in the hands of the oppressors.

"What can we do?" said the Pastor.

"Cease to do evil, and learn to do well," is what the Lord said. That is just what the Socialists believe in, and the only way to do that is to vote the Socialist party into power, and, by acts of legislation, take the entire plant we call capital, out of the hands of these oppressors and place it in the hands of the whole people to own and operate collectively.

So long as the churches stand for capitalism, which oppresses the poor, their prayer meeting and solemn assemblies are as much of a mockery as was those of the Jews.

These scriptures are simply to warn us; we, by act of legislation, uphold the conditions and we can undo them. God will have us do for ourselves what we can. Nor will he force us to do right, but if we do not heed, like the Jews and other nations of the past, we must suffer the consequence.

That the Lord stands on the side of justice, for the oppressed read this:

"The Lord standeth up to plead and standeth to judge the people."

Who was to blame for this oppression? Hear the prophet:

"The Lord will enter into judgment with the ancients of his people, and the princes thereof."

What had the rulers of the people done to incur the displeasure of God? Listen to him again:

"For ye have eaten up the vineyards."

And what else?

"The spoils of the poor is in your houses." (Isa. iii:13, 14.)

We read how the Lord entered into judgment with the Jews through the destruction under Nebuchadnezzar, and you know what come upon this country, because of the slavery oppression, during the late rebellion.

God has so fixed the economic laws that capitalism will bring its own punishment, and it will bare hard upon the innocent, as well as the guilty, unless prevented in time by Socialism.

The spoils of the poor, then, as now, consisted of the wealth produced by them and taken by the rich. True, the poor are allowed wages out of what they produce, but that can never equal the value of the product without destroying the wages system.

Pastor, the churches are now in the same state, many of them, as the Jews were, and, like Isaiah, you want to sound the alarm. I speak now of the church as a body; individual Christians are getting their eyes open to what the Bible teaches.

Of course, most of the non-Christian world are yet in the same position on the question of justice to the working classes, as the churches are.

"What mean ye that ye beat my people to pieces, and grind the faces of the poor? saith the Lord." (Isa. iii:15.)

Here God calls the poor his people. And these extreme accusations brought against the rich, such as breaking to pieces and grinding the face of the poor, only show the severity of the oppression.

As to how the daughters of the rich spent the spoil of the poor, let us read the following fashion plate of the daughters of Zion:

"Moreover, the Lord saith, because the daughters of Zion are haughty, and walk with stretched forth necks and wanton eyes, walking and mincing as they go, and making a tingling with their feet; therefore, the Lord will smite with a scab the crown of the head of the daughters of Zion and the Lord will discover their secret parts. In that day the Lord will take away the bravery of their tinkling ornaments about their feet, and their cauls, and their round tires like the moon, the chains, and the bracelets, and the mufflers, the bonnets, and the ornaments of the legs, and the head bands, and the tablets, and the earrings, the ring and nose jewels, the changeable suits of apparel, and the mantles, and wimples, and the crisping pins, the glasses, and the fine linen and the hoods, and the veils."(Isa. iii:16-23.)

All that display of fashion was made by the haughty daughters of the rich parasites in the streets of Jerusalem, and in the temple, and at the levees given by the Jewish kings and nobles, at the expense of the poor producers, whom they were spoiling, breaking to pieces, and robbing.

And now the prophet is sent of God to warn the nation that, unless it is stopped, the nation will be destroyed. Compare this with what you see around you today, on the street, and at the watering places, in the churches of the wealthy; how the haughty daughters of the men who have spoiled the poor, dressed in the finest apparel, wear diamonds, gold and jewels, live in the best hotels and mansions and ride in palace cars, etc., and you have an exact picture of what the prophet complained of. The Socialists are the prophets to warn the nations of today of this great wrong, and point the way out. This is the class who now feed the produce of the poor to pet dogs while babies starve.

Isaiah's remedy and ours are alike, he said: "Cease to do evil and learn to do well," and that includes all the Socialists are contending for, in a nutshell. It would seem that the prophet had us in view, as well as the people of ancient times, when he uttered the following:

"Woe to them that decree unrighteous decrees, and that write grievousness which they prescribe."

All that points to the bad laws made and enforced by

capitalists. What was the intent of these bad decrees?

"To turn aside the needy from judgment (justice) and to take away the right from the poor of my people that widows may be their prey, and that they may rob the fatherless." (Isa. x:1,2.)

Just what is being done today. The poor producer is defeated in the courts, and the fatherless robbed of everything, under mortgages and in various ways, while the cry of the widow may be heard on all sides.

Speaking of the churl or miser, in his day, the prophet said:

"He deviseth wicked devices to destroy the poor with lying words." (Isa. xxxii:7.)

The poor are still being destroyed by the lying words of those who are their political party leaders, who betray them in the interest of capitalism. God said to the prophet:

"Cry aloud, spare not, lift up thy voice like a trumpet, and shew my people their transgressions, and the house of Jacob their sins." (Isa. lviii:1.)

Follow this example and cry aloud against the oppression of today.

This is telling the agitator to be fearless in going on with the work of education. But, as you read on, you find that the Jews, like us, seemed to take daily interest in finding out the laws and ordinances of God, having their solemn fasts, afflicting their souls, and in pious pretense bowing their heads down like "bullrushes." (See Isa. lvii:2,5.)

All this pretense is carried on today by the people, both in and out of the churches, who make pretentions to justice or piety, but all this will not satisfy the Lord, who says:

"Is not this the fast that I have chosen, to loose the bands of wickedness, to undo the heavy burdens, and to let the oppressed go free, and that ye break every yoke?" (Isa. lviii:6.)

Come, Pastor, let us do as these people was told to do, take off the heavy burden which the capitalist system has bound on the toilers, who are producing all the wealth of the world, and giving it to others, while them and theirs go without. Let the oppressed in mine, factory and sweatshop go free, and break every yoke of the oppressor!

"But, how is the question to be settled?" said the Pastor.

By voting the Socialist party ticket, as I told you, and taking all capital, which is now used as an instrument of oppression, out of the hands of the oppressor, and administering it in the interest of the whole people.

"But is your plan like the one here suggested?" asked the Pastor.

As it was not possible under the law given to the Jews, to center all capital in the hands of the few, without violating the law, it was necessary, only, for them to stop violating it. But when he said:

"Is it not to deal thy bread to the hungry and that thou bring the poor that are cast out to try home, when thou seest the naked that thou cover him, and that thou hide not thyself from thine own flesh," (Isa. lviii:7.), he says just what we say. Socialism proposes that there shall be no more hunger, and will build homes for all, take away the curse of poverty, clothe all with the best garments science can produce, and regard our brothers as our own flesh. We are here plainly told what to do, how to do it is left with us.

Here is a passage that hardly needs any comment, to apply it to present conditions:

"Also, in thy skirts is found the blood of the souls of the poor innocents; I have not found it by secret search, but upon all these." (Jer. ii:34.)

The blood of the innocent poor is on the skirt of all the capitalists, and those who support them knowingly at the ballot box, whether preacher or laymen, in the church or out, and, as in the days of the prophet, this blood is not spilt in secret, but then, as now, the guilty pleaded innocence. (See Jer. ii:35.)

When your church has done its duty, as an instrument in the hands of God you can then do as here directed:

"Sing unto the Lord, praise ye the Lord, for he hath delivered the soul of the poor from the hands of evildoers." (Jer. xx:13.)

"But, you forget, he speaks here of the delivery of the soul," said the Pastor.

It is evident that the term "soul," in both this and the other passage, includes the entire man, body and all, for, otherwise, how could a "soul" suffer at the hands of "evildoers," unless still in the body. In this talk, we are attempting to deal only with what the Bible says of man's economic rights here, and not in the hereafter, which we both believe in. And many of these passages speak of things to come on earth, as already done.

Again, the Jewish oppressors of the poor are pointed to past history, which reminds us of what the lessons of the past ought to teach us. The frequency with which the prophets, and even Christ, pointed to Sodom and Gomorrah, makes it interesting to know just what was some of their sins. Ezekiel, speaking to Jerusalem, said:

"Behold, this was the iniquity of thy sister Sodom; pride, fullness of bread, and abundance of idleness was in her and in her daughters, neither did she strengthen the hand of the poor and needy." (Ezek. xvi:49.)

This abundance of idleness and fullness of bread was all at the expense of the poor, which lead to other vices. We have around us the same abundance of idleness and fullness of bread, among the rich at the expense of the poor. Under capitalism, which might better be called diabolism, we have today all the meanness going on in Sodom, in our American cities.

Speaking of a certain man in Jerusalem, God said:

"He hath oppressed the poor and needy, hath spoiled by violence, hath not restored the pledge," etc.

What disposition was to be made of this oppressor, in the general overthrow? Hear the prophet:

"He shall surely die, and his blood shall be upon him." (Ezek. xviii:12, 13.)

And, unless Socialism is peaceably established, the oppressor now, as in the days of the past, will be overthrown with great slaughter.

Such has been the well known fate of all the great oppressive nations of the days gone by.

But, probably, the most pungent of all the minor prophets on the question of "The Poor and Their Oppressor" was Amos, who lived and wrote about 787 B.C. His remarks were directed against several surrounding nations as well as the Jews. One of his indictments against the Jews was:

"Because they sold the righteous for silver, and the poor for a pair of shoes; they pant after the dust of the earth on the head of the poor," etc. (Amos ii:6.)

Do you know the righteous poor are still being sold into slavery in the silver mines and shoe factories? The panting after the dust of the earth on the poor man's head shows the intense desire to take everything from the worker. It was said of the rich then, as the Socialists say today:

"For they know not to do right, saith the Lord, who store up violence and robbery in their palaces." (Amos iii:10.) The same is still in the palaces.

So, when we say the rich are robbers, we agree with the prophet. How is this, Pastor?

"Forasmuch, therefore, as your treading is upon the poor, and ye take from him burdens of wheat: ye have built houses of hewn stones, but ye shall not dwell in them; ye have planted vineyards, but shall not drink wine of them. For I know your manifold transgressions and your mighty sins; they afflict the just, they take a bribe, and they turn aside the poor in the gate from their right." (Amos v:11,12.)

Who treads upon the poor, now, with their burdens? Who lives in the houses of hewn stone, today? Certainly not the worker, who built them. While bribe-taking is too common to excite much attention, today. Why don't you follow the example of the prophet and preach against it?

For all this oppression of the poor the Jews were threatened with destruction and the nations surrounding them, that had been destroyed for the same reason, was pointed to as a warning. Turning aside the poor from their rights in the gates referred to the court held at those places.

The parasite of that day was just like ours, spending their time in idleness. It is said of them:

"That (they) lie upon beds of ivory, and stretch themselves upon their couches, and eat the lambs out of the flocks, and the calfs out of the midst of the stall; that chant to the sound of the viol, and invent to themselves instruments of music like David; that drink wine in bowls, and anoint themselves with the chief ointments; but they are not grieved for the afflictions of Joseph. Therefore, shall they go captive with the first that go captive, and the banquet of them that stretched themselves shall be removed." (Amos vi:4-7.)

These oppressors lived on the fat of the land, in fine houses, at the expense of the poor, and the same things surround you on every side today, but you are silent about removing the cause of all this.

They had false teachers then, as now. Such was Amaziah, the priest of Bethel, who brought before King Jeroboam charges, saying:

"Amos hath conspired against thee in the midst of the house of Israel, the land is not able to bear all his words." (Amos vii:10.)

For pointing out these same evils, of which Amos complained, Socialists have often been charged with opposing good government. The substance of the complaint made by this truckling servant of the rich was as follows: "Amos saith Jeroboam (the king) shall die by the sword, and Israel shall surely be led away captive out of their own land." (Amos vii:11.)

Death by the sword, and leading away captive, has filled the pages of the world's history and will continue until Socialism ushers in the brotherhood of man.

The excuse that the land was not able to bear the word of the prophet against these rich robbers of the poor is on a par with some of the complaints of the same class today, when they are confronted with their deeds.

Amaziah, the priest, placed himself on a level with some of the priests of our day, when he said to the prophet Amos:

"Go, flee thee away into the land of Judea and there eat bread and prophesy, but prophesy not any more at Bethel, for it is the king's chapel and it is the king's court." (Amos vii:10-13.)

So we are told to take our complaints to other countries, where Socialism is needed.

Then, you know, these complaints disturb the peace of the courts of the kings, the nobles and the rich.

The chapels of the exploiters are not open to the kind of talk the prophet and the Socialists give.

We find the prophet did not obey the command to stop, any more than we do.

Remember, Amos, the prophet, was a poor sheep herder and gathered sycamore fruit for a living.

If the whole of what the prophets said on this matter of the class struggle between the rich and the poor should be considered, a volume might be written.

But we have pointed out enough to show that the Old Testament is, everywhere, on the side of the poor and oppressed.

"You have not told us what the New Testament says about the poor," the Pastor remarked.

At our next sitting I will try to show that Christ's gospel was a message to the poor.

In our conversations about "The Poor and Their Oppressors" among the ancient Jews, we have said nothing of other evils, such as drunkenness and prostitution, all of which are traceable to economic conditions, because time will not permit.

We think we have shown that Marx was right as to the existence of a class struggle, so far as it applies to the Bible, and that the Bible places God always on the side of the poor, and shows that all men are brothers, and offers justice as the only remedy for the struggle.

"What about love," said the Pastor.

Love and justice are two attributes of man that ought not to be separated in our consideration of economic questions.

XI

Christ's Gospel a Message to the Poor

Well, Pastor, at this sitting, we will try to show that the teachings of Christ is in harmony with that of the Jewish law and the prophets concerning the economic struggle going on between the rich and the poor. Indeed, Christ always appealed to the Old Testament as of divine authority. We shall see he repeatedly said that his gospel was a message to the poor.

When John the Baptist sent to him enquiring whether he was the one to deliver the nation, he said, among many other things, go tell him:

"The poor have the gospel preached to them." (Matt. xi:5.)

And, again, after he had been away from home for some time, and established a great reputation as a teacher, he returned to the little town of Nazareth, where he had been brought up, and on the Sabbath went into the synagogue, as was his custom, and read from the book of Isaiah, the following:

"The Spirit of the Lord is upon me, because he hath anointed me to preach the gospel to the poor, he hath sent me to heal the broken hearted, to preach deliverance to the captives, and recovering of sight to the blind, to set at liberty them are bruised; to preach the acceptable year of the Lord." (Luke iv:18,19.)

This was a quotation from Isaiah, the prophet, which Christ declared referred to him. For he began his discourse by saying:

"This day is this scripture fulfilled in your ears." (Luke iv:21.)

The method of appointment to office among the Jews was by the anointing of oil. So Christ said he was anointed by the Spirit of God to preach the gospel to the poor.

"I see nothing in that favorable to Socialism," remarked the Pastor.

Why did he not say the rich have the gospel preached to them, if the gospel message was not more to one class than another?

"Do not the rich have the gospel preached to them today?" asked the Pastor.

No! not in reality, for if the things we have been pointing out as the teaching of the Bible was preached to the rich, it would condemn them at once.

"Lift up thy voice like a trumpet, cry aloud and tell Israel her sins and the house of Jacob their transgressions," is what you are told to do; but, in most instances, the worst old sinner that ever robbed the poor can sit under the so-called gospel of today and not once hear of his sins. In fact, he is universally commended as the best of a Christian. You would have to have a microscope to find any gospel in what is now preached to the rich.

He was not only to preach to the poor, but to heal the broken-hearted.

We have seen how the hearts of the poor toilers of the past was broken by being robbed of their products, and having to suffer in poverty.

Around us, on every side, are heart-broken and discouraged men and women, some committing suicide and others dragging out a miserable existence.

This, almost without an exception, is the outgrowth of private ownership of the sources and means of producing wealth.

Christ cannot heal the broken-hearted without taking away that which breaks them.

As we have seen Christ's mission, according to Daniel, was to break in pieces all other kingdoms and establish one that would stand forever.

And John, one of his students, declared Christ came to destroy the works of the devil, which is the present industrial system.

Christ's method of healing broken hearts was by doing unto all men as you wish them to do by you, and none of us wish to be poor.

Hence the gospel was not a message to the rich, in the same sense as to the poor, for it promised the relief of the poor from their oppressors.

The rich have seized everything in sight, and to obey Christ they would have to make restitution and give up their method of exploiting the poor workers, which they will not do.

The gospel is a message of relief to the poor, because it would restore to him his products.

"Rather is it not a message that offers to us heaven?" said the Pastor.

Yes; but it offers to us the earth first, and heaven afterwards, and it is the earth we are talking about now.

As we told you, we accept all these things as well as yourself, leaving other Socialists to think as they like. But the average preacher is neglecting the earth altogether in his application of the gospel, and that is what we are trying to show in these talks.

Another thing Christ came to do was to deliver the captives.

"Yes, those held captive in sin!" said the Pastor.

Did we not in our investigation find sin to be the violation of the law laid down governing the relation of one man to another? The trouble is we talk too much about sin without telling what it is. The fact is that this whole capitalist system is a sin, or violation of the great law of universal brotherhood.

It is plain that the violation of this law of right social relations between man and man is what the Bible means by sin. Now we Socialists want to take away this great sin of the nations by destroying the cause—capitalism.

How many of the workers of the world are held captive in prison for taking back by stealth a small portion of the product of their own labor, which the rich have exploited them of under laws made by themselves? These captives Christ came to deliver by taking away the cause. There are occasions in which prisoners are treated as kindly as the circumstances will permit; but even these are exceptions and offer no solution of the problem of crime, which must be cured by removing the cause.

"Well, then, when he comes the second time this will be done," said the Pastor.

Why not be consistent, then, and leave all sins for Christ to put down when he comes. The same people said in the days of chattel slavery—wait till Christ comes and it will be put down.

No! He told men to go and preach this gospel to every creature, thus using men as his instruments. You remind me of those who contend that if Christ wants the gospel to go to others, he will take it himself. This gospel of Socialism must be preached to the people by men, and it will not fail to accomplish its purpose. The word gospel means good news, which is true of Socialism as a message to the poor.

"What about this giving sight to the blind?" asked the Pastor.

That was physical sight, but some of you are just as badly in need of intellectual sight, and it is the mission of the Socialist to open your eyes to read the signs of the times.

Another important part of his mission was to set at liberty those that are bruised. The wounds and bruises of the worker are all traceable either directly or indirectly to our present social conditions.

"Is not this the land of liberty?" asked the Pastor.

Land of liberty, indeed! Where a man can't live on the earth without buying or renting from some one else. Cannot work for bread to feed his family without the consent of some one else, and even then only by giving up the larger part of his products to some one who does nothing. Is that what you call liberty? Go tell these "bruised" ones in mine, field and factory that Christ came to set them free in this life, and then they can get time to think more about the future. These words about prisons are to be taken as literal as that about opening the eyes of the blind.

Under Socialism, the prison doors will all, in a short time, be closed forever, just as completely as the slave pen, which now only lingers, here and there, as monuments to our shame.

The trouble is, we preachers have been telling the people that the gospel has little to do with changing man's economic conditions, but he must look forward to happiness in the next world, when, in fact, the gospel was intended to make man happy here first.

Of course, we want to be fair in our criticisms of professed Christians by admitting that, relatively, just as large a number of those on the outside of the churches have not yet been brought to the light of Socialism as those on the inside.

It is a well-known fact that both Christ and his relatives were among what the Socialists call the proletariat or propertyless class of the country. And when he was out on his mission, he said of himself:

"The foxes have holes, and the birds of the air have nests; but the Son of Man hath not where to lay his head." (Matt. viii:20.)

His homeless and pennyless condition would subject him to arrest and imprisonment if he was here now, and that, too, under laws made by so-called Christian nations. The present capitalist system has no more use for Christ and his teachings than had the rich robbers of his day. The economic truths underlying Christianity as taught in the Bible, which is identical with those taught by the Socialists, cannot be destroyed.

"But the rich have as much use of Christ as have you Scientific Socialists," remarked the Pastor.

Without, at this point, further discussing the attitude of Scientific Socialists toward Christ and the Bible, let me say, they agree with him, as we have shown, in their plea for bettering the condition of the workers, by giving them their entire product, the very thing the capitalists oppose. I know Socialism to be a good thing, and in harmony with the teachings of Christ, and I will not oppose it because some opponents of Christianity favor it. The kingdom of heaven is promised to the poor:

"Blessed be ye poor, for yours is the kingdom of heaven." (Luke vi:20.) Again:

"Blessed is the poor in spirit, for theirs is the kingdom of heaven." (Matt. v:3.)

"But that refers to the spiritually poor," said the Pastor.

What do you mean by the "spiritually poor?"

"The humble, good, pure and upright," answered the Pastor.

Very well; then Socialism will give men a chance to be all that.

We referred to Daniel, a few moments ago, and here let us go back to him again and quote more at length what he says. It is evident that he was referring to the same conditions, to be ultimately brought about upon earth, here set forth in the New Testament and contended for by the Socialists, when he said:

"In the days of these kings shall the God of heaven set up a kingdom, which shall never be destroyed, and the kingdom shall not be left to other people, but shall break in pieces and consume all these kingdoms, but it shall stand forever." (Dan. ii:44.)

This new government, which the God of heaven was to set up, found its beginning in Christ, whose doctrine of the brotherhood and equality of man has from his day been engaged in the work of breaking to pieces the great robber governments of men, and Socialism is only another name for one phase of this great onward movement.

"But was not this kingdom wholly to be spiritual, and not physical, as we said?" remarked the Pastor.

Both, as man is composed of body and spirit, and no man can rob his fellowman of his product and be spiritually right.

John the Baptist, you will remember, said:

"The kingdom of heaven is at hand." (Matt. iii:1.)

That is, here on earth, not somewhere else; and are we not taught to pray:

"Thy kingdom come, thy will be done on earth, as it is in heaven." (Matt. vi:10.)

Mark you, all this refers to a condition of things here, and not beyond. This kingdom, set up within us, must take shape in better economic conditions to be of any practical use.

"I grant you this kingdom, or new condition, was to be set up in men's hearts, which is, of course, only another term for mind," said the Pastor.

That is true, and is the reason why we are trying to change the men's minds from capitalism to Socialism, or, what the Christian calls, from sin to righteousness. This passage tells us to pray for the same conditions to prevail on earth as prevails in heaven.

Do you think one set of persons own everything in heaven, and live at the expense of the others, as we do here? In fact, is not Socialism as pictured today, the nearest approach to what you believe prevails in heaven, than anything yet advocated by man?

"I thought you Socialists were opposed to kingdoms!" the Pastor said.

The term "kingdom of heaven," as we said, means a government entirely unlike the ones it is breaking in pieces. In this case, the Golden Rule will be the law, and Christ the invisible king, and the Socialists accept what he taught on economics. It is significant that Christ was not only among what the Socialists call the proletariat, or extremely poor, but his gospel was a message to that class, and, as we shall see, his church was founded among that class, and not among the rich. But the life of Christ harmonizes with the Old Testament scriptures, as we have seen, which invariably places God on the side of the poor and oppressed, representing him as destroying one nation to get men out of slavery, overthrowing others because of other forms of robbing the poor, and, finally, not sparing his own chosen people because they persisted in filling their houses with the spoils of the poor.

Is it not significant, again, that Christ was not only born among the poor, but that he lived all his life among them, gathered his followers from them, and thus instituted his church.

Other great leaders have used their power to get rich at the expense of their fellows; but he never did. Like others, we learn that the tempter offered him all the riches of the world to forsake this battle for the poor. (See Matt. iv:1-11.) But he did not accept it. The same temptation of the glory of the world's wealth is always offered by the rich to those who would fight the battles of the poor.

You and I, at least, recognize him as the Son of God. Why was he not born among the rich and noble, and why are we told that the angels, who announced his birth, was sent to the poor shepherds, in place of the wealthy and professedly pious priests of Jerusalem?

Whatever others may think of the life and character of Christ, these are very pertinent questions for those of us who believe him to be divine.

Lastly, why was his mother not one of the haughty daughters of the land, in place of one of the proletariat?

XII

Charity as a Solution of Economic Difficulties

"You must admit that among the most charitable people in the world are the rich, and that helping the poor is laid down in the Bible as a religious duty. And yet I hear you Socialists always denouncing charity and harping about justice," remarked the Pastor.

We are glad you raised that point. Any Socialist who has studied the Bible from the economic standpoint knows that it no more offers charity as a final solution than did the Socialist party when it sent several thousand dollars to the workers who had been robbed by the capitalists in the Pennsylvania mines.

So, you see, we only oppose offering charity as a remedy for economic difficulties. Charity, at best, simply means to give back to the worker when in the pinch of hunger a small pittance of what he has produced and been robbed of through profit on his labor; on goods, or by rent, or interest. But it is well enough, while we are on this point, to read a few of the many striking passages on this subject. Seeing the capitalist class, who exploit the poor, are fond of standing behind the scriptures, as a bulwark against the workers having all they produce, thus doing away with charity, let us look into the matter. One day Christ was invited to dine with one of the chief Pharisees and during the conversation said to his host:

"When thou makest a dinner or supper, call not thy friends, nor thy brethren, neither thy kinsmen, nor thy rich neighbor, lest they, also bid thee again and recompense thee. But when thou makest a feast call the poor, the maimed, the lame, the blind, and thou shalt be blessed, for they cannot recompense thee, for thou shalt be recompensed at the resurrection of the just." (Luke xiv:12-14.)

As we said, occasional dinners were given to the poor, but Christ said the poor and unfortunates were the only ones to be invited. The reason is apparent. Because having been robbed of all, they have nothing to pay with.

"But if the rich have been taking, as you Socialists say, from the poor, why should they be rewarded in the end?" said the Pastor.

There may be two reasons for that; one is that we all have to learn, and a large number of the rich, as well as the poor have not yet discovered the underlying economic cause of all this poverty and wretchedness. Another reason is that the few who know can't stop the thing by changing the system, single-handed and alone, if they wanted to, and can only go on insisting on a change and giving back a little now and then through charity, or, in other words, every man should do all he can to help others under the circumstances.

But do the rich, who are always insisting that charity will solve the economic problems, now confronting us, act on Christ's instructions here given, and throw open their mansions and dwellings only to the poor and miserable from the hovels of poverty, excluding the rich and opulent? If not, let them cease to talk about Christian charity.

Keep it in mind that the same Christ who recommended charity to relieve the immediate sufferings of the poor, which we showed the Socialist party believed in, also said.

"Thou shalt love thy neighbor as thyself."

Love thy neighbor as thyself would take away all necessity for charity. This relation, between us and our neighbors, can never exist under the private ownership of the earth, and its resources, which we have shown to be contrary to the Bible.

There is another kind of giving which Christ condemns, when he says:

"Take heed that ye do not your alms before men, to be seen of them, otherwise ye have no reward of your Father who is in heaven. Therefore, when thou doest thine alms, do not sound a trumpet before thee, as the hypocrites do in the synagogues and the streets, that they may have glory of men." (Matt. vi:1,2.)

The hypocrite who gives, not because he cares for the poor, but, that he may blow his trumpet through the Associated Press, to be seen of men, is to have no reward of the heavenly Father, for the reason that the reward he asked for was, the praise of men, and he gets that here.

"Another thing you Socialists seem to forget is, the great work of charity done by the churches, the Salvation Army, and other religious institutions," said the Pastor.

We would not stop you, but would have you understand the cause, which is capitalism, and vote the Socialist ticket so as to remove it and put in its place cooperation.

We suspect, however, that the rich from which you get your donations will shut down on you, when you begin to want to remove the cause, for it will conflict with their class interests. You are aware, Pastor, that most of the help the churches and the Salvation Army give the poor, are collected from the rich, who took it from the poor, who produced all the wealth.

Now, all this taking from the producer his product is contrary to the Golden Rule, and when you preach that, you will find that the rich will stop helping you, as a rule, and that, as Christ said:

"Ye cannot serve God and Mammon (wealth)." (Matt. vi:24.)

Or, in other words, you will discover that the class struggle, you hear the Socialists talking about, exists in the churches as well as in the factory.

Master and slave, before the war, all belonged to the same church. They met on Sunday and prayed together, and one church member sold the other the next day. So now, in many cases, master and wage-slave belong to the same church, meet on Sunday and pray together, and the one turns the other off from even the pittance he allowed him to take out of his earnings as wages or sets him out of house and home for non-payment of rent, or under mortgage, the next day. All that, notwithstanding the Bible says love both the brother and the stranger as yourself.

It took the abolitionist, in and out of the church, to show the inconsistency of slavery and force a division, as the Socialists are now doing.

"Yes," said mother, "I belonged to one of that kind of churches, myself, before the war."

"You will not deny that the ancient churches looked after the poor?" said the Pastor.

No. Paul tells us that when him and Barnabas went to the Gentiles they were to look after the poor. (Gal. ii:10.)

And he gathered contributions from other churches for the poor saint at Jerusalem. (1 Cor. xi:2.)

All that, as we have seen, was temporary, designed to last until the Golden Rule of Socialism is established.

"It seems to me that you certainly differ with the Bible, as to the cause of poverty," says the Pastor.

How so? Speaking of the sluggard or lazy man it says:

"So shall thy poverty come as one that traveleth, and thy

want as an armed man." (Prov. vi:11.) Again:

"The soul of the sluggard desireth nothing, but the soul of the diligent shall be made fat." (Prov. xiii:4.) Also:

"Slothfulness casteth into a deep sleep, and an idle soul shall suffer hunger." (Prov. xix:15.) Here is another one:

"The drunkard and the glutton shall come to poverty, and drowsiness shall clothe a man with rags." (Prov. xxiii:21.)

One more text while we are reading:

"He that tilleth his land shall have plenty of bread, but he that followeth after vain persons shall have poverty." (Prov. xxviii:19.)

Well, Pastor, what do you gather from these texts?

"I gather, first, that the Bible teaches that idleness is the cause of poverty, and we all know that drunkenness and gluttony, or riotous living is one of the prime causes of the poverty you Socialists complain of."

In a country where debts could not be created for the idle to live on, or interest or any increase demanded, nothing but laziness could prevent a man from having enough, so long as the laws were enforced.

But in these so-called Christian countries we are living in open violation of the biblical law against debt and usury, and the man who does not work gets the best of everything. While drunkenness is not to be justified, it brings poverty only because of the profit charged on the sale of liquors. Socialism is intended to prevent the idle from living at the worker's expense.

Socialism will compel the lazy man to go to work and help to produce or get nothing.

But you did not comment, Pastor, upon the passage about the man tilling his own soil.

That was alright in a country where the land could not be monopolized and held by the few, either under mortgage or by deed, as it is with us. Give the people the land to operate collectively and the same will be true now, they that till the land will have plenty.

So, then, we find, on examination, that the Bible offers charity, only, as a temporary relief and says:

"Do unto all men as you would they should do unto you." as the only solution of economic difficulties.

To do that, the Socialists propose to overthrow capitalism and build the Cooperative Commonwealth on its ruins. Every Socialist is asking for others what he wants himself.

"At our next meeting," said the Pastor, as he arose to go at a late hour, "I hope to get your views on the rich men of the Bible."

XIII
The Rich Men of the Bible

"I suppose you know that the Bible gives us accounts of some very rich men;" was the remark of the Pastor on seating himself at the table when we met the next evening to resume our investigation. "For instance, it is said:

'Abraham was a very rich man in cattle, silver, and in gold . . .' (Gen. xiii:2.)

"Now it is not at all likely that Abraham raised all the cattle, and dug all the silver and gold, he possessed, out of the mines himself. Indeed, we are told he had a number of servants, which doubtless, largely did the work."

Well, in the first place, Abraham lived before the law was given touching these economic questions. And, again, the bare statement that he had all these possessions is, in no sense, a justification of his method of getting them, any more than when a Socialist mentions the fact that a man is very rich, without referring to how he came in possession.

"But God greatly blessed Abraham and called him his friend," said the Pastor.

Certainly! and, doubtless, Abraham was acting up to the best light he had.

You have both the Bible, and the Socialists to enlighten you, and are you, like Abraham, acting up to the best light you have got?

"I suppose you would say that Job was another one of those rich men that lived before the law was given," added the Pastor.

"But, after enumerating his possessions, in the first chapter of the book, we are informed that the Lord gave Job 'Twice as much as he had before...'" (Job xiii:10.)

There is a sense in which God gives all men, whether good or bad, everything, and that is by creating all...

The book of Job, as we have shown in our previous conversations, you will recollect, contains some of the strongest denunciations of the exploitation of the poor to be found in the Bible.

These two men, Abraham and Job, lived thousands of years ago in the misty ages of the past, before the economic teachings of the Bible were fully presented.

The Bible, just as we are compelled to, deals with man just as it finds him, and not as he should be, and, therefore, all the lights and shades of his character shows as it is, good, bad, or indifferent.

It thus gives us a true life picture of man.

The earth, and all it contains, God gave to men collectively, and holds them responsible for robbing each other of their share of its produce.

"Was not the kings of the Jews rich, and did not the Lord give Solomon riches, wisdom, and long life?"

"I have, also, given thee that which thou hast asked, both riches and honor." (1 Kings iii:13.)

"Now, if he gave Solomon riches, why will he not give Rockefeller riches? For if gold and silver is an evidence of riches, then your richest men today are not to be compared with Solomon, who, it is claimed, handled fifty-five billion dollars worth of gold in the construction of the temple, and no modern prince ever had such palaces to live in," said the Pastor.

"We have shown that the Jews disobeyed God when they demanded a king, but, knowing that when they got into the land of promise and had grown corrupt, they would demand a king, he laid the following down as a rule by which they were to be governed:

"Neither shall he (the king) multiply wives to himself, that his heart turn not away; neither shall he greatly multiply to him silver and gold." (Deut. xvii:17.)

Such was the law to govern the kings.

They were to have but one wife, but, most of them notoriously violated the law, just as the same class do all laws that don't suit them now.

They were not to heap up gold and silver, but, who did more of that than Solomon? Now let us compare this law of God with what he said about giving Solomon riches. We are told that Solomon chose wisdom, and God said:

"I have, also, given thee that which thou hast not asked, both riches and honor." Let us examine this.

"Have" is in the past tense. That is, through being born the king of Israel he had come into "both riches and honor."

But the circumstance of birth is no sanction of the method of accumulating the fortune one inherits.

The law, just sighted, shows that God did not sanction Solomon's vast accumulation of fortune at the expense of the workers, any more than the wives he took to himself.

If God did not want men to lay up vast fortunes then, he don't want them to do it now.

Of course, so far as the temple is concerned, it was a public building belonging to the whole people, but it was often used for private graft. Notably: the bankers could not have got into the temple without giving the priest a rake-off. So Solomon violated the law as well as the other kings, in oppressing the people.

You will recollect reading that, when Rehoboam, Solomon's son, came to the throne the people rebelled against the oppression of the king's administration, and when he would force them into subjection, the Lord said:

"Ye shall not go up nor fight against your brethren the children of Israel, return every man to his house for this thing is of me." (1 Kings xii:24.)

It will be readily admitted that the Israelites were not seeking to set up Socialism, but they were revolting against oppression, and if the Lord was with them, why not with us now? These Jews, like the Socialists, revolted against the king's oppression, while you stand by Rockefeller in his oppressions. Not knowing their class interests they only chose themselves another master however.

A rich, young man came to Christ, one day, inquiring after eternal life, and when told to keep the commandments, he said he had done that. But when Christ said:

"Go, sell that which thou hast and give to the poor." (Matt. xix:2.)

That settled it. He did not want to give back to the people that which he had plundered them of, whereupon Christ proceeded to give his opinion of rich men, by saying:

"That a rich man shall hardly enter into the kingdom of heaven.... It is easier for a camel to go through the eye of a needle than for a rich man to enter into the kingdoms of God."

Then, seeing the astonishment of his disciples, he added:

"With man this is impossible, but with God all things are possible." (Matt. xix:24.) "Now hardly shall they that have riches enter into the kingdom of God." (Luke x:23.) There the material interest of the rich is clearly recognized as we do today.

If the literal needle is here meant, then, a rich man would be compelled to do what Christ told the young man to do, to get into the kingdom, that is: give back to the poor what he has taken from them.

"That is generally supposed to refer to the little gate in the wall of the cities through which the belated camel had to go on his knees after having his burden taken off," said the Pastor.

That would hardly better it, for in that case, our rich men, who are loaded with the spoils of the workers, would have to unload on this side, and go through on their knees, in order to enter the kingdom. We Socialists are trying to help them unload. Christ declared that it is possible for God to bring this about. That is, unload the rich of the plunder they are now burdened with, as a necessary step to their entering the kingdom.

The preacher of today is the representative of Christ, and when the rich, young man comes to him seeking eternal life is he told to go and get right with the poor?

The Socialist who stands up to plead the cause of the poor as against the rich, in that respect, stands with Christ. Of course,

I am glad to know, that there are exceptions to the rule among the preachers and that these exceptions are on the increase.

The influence of the Bible, and its teachings, has overleaped the confines of the church, and spread out among those who are not adherents of Christ.

You will remember reading that Christ said:

"There was a certain rich man, which was clothed in purple and fine linen and fared sumptuously every day; and there was a certain beggar, named Lazarus, which was laid at his gate, full of sores, and desiring to be fed with the crumbs which fell from the rich man's table." (Luke xvi:19-21.)

Around us today, on every hand, we see the same thing here referred to. The old, the lame, and the blind, begging at the rich man's door, or eking out a living from swill barrels, or fed on the crumbs from the table, of the men for whom their class have produced great fortunes.

The descendant of the rich man still lives in his mansion, while the children of Lazarus are at his gate full of sores; but Christ gives the beggar decidedly the advantage in the next world.

"That brings out my contention: why worry about these things? all will be right hereafter," the Pastor remarked.

Christ, however, thought it necessary to condemn the action of this rich man, and to give it as the cause of his punishment hereafter.

If the teachings of the Golden Rule is carried out, as it will be under Socialism, no such conditions of extreme wealth on the one hand, and extreme poverty on the other would be possible.

"If the rich man becomes a Christian, will he not be all right?" asked the Pastor.

Certainly! but Christ laid down the conditions to the young man, and that was:

"Go sell all that which thou hast, and give to the poor, and come and follow me and thou shall have the riches of heaven."

While you tell him, God has greatly blessed him, when, at the same time, the Bible denounces him as a spoiler of the poor.

You tell him that he can hold on to his riches and get to heaven, while Christ says he cannot, and yet you claim to represent Christ.

The first step for the rich man towards heaven is, to stop robbing the poor, which can only be done through Socialism.

It is significant that, when the rich man wanted some one sent from the dead to warn his brothers he was told:

"They have Moses and the prophets, let them hear them." (Luke xvi:29.)

We have shown that Moses and the prophets taught that:

"The land shall not be sold forever."

That they opposed interest or increase of any kind declared that the rich had the spoils of the poor in their houses, and they said:

"Thou shalt not covet anything that is thy neighbor," and "Thou shalt love thy neighbor as thyself."

Now, it is plain, that no man who lived as this rich man did, while his brother Lazarus was in the condition described, could observe the teachings of Moses and the prophets. This rich man was lost because he took what the poor produced.

As we said, the case of these two men is duplicated around us every day among the rich and poor, but, according to most of the preaching now, the rich man may rob Lazarus and die with his ill gotten gains, while the poor rots at his very gate, and be all right here and hereafter.

"What about this other rich man Zacheus, why did Christ commend him?" said the Pastor.

Because by giving half of his goods to the poor, and restoring to everyone he had cheated out of anything, fourfold, he was doing the best that could be done under the system of private ownership, then prevailing in the Roman empire. (See Luke xix:8.)

The truth is, while the Bible shows there were rich men then, as now, their methods of robbing the poor producer, in order to get rich, is everywhere condemned.

Anyone who reads the Bible carefully, will find it agreeing with the Socialist in fighting the battle of the poor.

"Some of your Socialists might not accept that part of the story of the rich and poor man, which relates to the hereafter," the Pastor remarked.

Perhaps not. But you and I do; and we wish to show that Socialism, by insisting on universal brotherhood, is only doing what everyone who accepts Christ must admit is necessary to future happiness; and, therefore, you cannot afford to oppose Socialism, as in opposition to Christianity, regardless of what any Socialist, as an individual, may say, seeing that the basic principles of Socialism are in harmony with the Bible.

XIV

Christ on the Accumulation of Wealth

You know, Pastor, at this time, the world is simply gone mad in the scramble for wealth, and the people who profess to be following Christ are no exception to the rule.

It seems to me it is about time Christian people made inquiry as to what Christ said and did about the accumulation of wealth.

To be a Christian, is to be like Christ; therefore, what he has taught on this subject ought to be authority among those who profess to follow him.

At the risk of being a little tedious, allow me to read you just what he did say on this subject:

"Lay not up for yourselves treasures upon earth, where moth and rust doth corrupt and where thieves break through and steal, for where your treasure is there will your heart be also.... No man can serve two masters, for either he will hate the one and love the other; or else, hold to the one and despise the other. Ye cannot serve God and Mammon (wealth.) Therefore, I say unto you, take no thought for your life, what ye shall put on. Is not the life more than meat, and the body more than raiment? Behold the fowls of the air! for they sow not, neither do they reap, nor gather into barns, yet your Heavenly Father feedeth them. Are ye not much better than they? Which one of you by taking thought can add one cubit to his stature? And why take you thought for raiment? Consider the lilies of the field, how they grow, they toil not, neither do they spin, and yet I say unto you that Solomon in all his glory was not arrayed like one of these. Wherefore, if God so clothe the grass of the field, which today is, and tomorrow is cast into the oven and burned, shall he not much more clothe you, O, ye! of little faith? Then take no thought, saying: what shall we eat, or drink, or wherewithal shall we be clothed? For after all these things do the Gentiles seek: for your Heavenly Father knoweth that ye have need of all these things. But seek ye first the kingdom of God, and his righteousness, and all these things shall be added unto you. Take therefore, no thought for the morrow, for the morrow shall take thought for the things of itself, sufficient unto the day is the evil thereof." (Matt. vi:19-34.)

Now, Pastor, what do you think Christ meant by this language?

"Well, I confess that there is some difficulty connected with this passage, yet, it seems evident to my mind, he could not have meant that we should not look out for sickness and old age. It seems to me the main thing to be understood here is, that our heart, or mind rather, are not to be placed on our earthly possessions, which are perishable," he replied.

In preaching, years ago, we found the same difficulty in this scripture, until we became Socialist, and that moment all seemed clear.

It was plain that Christ meant just what he said. That we should not lay up treasure here on earth, and that a man can not go into the scramble for wealth and serve God. That we should not worry about food, clothes, and shelter, any more than the birds, the grass, or the flowers do. It is impossible to harmonize with this with the present conditions of poverty, hunger and nakedness, however:

"Seek ye first the kingdom of God, and his righteousness, and all these things shall be added unto you."

What are the things he had just spoken of, but clothes, food and indeed, the best of everything; as is shown by his referring to the beauty of the flower, and the plenty of the birds.

You see that word "seek" indicates that it was a condition

to be sought, not in heaven, but upon earth at some future time. We would turn all the capital and resources over to the people to be operated collectively for the benefit of all. Then, give each man, as a reward for his labor his equal share of the best of everything science and skill combined can produce, in the way of houses, books, paintings, statuary, clothing, food, and all else he needs.

Next, we would feed, house, and educate the children, while getting ready to work in the departments of industry; and place the old on the retired list with the same income they had while at work. Do this, and you may cease to lay up treasures on earth, or worry about the morrow.

To seek his righteousness is to do what he says to do.

Men inherit, by birth, whatever the public owns without a will.

That the kingdom refers to a condition to come on earth, see the Lord's prayer:

"Thy kingdom come, thy will be done on earth as it is in heaven."

Certainly we have not yet got all the people to accept this condition on earth. You don't suppose that a few persons in heaven, like a few on earth, have got possession of everything and the rest will have to buy or rent one of the mansions Christ went to prepare? (John xiv:2.)

Christ said that the kingdom of heaven, he came to establish, was at hand, and left us to convince the people of that fact. Remember, earth and heaven are to do the will of God alike. Don't we pray for that?

When he taught them to say: "Thy kingdom come," he had not yet completed his work of organizing it, and starting it to breaking to pieces all other kingdoms.

Now, is it not a fact, that, both by precept and example, the rich professed Christians, as well as the non-professor, tell us to do just what both Christ and the Socialists say not to do: that is get rich at all hazard?

"It strikes me that you Socialists have very little of the gentleness and spirit of Christ in dealing with your opponents," said the Pastor.

I am not sure about that, in order to test the matter, allow me to read you one of the discourses of Christ, as given in the Twentieth Century New Testament, which is all the same, in substance as the version in common use, except the rendering is into the English of today, in place of that of three hundred years ago, and is, therefore, easier understood. It is as follows, and was preached to the rich and professedly pious people of his day.

"The Rabbis and Pharisees now occupy the chair of Moses, therefore, practice and lay to heart everything they tell you, but do not follow their example, for they preach but do not practice. While they make up heavy loads and pile them on other people's shoulders, they decline, themselves, to lift a finger to move them. Indeed, all their actions are done to attract attention. They widen the text which they wear as a charm, and increase the size of their tassels, and like having the place of honor at dinners, and the front seats in the synagogues, and being greeted on the streets with respect, and being called Rabbi by everybody. But do not allow yourselves to be called 'Rabbi,' for you have only one teacher, and you, yourselves, are all brothers. And do not call any one upon earth your father, for you have only one father, the Heavenly Father. Nor must you allow yourselves to be called 'Leaders,' for you have only one Leader, the Christ. The man who would be greatest among you must act as your servant. All who exalt themselves will be humbled, and all who humble themselves will be exalted. But alas, for you Rabbis and Pharisees, hypocrites that you are! because you close the kingdom of heaven in men's faces, you do not go in yourselves, nor yet allow those who are going in to do so. Alas, for you, Rabbis and Pharisees, hypocrites that you are! because you scour both land and sea to make a single convert, and when he is gained, you make him twice as ready for the Pit as you are yourselves. Alas for you, you blind guides! who say:

'If any one swears by the temple, his oath counts for nothing, but if one swears by the temple gold his oath is binding on him!'

"Fools that you are, what blindness! why, which is the more

important, the gold, or the temple which has given sacredness to the gold? You say too:

'If anyone swears by the altar his oath counts for nothing, but if any one swears by the offering placed on it, his oath is binding on him!'

"What blindness! why, which is the most important, the offering or the altar which gives sacredness to the offering? Therefore, a man swearing by the altar is swearing by it and by everything on it, and a man swearing by the Temple is swearing by it and by him who dwells in it, while a man swearing by heaven is swearing by the throne of God and him who sits upon it. Alas for you, Rabbis and Pharisees, hypocrites that you are! because you pay tithes on mint, fennel, and caraway seed, and have neglected the weightier matters of the law, justice, mercy and good faith. These last you ought to put into practice, without neglecting the first. You blind guides, to strain out a gnat but swallow a camel! Alas for you, Rabbis and Pharisees, hypocrites that you are! because you clean the outside of the cup and of the dish while inside they are full of the fruits of grasping and self-indulgence. You blind Pharisees! First clean the inside of the cup and the dish, that so the outside may become clean as well. Alas for you, Rabbis, and Pharisees, hypocrites that you are! because you are like tombs that have been whitewashed and look beautiful outside, while inside they are filled with dead men's bones and all kinds of filth. It is the same with you, outwardly, and to others, you have the look of religious men, but, inwardly, you are full of hypocrisy and sins. Alas for you, Rabbis and Pharisees, hypocrites that you are! because you build tombs for the prophets and decorate the monuments of religious men, and say:

'Had we been living in the days of our forefathers, we should have taken no part in their murder of the prophets.'

"In this way you supply evidence against yourselves that you are true children of the men who murdered the prophets. Fill up the measure of your forefather's guilt, you serpents and off-springs of vipers! How can you escape being sent to the Pit? This is why I sent you prophets, wise men, and Rabbis: some of whom you will kill and crucify, and some you will flog in your synagogues, and pursue from town to town, that upon your heads may fall every drop of innocent blood spilt on earth from the blood of the innocent Abel down to that of Zachariah, Barachiah's son, whom you murdered between the temple and the altar. All this, believe me, will come home to this present generation. Jerusalem! Jerusalem!! she who slays the prophets and stones the messengers sent to her—O, how often have I wished to gather your children around me, as a hen gathers her chickens under her wings, and you refused to come! I tell you, your house will be left desolate; for nevermore shall you see me until you say, blessed is the one who comes in the name of the Lord." (Matt. xxiii chapter.)

Time will not permit us to say all that might be said about this remarkable sermon but, remember, he was talking to the strictly religious people, just such as now fills many of our churches. He called them hypocrites, blind guides, whitewashed tombs, murderers, vipers, and children of the Pit. Read it over carefully, and then think if you ever heard a Socialist speaker use any harder language.

These people who then laid heavy loads on the masses, and wanted the chief seats at the feast, and desired everybody to call them Rabbi, was just like the rich class today, and, like your Master, you should treat them the same.

This sermon is a model for the minister of today when dealing with the same class.

"You don't compare those hypocritical Pharisees with the Christian people of today?" said the Pastor.

What is it that those Pharisees were doing that is not being done by some people today, both in the church and out?

"You talk about the gentleness of Christ."

Yes, we find that he could be all the gentleness of the summer zephyrs wooing the flowers when he was a mind to, and, then, on the other hand, when dealing with hypocrisy and sham, he could be all the majesty of the thunder storm uprooting the oaks. When he said their fathers murdered the prophets and they raised monuments to them, he accused them of just what the rich

The Bible and Socialism 181

are doing today.

The slave-holding capitalists murdered Lovejoy at Alton, Illinois in 1837, but he has a monument to his memory now.

The broadcloth mob tried to hang Garrison for preaching against slavery, and their sons raised a monument over him after he was dead.

Wendell Phillips was called a villain when battling against the wrong, and often had to speak with friends surrounding him to hold back the mob, but he is a patriot now that he is dead.

Frederick Douglass was often mobbed, was hated, and had to fly to Europe for his life. But when he died a nation rose up to do him honor.

So one generation hung John Brown and then vied with each other in raising monuments to his honor a few years later.[7]

So, leading Socialists was once banished from Germany, but their enemies are beginning to admit they represent the brains of the country.

Better to help living men do the work of the hour, than to build tombs in honor of dead ones.

Don't you know that it was the rich class he preached against and the misguided poor, who did not understand their class interests, that put Christ to death.

When you go home, read carefully the sermon we have been considering, and say no more about the bitterness of the Socialist.

Christ was among what the Socialists call the proletariat, and so was his early followers. And yet he did not teach that poverty was a good thing, but, quite the contrary, when he said:

"Your Heavenly Father knoweth that you have need of all these things; seek ye first the kingdom of God, and his righteousness, and all these things will be added unto you."

He meant if we do right; by setting up Socialism we will get all these things.

We gather from the allusion to the grass, the flowers, and the birds that there is nothing too good or fine for those to have who are willing to work for it. The fact is he wanted the willing workers to have all the good things the earth can afford and only opposed one man accumulating wealth at the expense of another.

When Socialism brings about the brotherhood of man, which Christ taught, we will create an abundance of the best things earth can afford for all, and the scramble for laying up fortunes will cease forever.

While we are on this point, did you ever notice the fact that Christ poured out all his denunciations against the rich of his day, and said: "The publican and the harlot enter into heaven before you do?"

It was not because he believed in the vices going on in the dives of Jerusalem, but, because like the Socialists of today, he knew that the accumulation of wealth in the hands of the few was the cause, and he aimed to cure the disease by removing it.

"Sin was the cause, you had better say," remarked the Pastor.

Certainly, the laying up of wealth at the expense of the workers is a violation of the law, "Love thy neighbor as thyself," and "Sin is the violation of law," remember; so these rich sinners are still driving the poor into vice by exploiting them.

XV

What the Prophets Said of Economic Conditions in Other Nations

Glad to see you, Pastor, after so many days of interruption in the investigation, was our greeting as he walked into the study. We feared you were offended at the plainness of our talk, or may be you had tired of the investigation.

"Oh, no! on the contrary, I have been much interested with the very novelty of it, then, too, it is putting the teaching of the Bible in a new light to me. However, I am not yet, altogether, satisfied that you are entirely correct in your views. I would have been on hand, again, sooner had not my church work been somewhat pressing," said the Pastor.

We had occasion to refer to other nations than the Jews,

during this investigation; but do you know that the denunciation of them by the prophets was almost wholly on economic grounds?

To undertake to read the numerous scriptures referring to other nations would take too much of our time, so you can read them at your leisure.

Are we not told that the people before the flood were destroyed because they had grown corrupt and filled the earth with violence and "did only evil continually?" (Gen. vi chapter.)

Violence, which doubtless, refers to war, and corruption among men, is traceable to the private ownership of the source and means of producing wealth.

Here we are told the earth was destroyed rather than permit such injustice to go on.

Trace this violence and corruption to whatever cause you will, the Socialist idea of Universal Brotherhood will take it away.

Curious, is it not, that many who claim to believe in the Bible, now make all sorts of excuses for violence and corruption!

"I want to remind you again, as I did before, that it will be hard to get some of your Socialists to believe in these ancient accounts of the Bible," said the Pastor.

We are talking to you who believe in the Bible, and insisting that you shall follow its teachings on this question of economics.

If the nations surrounding the Jews had a social system that robbed the producer, for which they were condemned, then the writers of the Bible done just what the Socialists now do. Nor are we, as we said before, concerned in these conversations with anything else the Book teaches.

While we are not told so, in the eleventh chapter of Genesis, yet, it is not at all improbable that the tower of Babel was being built by slave labor.

It was out of this Land of Chaldea that Abraham came to the country of Canaan.

Through him the world was to have, not only a new nation, but, also, a new social condition, for it is said of him:

"In thee shall all the families of the earth be blessed." (Gen. xii:3.)

Socialism is intended to bring a blessing to all mankind, and we have in all the ages past been growing toward it as economic conditions ripened.

Socialists everywhere, recognize that teaching should go hand in hand with conditions. While the Bible has not made new methods for creating wealth, yet it has spread the Socialistic teachings of the descendants of Abraham through the world.

It is significant that Karl Marx, the great Socialist writer, whose teachings are now quoted as infallible authority by Scientific Socialists, was himself, a descendant of Abraham, the man through whom all nations was to be blessed.

Therefore, the adoption of International Socialism will bring a blessing, through Abraham and his descendants, to all the families of the earth. The mission of the Socialist is to teach the workers to recognize what economic development is leading to.

"Do you mean to say that Marx was a Jew?" asked the Pastor.

Yes sir! that is what we mean. So he done the greatly needed work of reasoning out from the standpoint of the philosopher, what his ancestors, the writers of the Old and New Testaments, had already done from a moral and religious standpoint.

"Wasn't Christ, the son of Abraham, through whom all 'the families of the earth' are to be blessed!" said the Pastor.

Certainly! but you can't carry out the economic teachings of Christ without adopting Socialism.

It seems to me, however, that we have wandered from the subject of the evening, somewhat.

In the fourteenth chapter of Genesis, with which you are too familiar to need that we should take time to read it to you, the kings of the Canaanites were plundering the working people through war and Abraham's nephew, Lot, was carried away, together with his goods and those of others. You will recollect reading that Abraham, and his men, pursued these robbers, re-captured the goods and the people, but refused to take anything for their services, evidently so as not to be involved in that kind of injustice. Those kings was doing just what the ruling class are still doing, and the Socialists think the spoils ought to be taken out of the hands of the oppressors now, as the Bible here teaches.

When you go home if you will read carefully the eighteenth chapter of Genesis, you will find there a history of the destruction of these same people of Sodom and the surrounding plain.

"Do you believe the account, yourself?" asked the Pastor.

Certainly! but what we are here concerned with is, that the narrative places the Bible on the side of justice. The meanness of these people, among which was robbery and oppression, and their consequent over-throw, is held up to evil-doers throughout the Old and New Testament. We, Socialists, teach that the injustice and oppression of the poor producer always leads to destruction, unless prevented.

The wealth these robbers plundered the people of could only be produced by labor then, as now.

In the narrative, regarding the destruction of these oppressors, the Lord said of Abraham:

"I know him that he will command his children and his household after him, and they shall keep the way of the Lord to do justice and judgment." (Gen. xviii:19.)

The reason the Lord gave Abraham for destroying these people was, because, as he said:

"Their sins is very grievous." (Gen. xviii:20.)

The difference between Abraham's household and these people was, that one was just and the other was not.

One of the grievous sins of the times was the exploiting of the poor. According to account there was not ten righteous persons in the city.

These things ought to be condemned now, as they were then, and the justice we advocate is the only remedy. The Bible, you know, says:

"Cease to do evil and learn to do well."

Profane history, as deciphered from the monuments and recorded by ancient Greek writers as well as the Jewish prophets, informs us that Egypt did her mighty work of building pyramids and palaces, temples, artificial lakes and other vast internal improvements, through the slavery and exploitation of the working class.

Egypt was what, in this country, is called a great world power, and a prosperous nation, but it was all in the hands of the few then, as now.

Against this the prophets thundered, in place of sanctioning it as do most of the preachers today. Read Ezekiel xxix and xxx chapters.

"I thought you Socialists taught that the centralization of wealth in the hands of the few would bring Socialism, why didn't it in this case?" asked the Pastor.

Centralization of wealth can only bring Socialism where the producer is in a condition to be reached and taught to take advantage of the conditions. At that age the wages system existed, yet, most of the wealth, was produced by slaves among the nations who were not far enough advanced to take advantage of the situation, consequently national decay and destruction was inevitable. Another reason was, the crude methods of production kept all workers employed.

Today, as economic conditions develop, we find a people that the Socialistic propaganda can prepare to set up the Cooperative Commonwealth, when the time is fully ripe, because modern machinery, with its rapid creation of wealth, lessens the demand for labor. Machinery workers would not bring Socialism without the teachings of the people; but the destruction of the nations would follow instead.

"When Joseph, under the direction of Pharaoh, during the seven years of plenty, stored up the grain and then sold it to the people; getting first their money, next their cattle, and lastly, their land turning the same over to the king, in whose hand was the government, wasn't that something like what you Socialists want?" asked the Pastor. (Gen. xlvii:13-26.)

We learn from this that the people of Egypt had private ownership of land in B.C. 1700.

This transaction, in place of being anything like Socialism, was very much like what we are doing now. The people who produced this grain had it taken from them by those who never produced any of it. Do we not turn everything the worker produces over to the non-producer, outside of a bare living, and then the worker buys it back at the sacrifice of land, money, and everything else?

Pharaoh and his nobles governed the country just as the same class do now.

"Then you don't think the transaction was right," said the Pastor.

No! The Bible don't say it was right; and the subsequent punishment of Egypt for enslaving the Jews, and the law following which prevented the land from passing into the hands of the few, condemns the whole thing.

Socialists, as we have shown, don't propose to put the land into the hands of one man, but in the hands of the whole people where the power to make all laws by direct vote will rest. It was the laws of Egypt, that gave everything to Pharaoh and not the laws of the Jews.

Ezekiel, as you will find by reading what I told you, said of Egypt:

"It shall be the basest of the kingdoms, neither shall it exalt itself anymore above the nations." (Ezek. xxix:15.)

As a result of economic injustice the glory of Egypt has long since departed, and owls, bats, and dragons, now live in their fallen palaces and temples. Let these teachings be presented in the churches, with proper application to the conditions in the nations of today.

Daniel's account of the Chaldean and Persian Empires may be studied in the light of present day conditions. We refer, now, to the historical part of the book. At the same time read, along with this, the accounts given by great historians, and the two will show how the rulers of Babylon carried away the wealth created by the workers of other nations, and forced the poor to build walls, palaces, temples and hanging gardens.

Nebuchadnezzar's gold image, mentioned by Daniel which the three Jews refused to bow to, was stained with the blood of the poor. There was about as much sense in bowing to that image as there is now of believing in the virtue of the gold reserve in the Treasury vaults at Washington. We commend the example of the three Jews, who in the face of the king and the assembled multitude, refused to bow to the power of wealth, to the preacher and statesmen of today, go and do likewise!

Go! say to these oppressors of today, as did Daniel: to the King of Babylon: "Brake off thy sins by righteousness, and thine iniquities by showing mercy to the poor." (Dan. iv:27.)

The way to show mercy to the poor is to abolish poverty. Isaiah said of this city:

"Babylon, the glory of kingdoms, the beauty of the Chaldeans excellency, shall be as when God overthrew Sodom and Gomorrah," etc. (Isa. xiii:19-22.)

So wonderfully eloquent and touching is Ezekiel's description of the great Phoenician city of Tyre that it would be a pity, Pastor, to spoil it by just reading a verse now and then; but read it at your leisure in your own study. Read and study the twenty-seventh and twenty-eighth chapters and you will find her trading with all nations, and in every sort of thing, from animals to the persons of men. Her kings and princes lived in a style that eclipsed anything in this day, and yet the prophet denounced this traffic as wicked and said it would lead to destruction, which it did.

Now, Pastor, if this imperfect sketch of what the prophets of the Bible said of the nations who exploited the poor, in their day, will cause you to speak to your congregation in the same way of the nations of today, in place of calling them Christian nations, we shall be satisfied with our evening conversation.

There are many other nations mentioned by the prophets in much the same strain.

"Changing the subject a little, what is this?" said the Pastor, picking up from the table a manuscript.

That is a lecture delivered by the late Rev. Annie R. Woodbey, and it just comes to hand. Pass it to me and we will read you something she said about these nations, as a fitting close to this talk.

"I have heard of her, and would be glad to hear it," remarked the Pastor.

"Ezekiel uttered the doom of this renowned city (Tyre) when he said:

'And they shall destroy the wall of Tyrus and break down her towers. I will also scrape her dust from her and make her like the top of a rock. It shall be a place for the spreading of nets in the midst of the sea, for I have spoken it saith the Lord God, and it shall become a spoil to the nations.'

"At the time the prophet uttered these predictions Tyre was the greatest commercial city of the world. All nations traded in her streets, the ships from every country anchored in her harbor, and she flourished like an evergreen.

"Her wise men were renowned throughout all the world. Why should it not stand forever?... Has this prophecy been fulfilled? Mr. Volney (not a believer in the Bible) quotes it and applies it to Tyre, and then says:

'The vicissitudes of time, or, rather, the barbarism of the Greek of the lower empire and the Mohammedans have accomplished the prediction.'

"Passing over the destruction of Tyre, by Nebuchadnezzar and, also, by Alexander, when her timbers and dust were thrown into the sea to make a bridge to New Tyre, Mr. Volney says:

'The whole village of Tyre consists only of fifty or sixty poor families, who live obscurely on a trifling fishery.'

'The port of Tyre,' says Dr. Shaw, 'is choked up with sand and rubbish to that degree that the boats of those fishermen who now and then visit this once renowned emporium and dry their nets upon its rocks and ruins, can, with great difficulty only, be admitted.

"So complete has been the ruin of this city, according to the prophecy. Such is the testimony of those who have visited these ruins in our own day.

"Where Tyre, the Queen of the Sea, once stood, fishermen are spreading their nets on the desolate rocks, and mighty waves are rolling over her marble columns.

"In the empty apartments of Edom the fox makes his den, and the light, flying sand of the desert is sifting over the splendid, but now forsaken, ruins of Palmyra.

"Owls and bats live in the ancient halls of kings, and the night winds make sad music through rents of their once gorgeous palaces.

"The Arab stalks along the streets of Jerusalem, and contemptuously laughs at the weary pilgrims.

"The Musselman's voice sings mournfully over the tombs of the prophets, while time heaps rubbish over the places where once flourished the Seven Churches of Asia."

"I hope these words may never be said of our fair land," said the Pastor, earnestly, as he arose to go.

It is either that or Socialism in the course of time, we replied.

XVI

Attitude of the Socialists Toward the Churches

It was evident that the strong language we used in our application of Bible teachings to the practice of the churches of our day had given the Pastor considerable concern, so much so that when we next met his first question was:

"Why do you Socialists always attack the church so bitterly, giving it no credit for anything?"

We can not speak for all who claim to be Socialists, but as for ourselves, we think we give due credit to the church for all the good it has done. The church is not true to the economics of the Bible.

Before the church was organized by Christ, we have seen during these conversations, the only real followers of God were the prophets. They taught the true principles of economics, and though often hopelessly in the minority, pleaded the cause of the poor and oppressed and had their followers just as the Socialists of today have.

Nor has their work been lost, for the Socialism we are now about to set up is the result of the growth of ages of teaching and economic development.

It was through these ancient advocates of the cause of the oppressed that we have the law and the prophets.

The only truly loyal citizens of ancient Israel were those who abided by the laws of the nations, including those against interest, and oppression of all kinds. Although, as Christ said, they were persecuted, and often murdered, for their advocacy of the cause of their class, yet they were the only true people of God.

As it is today, so it was then, many of the people had to be taught the rights of the working class by the speaking and writings of the prophets. A prophet then was, in many respects, what we call an agitator now, and should you put their words on economics into every-day English and speak them from a box on the street corner, the capitalist press would denounce you as a Socialist agitator.

So far, then, from discrediting the Bible, we give it credit for setting up the only commonwealth in the days of antiquity, that has lead up to what we Socialists are now contending for.

"All that applies to the Old Testament, which, if I rightly understand you, came through a class of men and women who, on the relation of the rich and the poor, believe as you Socialists do," added the Pastor.

You understand us exactly. What we have said applies just as well to Christ and his teachings as to the old dispensation.

Certainly, no one will claim that one can be a Christian and not do what Christ said, as near as his knowledge, after diligent study, will allow him.

So far from undue criticism of the church, we give the founder of it, credit for teaching the same doctrine Socialists now advocate.

In due time we will show that Christ founded a cooperative institution, which he called his church.

"My objection to your position relates more immediately to your criticism of the churches of today," said the Pastor.

The early Christians, we shall see as we proceed, more nearly resemble the Socialists of today on economic questions, than our modern church people.

The great effort today on the part of the opponents is to lead the Socialists off after something other than the Cooperative Commonwealth, and thus prolong the struggle.

If the Socialists could be divided into warring factions the work would be hindered.

So the early churches, with their doctrine of universal brotherhood, were divided into different warring factions at last, by the wealthy class, who finally gained control, and thus, as we shall see, they lost their ideas of cooperation for a time. But—

"Truth crushed to earth will rise again."

So, in the Socialist movement, these same great truths are coming back with redoubled force and this time to win.

Among the greatest good the modern churches have done along economic lines is to translate, publish and circulate the Great Book, containing these teachings we are reviewing, night after night.

The right to think and speak as you please on all subjects, subject only to the criticism of others, was advocated by millions of Christians, though it cost them their lives at the rack and the stake.

Due credit must, also, be given to those who were not Christians on that score as well.

Then, as the light of Socialism is turned on the situation, we will find out which are the true churches, and which are the false ones. It is my belief that when the light of the Bible the churches profess to believe in, is turned on them, all that naturally belonging on account of their class interest to the Socialist movement, will come over.

Those whose class interest carries them the other way and who, at the same time, know the influence of the Bible among professed Christians, will, in all probability, try to show that the Book is on the side of the oppressor. Some tried that during the days of chattel slavery. We have, in the library here, some of the ablest books written on both sides of the slavery controversy and we find most of them written by professed Christians. This caused a split in the churches, and the true followers of the master stood for the rights of the poor and oppressed, as many of their fathers did in the past, and the same thing will, possibly, occur again. However, with some honorable exceptions, this dissension in the churches was along the line of material interest.

No! We are not opposed to the churches; we only ask that

they take up the study of Socialism in the light of the Bible they professed to follow, and having found the truth, advocate it, and vote for it. Some Socialists have opposed Christianity as such, because the churches have not fairly represented the economic teaching of the Bible.

Let the church stand on the side of this class struggle, that Jesus Christ would stand on were he walking the earth today, taking the Bible to settle where it is like he would stand, and the Socialists are willing to risk the results. The Bible is harder on the churches than the Socialists are.

We are not at all pessimistic, because the outlook for the establishment of Socialism is too bright for that. The churches have, of course, favored education, such as it is, and the ability to read and write opens the way for the Socialist propaganda. This is not saying that we will not have much of our present education to unlearn.

XVII

The Ancient Churches Cooperative Institutions

It is significant that Christ, being poor himself, gathered around him a number of poor fishermen and others of the working class, and, out of them, formed his church, the institution that was to keep alive his teachings and spread it to the end of the earth.

In the first centuries of the Christian era only now and then a wealthy man could be found connected with the church.

When Christ preached, it is said:

"The common people heard him gladly." (Mark xii:37.)

The evident reason was, because he was, himself, one of them.

Suppose, Pastor, we inquire what kind of an institution the early church was, so far as it touches the economic questions the Socialists and capitalists are now struggling over.

We Socialists think that cooperative ownership and operation of all industries should take the place of private ownership and operation.

Now, the fact is, the church was organized on a cooperative basis, in which all shared alike.

"And the multitude of them that believed were of one heart and of one soul, neither said any of them that ought of the things which he possessed was his own, but they had all things in common." (Acts iv:32.)

Here they ignore the so-called right of private ownership. But every church in the country now stands for private ownership. Had not the deadly doctrine of private ownership of capital laid its hands upon the church it would be hand in hand with the Socialist in advocating the common ownership of the earth, and the tools of industry, which is but carrying into the state the same principles then practiced by the church, as near it could.

"They had all things in common."

That is, they had economic equality.

"Neither was there any that lacked."

Or, in other words, there was no poverty, as there need not be where the people cooperate in place of competing. This tells us how it was done:

"For as many as were possessors of lands, or houses, sold them and brought the price of the things that were sold and laid them down at the feet of the apostles, and distribution was made unto every man according as he had need." (Act iv:34,35.)

"But this voluntary method is not the way you Socialists propose to get possession," said the Pastor.

These church members were, at the time, subjects of the Roman government, where they did not even have a vote, and were, therefore, doing the best the circumstances would allow by voluntary cooperation. We now have the vote and should use it.

The price of these possessions was not given to the apostles for their own use, as it is often to preachers now, thus placing them in a class to themselves, so far as income is concerned as compared with the poor in the churches. But it went to supply the needs of each one as their necessities demanded.

One man, Joses, is mentioned by name, who sold a farm and gave the price to the common stock, while another man and his wife, by name Annanias and Saphira, we are told, were struck dead for lying about their possessions. This ought, at least, to be a warning to those of us who believe in the Supreme Being and the brotherhood of man, not to tamper with things intended to better the condition of humanity. This account of the death of these two people places God, again, on the side of those who believed in cooperation and common ownership. (See Acts v:1-11.)

It seems that the whole burden of distribution, as well as preaching, was, at first, laid on the apostles, but when complaints arose about some widows not getting fair treatment, the apostles called on the whole people to appoint seven agents, known for honesty and goodness, to take charge of the goods; one of the prominent features of the coming Cooperative Commonwealth. The people must govern everything and settle their own disputes; appoint their own men to take charge of the cooperative stores of the nation, and distribute their goods. Since the churches have ceased to be what they should be on the question of economics, these officers, known as deacons, in other parts of the scriptures, have become largely useless. (See Acts vi:1-6; 1 Timothy iii:8-13.)

"It seems to me that the whole thing, you refer to here, related to a condition of things that do not now exist," said the Pastor.

Why is not cooperation as much necessary now as then? I am sure there is as many needy ones now as then and as much need of abolishing poverty.

"That condition was not continued in the churches, because it was impossible for it to be otherwise than temporary, as they would soon consume all they had and starvation would be the result," said the Pastor.

You don't suppose that the people quit work, do you? That other churches outside of Jerusalem were all cooperative institutions is evident from the fact that, the same men organized them in other parts of the country. And what is said of one of them will throw some light on the subject.

Paul, writing to one of the same kind of churches at Thessalonica, said, on this subject:

"For even when we were with you this we commanded that if any would not work, neither should he eat." (2 Thess. iii:10.)

In the ninth verse he had declared that while with them he labored with his own hands, that he might not be a burden. That Paul had reference to the common stock of the church, when he said: "If any man will not work, neither shall he eat," is evident, for the very good reason that the church had no power to prevent those outside its membership from living at the expense of others.

These cooperative churches then, kept the institution going by each one contributing to its support by work, and Paul set us preachers an example by doing his part.

Socialism, which advocates common ownership, is not opposed to private ownership of wealth which is the product of labor.

So, when the goods was distributed by the deacons or agents of these churches, to the people, who had done their part of the work, they at once became their private property as will be true under the Cooperative Commonwealth which we propose.

So it was the duty of each member to work to keep up the common stock that he might not be a burden to the rest. And if he would not do that, he was not to be allowed to consume the product of other people's labor, and so we say.

"How long did this condition of things continue?" asked the Pastor.

Were it not that our investigations are confined to the teachings of the Bible on the economic questions of the day, we might show from the church writers of the first three hundred years, known as the Ante-Nicene Fathers, that these cooperative churches lasted for three centuries.

"It seems to me you overlook the more important spiritual work of the church," remarked the Pastor.

No! I have come to the conclusion that we cannot be wrong in our relation to our fellowmen in this world, and at the same time, right in our relations to the next, the two are too closely connected to be separated.

It is this curse of private ownership of the means of production and distribution that stand in the way of the progress of the church, and Socialism will enable her to return to her ancient moorings.

The fact that the churches did not maintain, successfuly, a cooperative system, surrounded by private ownership of the means of production and distribution, hampered by the governments of the world, shows the truth of the Socialists' contention, that we must seize the powers of government and establish international Socialism to make ourselves sure.

Socialism, as a principle, is not at war with the Bible and Christianity, on the question of economics, as we have shown, but in harmony.

The churches, themselves, are out of harmony with the Bible, and Christ, himself, on this question. So long as the churches forsake the teaching of their Book and founder for capitalism, they may expect the opposition of the Socialist. But, as we said, we do not oppose those who follow Christ.

"But, I find in the literature circulated by your party, attacks on Christianity, as such," said the Pastor.

As to whether Socialism, which is the common ownership and collective operation of the earth and its resources for the benefit of the whole people, on a basis of the equal distribution of the wealth produced among the workers; is the thing best for the people, does not depend on any mistake any individual or party may make, in their zeal to teach the people. Most persons condemn Socialism from some preconceived prejudices, without giving it a fair hearing. Especially is this true among professed Christians when they find Socialism associated with those who oppose Christianity, as such. On the other hand, some Socialists oppose Christianity because of the people who pretend to be Christians, without giving its fundamental principles a thorough study.

In our opinion, both sides are at fault, in not seeking to better understand the economics taught in the Bible and the Socialist philosophy, so as to find their relationship.

Both Christianity and Socialism must stand or fail on their own merits, regardless of the character or mistakes of the persons who profess to adhere to either.

In spite of Christ's teaching us to love our neighbor, and not resist evil with evil, to put up the sword as he that fights with it shall perish by it, yet some over-zealous, but mistaken advocate of Christianity have used the sword to spread his doctrine. (See Matt. xxvi:52.)

"But what about this passage:

'Think not that I am come to send peace on earth: I came not to send peace, but a sword. For I am come to set a man at variance against his father: and the daughter against her mother: and the daughter-in-law against her mother-in-law. And a man's foes shall be they of his own household.' (Matt. x:34-35.)"

Said the Pastor:

These words were spoken to those Christ was sending out to teach this new revolutionary doctrine. And has not the attempt to plead the cause of the masses, against those who are robbing them, always brought out the sword to put the advocate down?

Is not that true today?

Do not these revolutionary questions divide kin folks against each other now, as in the past?

This same thing cost Christ and his apostles their lives.

Standing firm for principle, is what is meant by hating father, mother, wife and children, for Christ's sake and the gospel.

Is it not uncommon for families to become enemies over Socialism now, just as in the early days people did about Christianity.

In spreading his doctrine, Christ, like the Socialists, taught his followers to let their foes do the resorting to the sword.

The fact, then, that some have brought disgrace on the cause of Christianity by using the sword, no more proves Christianity not to be right than the indiscreet attack of some Socialist writers on Christianity, prove the principles of Socialism not to be right. We are ready to admit, that some Socialists have given no more study to the teachings of Christ and the Bible, than some Christians have to the principles of Socialism. We often hear the Bible condemned because it points out the punishment of bad people and in the next breath because they were not punished.

That is true, although the Bible and Socialists agree on economics.

All the twenty odd millions of church members in this country will not become Socialists, nor will all the Socialists become Christians. But a large majority of the church people belong to the proleteriat class and must, eventually, come to us.

I submit to you, Pastor, that the church will stand a far better show to convert these people, she finds so hard to reach now, by helping to down capitalism at the ballot box and setting up Socialism.

"Don't you think that the people are getting about what they are worthy of?" said the Pastor.

The wickedness of men, is no reason why any one should rob them of their right to live on the earth, and have what they produce.

In teaching us to love our enemies, Christ gave this as a reason:

"For he maketh his sun to rise on the evil and on the good; and sendeth rain on the just and the unjust." Referring to God. (Matt. v:45.)

Do you profess to follow God, and then set up a different standard from him? That which is opposed to what Christ taught is not Christianity, and that which is opposed to the Socialist platform is not Socialism, as we have shown.

"So you think those of us who do not accept the Socialist ideas are not Christians," remarked the Pastor.

Any organization claiming to be Christian and yet, knowingly, setting aside the economic teachings of the Old and New Testament, which lays at the foundation of the Christian religion, is no more of a church than is an organization claiming to be Socialist and at the same setting aside the platform of Socialism, really a Socialist party.

To be a Christian one must accept these foundation principles. Just as to be a Socialist one must accept the foundation principles of Socialism. And as the two are alike on economics (on that point) to accept one is to accept the other.

"But, I am told by some Socialists that no one can find out just what the Bible does teach on this question, because there is such a difference of opinion about it," remarked the Pastor.

Any one who can understand what Marx taught on the subject of economics, certainly ought to find no difficulty in understanding what Moses or Christ said on the same subject.

"But, they say there are differences of opinion among Christians," continued the Pastor.

So, we must admit that differences arise among us Socialists, but differences does not disprove either the truth of Socialism or Christianity.

"Well," said the Pastor, "I assure you that I had no idea that the Socialist philosophy and the Bible are so closely allied. But, then, truth will always claim relationship wherever it is found. While in college I gave a few weeks to the study of economics, I recollect, and accepted, with but little question, what I found in the text books of the time, because they were placed there by those thought to be the highest authority on the subject. Indeed, I remember very little about what I did learn, and hardly recollect who wrote the text books I used. I have since been so engrossed, during my ministry, with other things pertaining to the Bible, that I have given its economic teachings only a casual notice, now and then."

We are told, Pastor, to grow in the knowledge of the Lord Jesus Christ, and he said that knowledge was to be found in the scriptures, which testifies of him. (John v:39; 2 Peter iii:18.)

This is an injunction to those who are already Christians, to go on learning. Only a few days ago most of the persons who are now Socialists knew nothing of it, and millions more are learning, both in and out of the church.

And many preachers, like the rest, have yet to learn more about Christ and the Bible on these economic questions. Of course, as we said, the various organizations known as churches, have been the instruments through which the Bible has been preserved, whether they adhere to its economic teachings or not.

"When I took my theological course," the Pastor continued,

"my attention was called mainly to what was deemed the spiritual side of the Bible teaching, and most everything was explained in that light."

"There may be exceptions to this rule; but I think what is true in my case, is true in the majority of cases of those engaged in the ministry, and like other men, they need their attention called to these things."

"Indeed! If I understand you rightly, you think the Bible in teaching these things, was laying a foundation for the future, and that the economic conditions are now ripening to carry them out."

"But, I need not tell you about the training and life of the average minister, as you have been twenty-eight years in the ministry, and still retain your standing."

"This, of course, ends our very interesting evening conversations and, being convinced that Socialism is but the carrying out of the economic teachings of the Bible, I shall endeavor to study it and lay it before my people to the best of my ability."

"So, Good Night!"

The
Distribution
of Wealth

1910

Preface

This book is written to show those who are anxious to know, how it is possible to distribute the wealth produced by collective labor, after Socialism has overthrown the capitalist method of distribution. It is written not so much for Socialists as it is for those who would be if they could see any possible way of distributing wealth better than what we now have. I have therefore written in the plainest words at my command. I have dismissed all technical terms at the risk of being considered unscientific. Science is nothing more than systematized knowledge, and is none the less science when put in the simplest language. While I have written for the purpose of making Socialists out of those who are not; yet if what I have written will do anything to help Socialists to a better understanding of the subject so much the better. Socialist speakers and writers differ not as to what Socialism is, but as to what answers should be made to these questions regarding its future. But having thrown themselves open to the answering of questions, it is not possible to avoid some sort of a reply. The writings of Karl Marx were at the time a deduction as to the final or future outcome of capitalism, and the setting up of collective ownership in its place. So others may now make deductions as to the final outcome of Socialism. And these conclusions will stand or fall just in proportion as they are scientific. Among those who are best read in Socialist literature, almost every one has some one or more favorite authors whom they believe to be the best thinkers in the movement. To this I have no objections whatever. But I will here ask the reader's attention to my own idea as to what constitutes the best thinkers. To my mind the best thinkers are those who will to the best of their ability investigate both sides of a subject, and then be independent enough to say what they think and honest enough to carefully listen to the opinions of others, however much they may differ from theirs. And common sense enough to know that neither they nor those who differ with them are infallible. So that much of what either of them may predict might prove to be a mistake. Nevertheless we are so constituted, that we are compelled to try to forecast what will be the final outcome of a definite course of action. And if our reasonings are sound, we may arrive at the truth about what will be the future outcome of Socialism, as some Socialists of the past have, as to what we are now passing through, under capitalism. So let us have the broadest liberty of thought upon these questions of the future. If the Socialist movement is based upon truth, it cannot be destroyed by the utmost freedom of discussion, nor is the movement or the party necessarily in danger, because your views or mine are not at once adopted even should they be correct. Recollect that mistakes are human, and may be corrected. All I ask of the reader is a fair, honest consideration of what I have written.

Letter I

San Diego, California

Mr. J. Jones.

Dear Friend: When I last visited your ranch, you said that you were ready to accept Socialism, if you could only see any possible way by which the wealth of the people, when they all work together, can be justly distributed among those who produced it. As I didn't have time to give you my views on that very important subject then, you made me promise to write, which I now proceed to do. As my excuse for not writing sooner, I can only say that I have been too busy lecturing on Socialism to find time. If I cannot say all that I wish in a single letter, I shall continue them until I do.

Let me start with what we can agree about. We agree that it would be best for the whole people to own the entire earth, and working together produce all they need. Thus working they would produce common wealth, from which each individual could supply all of his needs. As we agreed, in different departments you produce common wealth on your ranch. There is your son William, who together with a number of the younger boys seem to have a natural liking for looking after the orchard and vineyards. Then there are Thomas and John, who never tire talking about the splendid crop of grain and hay, while I am sure that none of them could be prouder than Peter with his effort to produce common wealth by raising the hogs, cattle and horses.

Your daughters, too, I could see, were delighted with their work in which one does the sewing, another the cooking, while still another does the sweeping and general house work. And as if to make the thing as complete as may be, these children whom you have raised and educated, have put you and Mrs. Jones on the retired list, and are thus repaying you. All the wealth produced on the ranch belongs to your family in common, and each member is expected to consume all he or she needs, after you have taken care to produce abundance. Now if you will only think of the world of mankind, as one great family owning the whole earth as you and your children do the ranch, and in different departments producing all kinds of things in abundance, and then using them, you will see the Socialist commonwealth in a nutshell. You are doing all this in a small way on your ranch. So this larger family including all mankind, can produce and consume in the same way only on a larger scale.

Then too the old folks can retire, as you and Mrs. Jones have done, and let the children of the nation, which they have fed, clothed and educated, out of their labor, repay them by caring for them with the best of everything in their old days. All this is entirely different to what we are now doing in the world generally, in any place outside of the family. We are now living under capitalism, which means the private ownership of the land, factories, mines, railroads, steamships, steam boats, and all that we now call capital, by a few of the people, operated by the labor of the masses, for the benefit of the few owners. We call these things capital, because they are used to take away what the worker produces. These owners we call capitalists, or owners of capital.

Socialism means that the whole people shall own collectively all of those things we call capital, and work together in different departments like you do on the ranch, and keep what they produce for their own use. You get an idea of the difference between private ownership of capital, or what I call capitalism, and collective ownership and operation of this same thing I now call capital, when I say the wagon road belongs to all of us while the railroad belongs to the few. I am here simply trying to refresh your mind about what we talked over at length. As we agreed so well about these things, I wouldn't stop to call your attention to them at this time were it not for the fact that I wish to refer to them as a foundation for what I have to say on the distribution of wealth under Socialism, the one thing which you say prevents you from accepting the theory. I am aware that this question is everywhere pressing for an answer, because it is being put to me during my lectures from ocean to ocean. The inquiry is not, how will you distribute the wealth under Socialism when it comes? but whether it is possible to do it at all, any better than it is now being done, under present conditions. I will not stop here to say how it is possible to get possession of the industries and operate them, as you have read my book, *What to Do and How to Do It*.

Keep in mind that I said, wealth is that which man produces for his use by the application of his labor to the raw material around him, and he finds the whole earth one vast storehouse of such material, ready to his hand. But nothing which lies around him is wealth until he prepares it for his use.

I admit, as I told you, that as fast as the people learn we want them to take the entire plant of industry and operate it collectively for their own benefit, they next want to know how it is possible to distribute the wealth thus created. This I deem a perfectly reasonable inquiry. While we may not be able to decide for the future, any further than the effect of our teachings will go, yet it is possible to greatly affect what will be done in the future in that way. There is more than one way by which wealth might be distributed. I shall proceed to outline these different ways at your request and speak at some length of the one I deem best and hope to see adopted.

It is even possible to say just how some things will have to be done under Socialism, because there is only one way to do them outside of what we are now doing.

You say that some have dismissed your inquiry by saying that no one can tell just what plan will be adopted for the distribution of wealth under Socialism, and therefore it is no use trying to show how it can be done. I agree with you that such an answer is entirely unsatisfactory and that it is likely to make the inquirer refuse to help bring about a thing he can see no possible way of doing. If we start to build a house we have a plan at least in our mind before we begin gathering material; and so with other important things. To think about Socialism taking the place of capitalism, is to force upon the mind some idea about how the thing will be operated. Plans may be modified or changed entirely, but that doesn't say there is no use of one. Is not Socialism itself being discussed as a plan or system to take the place of what we now have? It may be considered as a plan of ownership, which we offer to take the place of private ownership. So if we are not to discuss plans for the future, then we should not discuss Socialism, for it is a plan to be adopted in the future. And if the people must inevitably adopt Socialism then the agitation of the matter is useless. I hold that the centralization of wealth in the hands of the few, by the use of modern machinery, which forces upon us an unemployed problem, together with systematic agitation, are all necessary to bring about Socialism. Ancient nations, such as Egypt, Chaldea, Rome and others had the concentration of wealth, but they did not get Socialism because their crude method of production required the employment of all the workers. Agitation is necessary to keep the people from doing what the Chinese claimed to have done, destroy the machines and go back to crude methods of production.

I am not expecting the world to go backward. International Socialism is now too far advanced. But at the same time if we Socialists say the people should own and operate the industries collectively, then it is up to us to show how it can be done so as to distribute the wealth in such a way as to serve the best interests of all concerned. And, as you say, now is the time to discuss the plan for distribution, just as we do Socialism, and let the votes of the future settle the matter. If we discuss the question now, however, it is more than likely that the people of the future will follow what they have been taught, as has often been the case before, and it will give them less trouble in the final settlement. You say that one Socialist speaker in reply to your question, said the fathers of this republic had no plan in mind when they carried on the agitation, which lead up to the adoption of the constitution. But he couldn't make you believe that it was necessary for us to do the same, even if it were true. I think you are right. But is it really true that they had no idea what they intended to do? Does not the history of those stirring times show that the framers of the constitution had it in their mind to follow the model of the English government, as near as the circumstances would permit? The President takes the place of the King, the Senate the place of the house of Lords, and the House of Representatives that of the Commons, and I will leave you to trace out the rest of the similarity at your leisure.

Did not Jefferson, although not a member of the constitutional convention, have it in his mind that: "All just governments derive their power from the consent of the governed," and was he not therefore broader than any other man of his time?

Do you think that Hamilton, who made a long speech before the convention outlining what he deemed a strong government, has never thought of the matter before? It is evident to my mind that these men had thought over what they intended to do, providing they were successful in their agitation. While none of them got all they wanted, yet the constitution bears the impress of what was in the master minds of that time. And the same thing will doubtless be true when Socialism is established. But this letter is already longer than I intended when I started in to write. So believe me yours in the cause of Socialism,

G.W. WOODBEY

Letter II

San Diego, California

Mr. J. Jones.

My Dear Friend: Your reply came duly to hand, and you say that my letter didn't succeed fully in removing the difficulty from your mind. That letter was only introductory to what I wish to say on the subject. I shall devote this letter to one of the possible methods of distributing wealth under Socialism. As you know, the capitalists own nearly all the things the whole people should possess. Money under the capitalist system is an absolute necessity as a method of distributing the wealth among the consumers, as well as settling obligations between independent industries. In the ages gone by the people have become so thoroughly accustomed to this method of distribution through the money system that it is now one of the hardest things imaginable to make them realize that anything else is possible. As you say, the money system under present conditions is deceptive, making the workers think they are getting all that they earn, because the value their labor will produce is never mentioned when they hire out for wages. The worker, not being an owner of capital, must either get as wages some of his own product, or its equivalent in money, in order to enable him to buy back enough to keep him alive, so as to produce more and feed his children that they may take his place. This is always true unless one happens to be producing on a small scale for his own use, and even then he must turn the surplus into money in order to exchange with others for what he does not produce. Money is only necessary under private ownership. But if all the industries belonged to one great trust composed of a few men, the members of it would need no medium of exchange among themselves. But exchange would still exist between the trust and the workers. No member of such a trust would sell his holdings because there would be nothing else to invest in. It seems evident that such a day of complete monopoly is fast approaching and with it the doom of capitalism.

It is not our purpose to discuss the capitalist system any further than to show why under it we are compelled to use money. Complete private monopoly such as I have hinted at must ultimately collapse for want of profits; because after the wants of the members of such a trust had been supplied out of the wealth created by labor, there could be no market outside of the worker with his wages, and these wages would constitute the worker's only purchasing power. A complete monopoly could never get back any more money than it payed out. At present however the big concerns not only get back what they pay out, but they are fast eating up the little middle men as the big fish eat up the little ones. But this must come to an end, and then like Alexander the Great there will be no more worlds for them to conquer, which will usher in the Cooperative Commonwealth.

If a few capitalists, by owning the entire plant of industry, would not need a medium of exchange, it is evident that the larger trust to be known as the Cooperative Commonwealth, consisting of the whole people, will not need one. This I believe is the common opinion of most Socialists. But nevertheless, if at the time of the setting of the new Commonwealth the people find themselves so much attached to the money system that they are loathe to give it up, and want to pay themselves off in their own money for doing their own work, which would be good at their own stores for the wealth that they themselves have produced in their own plants of industry, I can see no reason why they could not do so.

It would not be impossible for you to institute a kind of money system in your little cooperative commonwealth on your ranch, paying each member of the family in a kind of money which would be good for anything you produced. This, however, you will not do so long as you have no fear that one member will get more than another, and there is an abundance for all. You don't seem to fear that some one of the family will get something he does not work for. You are very well satisfied with your present method on the ranch so far as it relates to distribution, which is a model for the new Commonwealth. But after having this example before their eyes if they are still afraid to trust each other, when Socialism comes they can pay themselves off in money according to what each has done, which will be good for anything produced in the nation. So, my friend, should the money system be transferred to the Cooperative Commonwealth you need not fear but what each man will get what is due him, or so nearly so as to make no appreciable difference. So you see this is one way by which the distribution of wealth might be done. I tell you now plainly, I don't think that is the best way of doing the thing. There are those among Socialists however who think that it is just the thing that should be done, and they have a right to their opinions, as much so as I have to mine. It is my opinion that all possible plans should be discussed so that the best will ultimately be arrived at. I will now proceed to point out some of the objections to the continuation of the money system.

    1. It will tend in a measure to perpetuate that fear each man now has of his brother getting more than he, which is the heritage of capitalism, and retards that regeneration of society which Socialism is designed to bring about. To say as some do that we must continue the money system until the people are all ready for something better is the same thing that some tell us about Socialism. We must wait until everybody is ready for it, and not push it on by the rule of the majority.

    2. The idea that each person is an equal owner, in all of the industries of the country under Socialism would have but little chance to fasten itself upon the people, so long as each worker was paid off in money as he is now, and had to go to the store and buy as he always did. In place of the idea of common ownership growing in the mind, the purchaser would likely continue feeling that the departments of industry are independent of each other, as they are under a competitive system. This is the very idea that Socialism is designed to destroy.

    3. If the industries are to belong to the whole people, then by using money the purchaser would make himself laughable by setting a price at which he will sell himself his own goods.

    4. Then again, if he happens to lose his money or is robbed he can't get his own goods out of his store. While on the other hand the man who finds the money can get the goods he never worked for, providing he is dishonest enough to do so. And if men will cease to be dishonest under Socialism, as I contend they will, then we can dispense with money.

    I admit that money would be a good thing to keep account of what each one has done in the various departments of the new Commonwealth. But I shall try to show that it is not necessary to keep any account, and that it would simply be a waste of labor. And further that this loss of labor in coining money and bookkeeping would be greater than the loss from those who it is supposed will not labor. So now, my friend, you have before you one possible way by which the distribution of wealth may be made, and in my next letter I will point out another method.

Yours in the cause of Socialism,
G.W. WOODBEY

Letter III

San Diego, California

Mr. J. Jones.

Dear Friend: You say in your last letter, that you are aware that some Socialists are in favor of the money system being transferred into the Cooperative Commonwealth, but the idea is as unsatisfactory to you as it is to me.

Very well then, as I said, there are different ways by which the wealth might be distributed. I will in this letter point out another way by which the thing may be done. We will call this for convenience the labor check system. You will find it discussed on page 33, Chapter XVII, of: *What to Do and How to Do It.* At the time when the book was written, in 1904,[8] that was almost invariably the answer given to the inquirer, when he asked how it is possible to distribute the product under the new system. I there outlined how a time-keeper might be appointed by the workers in any one of the departments of industry and checks be issued according to the hours put in. These checks to show the hours and minutes put in by the worker; the products of all industry being so marked as to show the amount of labor expended in its production, so that the purchaser might have the amount of hours and minutes punched from his check, that it took to produce the article he wishes to buy, whether that be a house or a yard of cloth. I also said the money system could be continued. And further that mothers and children, the old, the indigent, either mentally or physically, might be supplied through the check system in the same way. I was told in the first place by those older in the movement than myself that when anybody asks me how the thing could be done to reply that no one could tell; the whole thing is a matter of the future. I found, however, that when these same persons were under the fire of the questioner, they resorted to this check system as an answer, and I followed suit. The fundamental basis of Socialism is fixed. We the workers must own and operate the industries and keep the wealth we produce. The chattel slave must be freed, said the abolitionist. Just how, was open to discussion. Some said it would be done by a gradual process, others said they would be bought, others as far back as the days of Jefferson, said that it would bring on a war; so different persons had their ideas, and it was well enough.

So more mature thought along this line, has at last brought me to the conclusion that while this check system could be used, yet it is not by any means the thing to do. It is open to almost all the objections of the money system. There would be the strange anomaly of the owners of the industries hiring some one to look after them to see how much time they put in at their own work. Under capitalism, as we have it now, bosses look after the workers who have no interest in the places where they work, but not after the owners. A man even today, who goes out to do his own work never thinks of hiring some one to look after him. Here again comes in the waste labor of bookkeeping, and marking of goods.

All this matter of the credits of the individual citizen, might be done by bookkeepers, like we have now. Only they would be simply agents of the people. Then again this check system might be so arranged as to have one advantage over the money system. It might be re-issued if lost by notifying the bookkeeper. All this, objectionable as it is, may yet be done in such a way as to give satisfaction to the worker, by insuring him the product of his labor. The adoption of this check system then is among the possibilities of the future.

If the people start in with anything that don't work to suit them, they will no doubt change it for something that does suit them better. For everything would then be subject to a referendum to the whole people. You want to know what the Socialist Party has to say on this question of distribution. It has said nothing about any method of distribution contending only that the producer must have the full product of his labors. But the speaker who is expected to answer questions must make some reply to this and many other things on which the party has made no official utterances. And this must continue so, or we must cease to answer questions. This is the reason I am trying to answer you; because like others you are eager to know if there is any possible way of doing the thing we Socialists say can be done. With a promise to write you next time about what I deem a much better way than either of the others, which I hope and believe will be adopted, I remain as ever yours in the cause of Socialism,

G.W. WOODBEY

Letter IV

San Diego, California

Mr. J. Jones.

Dear Friend: It is with pleasure I again write you on the great question of distribution which is now more and more becoming the question of the hour. And I am only the more eager to do so, because in your last you say you have found my letters worth reading to your family, and that they are favorably impressed with them.

We come now to what I call the natural, common sense method of distribution. The Creator has been very lavish in the distribution of the sources of wealth around us on every side. The earth is a vast storehouse of raw material, ready to our hand. So like the birds, the animals and the insects, man is invited to help himself to a bountiful table, requiring only that he prepare it for use. This his intelligence should teach him to do with the least possible labor. You admit that if all who are able were collectively producing wealth with modern machinery, there would be a superabundance of all the good things earth can afford for the entire people. And we are in all probability yet in the infancy of invention.

You will readily see that if each individual can be trusted to do his duty in the performance of the small amount of labor required of him, he may be allowed to help himself to all he can use of the best; as there need be no lack of anything. In fact, as I said, that is just what you are doing in your little commonwealth on the ranch. In your case the check and money system is not necessary. It is my purpose to show that such would be the effect of the setting up of the Cooperative Commonwealth.

Before I get done with these letters I shall show that the disposition not to work is the necessary outgrowth of the present method of creating and distributing wealth and that like all other things, to remove the cause will take away the effect. Nor should a few incurable cases in the first generation any more prevent the immediate application of the best remedy for an economic disease, than for a physical one. The fact that some patients in an epidemic are bound to die should never prevent the board of health from removing the garbage and filth from which the trouble arose. Indeed they should only be the more ready to apply the very best remedy at once. And society should hold them criminal for not doing the best thing without hesitation. Not using some temporary remedy, until the suffering people are ready for something better. What we want here is to find out, if possible, just the best thing to do. The food supply is as abundant as the air and the water. It lies all about us on every side. And we are blessed with a skill that makes it possible to produce wealth rapidly and abundantly, and yet many are perishing in spite of all this. This matter of distribution is the most important question connected with the Socialist movement. It is not, then, the sources for producing wealth we have to settle, nor our ability to produce it, but how best to distribute it. The land supply is abundant were it not monopolized by the few, and so with the air which is incapable of being monopolized. And so the supply of wealth will be abundant for the free and unrestricted use of all, when we get sense enough to work together.

You seemed anxious to know what the plan is that I am so much in favor of. Well in short it is this: Let the whole people own the earth and work together collectively, with the most advanced tools their skill can invent, making sure that they have produced each year all of the best of everything that they can use, providing for themselves public accommodations as well as private of all sorts, and then freely help themselves to what they have collectively produced, as you and your children do on your ranch.

The idea may be somewhat new to you, yet I am sure that the tendency is in the direction I have indicated in the use of public things. Having laid the plan before you that I think is the best one, I shall wait to hear from you, and in my next proceed to tell you why I think the people are likely to adopt it. My regards to each member of your little commonwealth.

Yours for the social revolution,
G.W. WOODBEY

Letter V

San Diego, California

Mr. J. Jones.

My Dear Friend: I see that like many others you are suspicious lest my declaration about the people providing themselves with all kinds of accommodations should mean the end of private property. On the contrary it means that all that the public does not collectively use, will be the private property of the individual. Such as his house, library, pictures, etc., etc.

There will of course be more public accommodations under Socialism than we have now. All publicly owned things are just that much Socialism so far as the ownership is concerned, lacking only the right of the people to manage what they own in their own interest. Were the Socialists elected to power there would never be any act to turn the roads, schools, and post office over to the people for example; as is necessary in the case of the things now owned by the capitalist. The trouble then is not with the ownership of the public things we now have, but is to be found in allowing the capitalists to manage them.

Under present conditions the working people furnish all accommodation and let the capitalists charge them a profit for the use of them, while under Socialism they will still furnish themselves with these accommodations without paying the capitalist for the use of them. Notwithstanding the mismanagement, some of the uses we now put public things to may throw some light upon what the people will do when all they have to use collectively belongs to them.

As representative government is the outgrowth of private ownership of the industries, so collective ownership will be followed by direct government. Upon this we are agreed, and we need discuss it no further.

The lands, mines, factories, railroads, and all capital yet remain to be taken over by the whole people in addition to what we now have. I believe under Socialism we will have the use of the railroads, hotels, stores and other things, just as we now use the wagon roads, streets, parks and libraries. I mean the free use of them, our labor having built them for that purpose. Public things are now supposed to be kept up by a tax resting mainly upon private property. But in the last analysis everything is paid out of the product of labor. So in the very nature of the case those who do not produce anything cannot pay anything.

Those things which the public owns and attempts to pay itself a fare, or buy stamps from itself—is exactly as if you should attempt to pay yourself for the things you produce on the ranch.

This attempt to pay ourselves for the use of the things that we, the public, own, is a part of the capitalist system transferred to public things, and will disappear entirely when we own everything. But the main thing I want you to notice here is that while every one is supposed to have contributed his share toward keeping up public things, when they come to use those things, on which fares are not paid, they don't have to show that they have done anything toward keeping them up, even in a community where they are unknown. All that is taken for granted.

Should I conclude to travel, from my home in San Diego over the wagon road to New York City, I would pay no fare, nor would any officer of the law, or agent of the people, be authorized to ask me whether I had done anything toward keeping up the roads over which I am traveling. I get to New York and freely use the streets the same way, without being once questioned as to whether I have done anything to keep up the streets either there or where I came from. Indeed, the authorities are not even concerned about where I did come from. I use the park and the library, and my children, who come with me, start to school the next week, and I am not asked what I have done to keep up either one. Of course it is my duty to help maintain all of these things (as I said), and the strange places through which I traveled took it for granted that I had done so, without troubling themselves to look after me. If I pay tax, or in any way help to furnish these public things that I am so freely using, that is done in my community, and not in the other states and communities through which I traveled, nor at the place where I just landed. And whether I did so was something entirely unknown to the strange people which I met on the way. No one fears when he sees the stranger using these public things freely that he may be getting something he didn't work for. The other man is content with the fact that he can enjoy the same privilege himself. When you come to think about it, a very large number of people are using public things without doing anything toward keeping them up. I refer to the rich, who do nothing but live at the expense of those who toil. But the worker needs no looking after, for the reason that he cannot avoid contributing his share, either directly or indirectly, to the keeping up of these things. For without him everything would stop. And under Socialism there would be no rich idlers to look after. Yet with all of this shirking of responsibility, we have never found it necessary to look even after the stranger lest the community should be cheated in the use of those public things upon which we do not pay fares or buy stamps.

We will suppose I start back from New York to San Diego, after the Cooperative Commonwealth is established, and this time I take the railroad which is now one of the great public highways of the nation. Why should I not use the railroad without paying a fare, just as I did the wagon road? For both of them have to be built and maintained at the expense of the people, of which I am part. And if the people can trust me to use the wagon road freely, believing that I will do my part without looking after me, they can trust me to use the railroad the same way. If we had always been paying fares over the wagon roads and streets, and I was just now advocating the throwing them open to be used as we are now using them, don't you think you would say the same thing you do about the way I want the railroads and other things to be used?

When I get back to San Diego and the people (myself included, now under Socialism) own the stores, hotels and restaurants, why may I not be trusted to freely use them as I now do the streets, parks and libraries? Stopping at the hotel, and getting what I need from the store, all on the theory that as one of the citizens and owners, I am performing my duty in some one of the industries of the great Commonwealth; just as they do now with the streets? I should, of course, do my duty toward keeping the hotels and stores well supplied, and the public railroads well equipped, and all this can be taken for granted, just as it is now about what we have already got. Nor should I have to have any checks, money, or anyone to look after me then any more than now.

The man who opposes this plan cannot consistently do so without first taking the ground that we are already being cheated by allowing the individual to use the wagon roads, streets, parks and libraries, as they are now doing, without making them show in every strange community, that they have done something to keep these things up, or paid a fare. If society can trust me to have done my duty in the community where I just came from, in the one case, it can in the other. It seems to me but reasonable that what we are now doing with the things we already have we will continue to do with the things we are going to have. I am sure that is just what I would like to see them do. But I must bring this already too long letter to a close.

Yours in the cause,
G.W. WOODBEY

Letter VI

San Diego, California

Mr. J. Jones.

Dear Friend: Just as I expected, you raise the point that the wagon roads, streets and parks, are still left the same after we use them, while we consume the clothes and the food. You are mistaken in this. Nothing ever remains the same after using it. That is the reason we cannot use the roads, the streets, or the accommodations in a park without wearing them out so that they have to be repaired. Otherwise, they would remain forever. And were it not for the profit system the cost of a suit of clothes or a meal of victuals would hardly be noticed.

Allow me to repeat here, so that you may not lose sight of it, the main objection to this plan is the old, worn out one, that men will not work under Socialism, which every Socialist speaker has had to answer over and over again. Take this away, and all must admit that it is the ideal plan. I am sure, however, my friend, there will be little or no danger even in the first generation which adopts Socialism, and none in the next. But let us leave this matter of the coming generations for the present, and consider the one by which Socialism will first be adopted.

Let us admit that there might be a few who would not want to work, when Socialism was first established. Such would only be the natural effects of their education and environments. The number of such persons, even to begin with, would be comparatively insignificant, while all they could ever get at the expense of the public would be what they could use on themselves personally and a chance to travel. If today all that the capitalists cannot use upon themselves, in way of food, clothes, travel, etc., was left to the workers, there need be no lack of anything or any suffering in the land. They not only use all that they can on themselves, but lock up through private ownership, what they cannot use, and let it rot while we starve. Of course it is not proposed that under Socialism anything shall be done for the idler.

Those who as a majority set up Socialism, will do it because they think all who are able to should work, and they will need no looking after themselves. Then the largest portion of the minority, that will at the time it is set up oppose Socialism, will do it, not because they don't want to work, but for other reasons. For this minority itself will largely be working people, leaving only a mere fraction, who will vote opposed to Socialism because they are wealthy enough to live at the expense of the rest. It is from these, who are now considered gentlemen because they do nothing useful, that we will largely get our idlers in the first generation under Socialism, if any. But when we have set up the Cooperative Commonwealth we have also changed the idea as to what constitutes a gentleman. Now, suppose I live in a community where everybody else is at work, and yet I will not, but must go to the public store for what I want, will not the whole community have me spotted? And what will be my standing? At present I can live at the expense of others, and be respected for it a great deal higher than if I worked. Under the new conditions I am lower than the tramp. I would not dare to ask any one to give me anything, for they would tell me to go to work, as there would then be plenty of it. So as an idler in even a strange community my condition would soon be unbearable. My opinion is that the hours of labor will be so short, and the conditions so pleasant, that few even of the descendants of the wealthy would brave the disgrace rather than do their part. If after all we have still a few idlers, I can see no reason why society should not make them work, seeing it would be for their own good, as they would then be getting the full product of their labor. We often make men work now under the most disagreeable circumstances, and give them nothing for it. And mark you, this could only be necessary, if at all, in the first generation immediately after the adoption of Socialism.

The very fact that Socialism is to be set up in the first place by the rule of the majority is evidence that sufficient force is still to be used to protect society. And if society finds it necessary to protect itself, by seeing that these few derelicts do their duty when they are to be the ones benefited, then it should be done.

We make men go to war now and kill each other for no benefit to themselves whatever. Any attempt to use money or the check system, as we pointed out, would cause us to have to watch every one in the nation, and would be more loss in waste labor by far than the idler would ever get. It would, in fact, be a continuation of what we are now doing, wasting our labor. For none of the persons employed to look after the idlers would be producing anything.

I referred you to the fact that the foreigner now has the free use of all the public things on which no fare or stamps are used, and no one complains that he is getting something that he does not work for. Indeed, he has more privileges than the citizen who is supposed to pay tax. If the public owned the hotels, and stores, the man from another country might just as well be allowed to freely use them as the things he now uses at the expense of the public. Under Socialism there will be no longer any strangers and foreigners. But every man will be at home anywhere on the globe and find brothers.

You may think there will still exist the old time fear that someone will get more than another if we take over the entire plant of industry. But it doesn't work that way with what we have already got. Who ever heard of one citizen getting into an altercation with another because one drove up and down the streets more times than the other, or because one had children in school while the other had none? Instead, the man who has no children, but plenty of property, doesn't oppose the education of the children of the man who has no property. A friend of mine thought that under this unrestricted system men would take out more produce than they could use. But there could be no speculation then, as all would be supplied in the same way, and no one would be doing any business on his own account, as nothing could be sold at a profit, and those you would sell to would have nothing to buy with.

The fear of want will then be gone forever, and with it the disposition to hoard up wealth. We will then have no more fear about what we are going to eat or wear than we have whether we can go down the street. And literally the command of the

Master, "Lay up not for yourselves treasures on earth," will be obeyed.

Socialism will, of course, have to be set up by the majority against great opposition, just as slavery was overthrown. But the great advantage of it will be so readily apparent that the opponents will fall into it when adopted even more rapidly than they did the new conditions following the emancipation of the slave. When I say the opposition will be tremendous, I don't mean to intimate that we must necessarily have a war.

So on the whole, my friend, I have no fear of the man who you think will not work under the new conditions, and I will now close by promising you to consider in my next letter why some men will not work under present conditions if it can be avoided.

Yours in the cause of the revolution,
G.W. WOODBEY

Letter VII

San Diego, California

Mr. J. Jones.

Dear Friend: I am glad to hear of the eagerness with which the members of your family look forward to the reading of these friendly letters of mine. It makes me think that they may do more than a mere passing good after all. I think, like you, we should talk over these great questions of state with our families.

I promised, I believe, to devote this letter to the reason why some men don't want to work. Under present conditions we have some who don't have to work, others who don't want to work but have to, and still a larger number that want to work but can't get to. The rich don't have to work because they can force others to support them through rent, interest and profits. Those who don't want to work but have to are influenced by the fact that they see the rich living at their ease in mansions, while the poor who work are in shacks and clothed with rags. Many of the poor cannot work because the rich, who own everything, will not let them. When I say work, I mean productive labor, of course. Many of the rich work hard at various schemes to get the wealth the poor produce, leaving them only a wage barely sufficient for their keep. The poor man who follows the example of the rich and will not work is always an eyesore to the rich idler, for the reason that of all the men that the rich can't get any profit out of, he is the one. He is like the slave that would not work. The master class beat the one to death, and now imprisons the other for vagrancy.

I hope, my friend, you now see why we have men who don't want to work, but lest you do not, I will go on to make it plainer. Again, what is the standing of the man or woman who works, in capitalist society? Do they rank as ladies or gentlemen? And yet is not capitalist society the ideal that we are taught to look up to? Why should the average person want to work under such teachings? Indeed, it is only necessity that will cause one to do so. The idea not to work if it can be avoided is instilled into the child. As I have just said, the average capitalist does not have to work. But is that the strongest reason why he and his children don't wish to do what is known as productive labor? I think not. Let us go back, for instance, to the slaveholder, by the way of illustration. He declared that he would go to war before he would permit himself and family to labor like the Negro slave and live in poverty, rags, and ignorance. He had been taught to believe that that was the necessary outgrowth of labor. And I submit that the condition of labor under chattel slavery was a poor school in which to teach the child of the master a desire to labor. So the capitalist of today and his children look upon the workers as he has them in the sweatshops, mines and factories of the country, putting in long hours for a bare existence, under the most unsanitary conditions, living in the worst of places, and eating of the worst of food; and, like his brother, the slaveholder, he is determined that he and his shall not be reduced to such straits. It has not yet dawned upon him that when the people who work own the industries in place of him, all of these disagreeable conditions will at once disappear. That the worker can and will make work a pleasure, under surroundings as pleasant as the skill and science of man can make it, is certain. That those who build the fine houses will then live in them, those who weave the fine clothes will wear them, those who raise the best of food will then eat it, and so on, is also true. It is my opinion that, notwithstanding the false education of the children of the wealthy, even they in the first generation will have so much of their distaste for labor taken away that we will have little or no trouble with them when the majority have changed conditions. They think that labor must always remain in the conditions they now behold it, so little do they know about economics. The present condition of labor teaches even the child of the working man not to work, although he is almost sure to have to. He is told to be on the continual lookout to get out of work and shift the burden upon some one else. And as a rule he ceases his vigilance late in life, and then toils through the rest of his days, and is cast by this system upon the scrap heap, filled with regrets over what he deems his neglected opportunities to have gotten rich at the expense of his fellow man and quit work. Men love the respect of their fellows, and the way to get it, under the present conditions, is to keep out of hard work. A boy is born into a family of a working man, and almost the first thing he can recollect hearing his mother say to his father was expressing the wish that he might some day get so he would not have to work, by getting houses to rent, money to loan, or stocks in some concern. So the boy comes to the conclusion that it is not a good thing to work. Then he soon learns that the boys of his acquaintance whose fathers don't work are able to give them nice things that his father can't give him because he is only a working man, and again he is determined not to work. Next the boy goes to school, and even in old, prosy arithmetic he learns that a merchant bought a bill of goods for $1,500 and sold them for $2,000, and is asked how much he gained. He figures it out and his eyes sparkle at this idea of living without work, by getting something for nothing. So you see the school teaches him not to work if possible.

We next find our boy on the busy streets, standing on the corner watching the hurry and scurry of trade. In the store he has noted the obsequious bowing and cringing of clerks at the appearance of the lordly merchant which in the school he had been told bought and sold goods at a profit. Here he gets another lesson how nice it is not to work, as he sees a working man, all greasy and dirty, going toward his filthy shack in the outskirts of the city, or to some lodging house, with his dinner pail in his hand, from which he ate his cold lunch somewhere on a pile of lumber or in a back alley. And when the boy inquires who that is, he is told it is old Bill going home from his day's work. But in a few minutes more another man comes dashing by in his auto, with his diamonds flashing, dressed in the latest style. Now, which one of these two men do you think our boy would prefer to be, Bill, the working man, or the gentleman in the auto, whom he is told Bill works for? The truth is, Bill works in one of the auto factories, but never rides in one of the machines. Now, the boy has heard his father and mother intimate that if times get much harder they will be compelled to take him out of school, and put him to work in one of the factories where so many other children are at work. So it comes to him to stroll down there and take a look. He finds the place ugly, dirty and dingy; the children look careworn and haggard, hardly daring to look up, with a brutal-looking boss keeping watch over them. So he inwardly wishes not to be sent there.

Now, friend Jones, you know as well I do that in the schools of the country the children are taught the glories of capitalism, and how nice it is to live at the expense of the other man. You farmers are a good example, as well as the mechanics, of what it is to be disrespected by the class that you are working to enrich. How much better, as you admit, it would be to have the land owned by the public, while you farmers run an agricultural department for the benefit of the nation, as others run the public school department, every one being equal owners in all of the departments, like the departments on your farm, to which reference has already been made, where your boys work in different departments, but yet make no exchange between each other because they are all one in ownership.

Today the hours of labor are long, and in most cases the work dirty and disagreeable, and the pay poor. Such is the cause of men not wanting to work. Remove this, and make labor a pleasurable recreation, and no one will refuse to work. This I shall try to show you can be and will be done. But I must reserve it for my next letter, and subscribe myself yours for the Cooperative Commonwealth,

G.W. WOODBEY

Letter VIII

San Diego, California

Mr. J. Jones.

Dear Friend: I am glad to learn from your last reply that not only you but the rest of your family have come to the conclusion that the farmers would be better off by running an agricultural department for the entire people, themselves included, than they are now practically doing the same thing, and paying interest to the few capitalists who hold the mortgages on their farms. But let me remind you that it would be better for the working people to do the same in all other departments of industry.

I am glad also you think I have made myself clear in giving the reason why people don't want to work, under present conditions. You seem equally anxious, however, to know why I think people will work better under Socialism than they do now. I am writing to you because you are not the only one who is asking questions about this matter. The idea that all should do their part of the necessary labor is being instilled in the minds of the people and will be one of the prime reasons for adopting Socialism. The majority, who will first bring about Socialism, will feel it incumbent upon them to make good their teachings by starting at once to house, feed and clothe the people with the best that the resources and machinery of the world can afford. The majority must do this to show that its predictions are not a failure. But how long it may take to adjust these things we must leave for our next letter. Having said enough about the generation which will adopt Socialism, let us talk about the children following its adoption. The boy born under the changed conditions will find himself surrounded with all the comforts that science and skill can produce. He finds his father working in the collective industries, along with others, all equally respected, and that he can get all he wants from the common stock that his father is helping to produce. He hears his mother inquire of his father, how he is getting on with the invention he is trying to get out for the benefit of the commonwealth. She declares that his success will not only mean the cutting down of the hours of labor, but will carry his name around the world, as a great benefactor of society. Unlike the other mother we mentioned under capitalism, who wished her husband could get out of his continual grind of hard toil, she heaps praise upon the short hours and splendid conditions under which he works, and the little boy mentally resolves to grow up and follow the footsteps of his father, just as the other boy did. The first boy was taught by his mother's remarks the low, brutal incentive of piling up dollars and cents at the expense of his brother man, while the last boy is taught by the remarks of his mother, that higher incentive based upon love for his fellow man and the praise of doing good.

The incentive for doing good is as much above that of rent, interest, and profits, as the heavens are higher than the earth. The schools are now pervaded with this new incentive, and our boy steps into the very atmosphere of it the moment he enters school. He reads in his books a contrast of the old with the new, and is horrified at the barbarism of the system just past. He reads how all this change was brought to pass, and shudders to think what he might have been. And he thinks what a fine thing it is for every man to be "his brother's keeper." He is taught that all men are brothers, and that there are no longer any strangers and foreigners, but the world is one great family, producing for its own good. He is taught in the schools that all the industries belong to him as much as to any other citizen. And he wonders why any one ever thought of any other way of doing things than the one under which he now lives, which runs so smoothly, and all are now so happy. The first boy was taught, as we said, the glories of capitalism, and he accepted it, and so will this boy accept what he is taught. One is taught the true dignity of labor, and the other the supposed dignity of idleness. These two boys are representative of the two systems of economics. The Socialist schools will not teach percentage, or how to live out of profits taken from your neighbor, because the new industrial system does not require it. When this new boy stands on the streets of the beautiful city in which he lives he, too, sees a man go dashing by in an auto, or in his flying machine, and on asking who it is, he is told that is one of old Bill's sons. He helps make these machines, but, unlike his father, he also rides in one as well. His machine is fine, and he is nicely dressed, and on his way to do a few hours' pleasant labor in the factory. The old rookery once called a factory, in which little children were ground up for profit, has now given place to one of model architectural beauty, within and without. It stands in a park, and the grounds are laid off with taste, with grand old trees, beautiful walks and fountains, more tasteful than some of the capitalist offices are now. These places show that the workers have an eye for the beautiful and the sublime, and they would put all this in the places where they work, even now, were it not prevented by the profit-making of the capitalist. But things have changed, and these and all other places where the work of the world is done, now belong to those who do the work. The floors are of the finest and best material, and the walls are decorated with the masterpieces of the painter and the sculptor. The ceilings are high, the machinery far apart, and every possible safeguard is used for the protection of life and limb. Superb dining rooms are attached, in which the best things of the land are served to the workers. No more workers are eating a little cold food out of a dinner pail in a filthy back alley. Bath rooms are attached, and also robing rooms. It was to such a place that old Bill's son was going in his machine when our schoolboy saw him. Now the boy has been told that he is to go to work in the factory when he has graduated from his school, which is preparing him for the place. He, like the other boy I pointed out under capitalism, concludes he will pay a visit to the place where he is to work. When he takes in these surroundings and enters in and looks upon this gay throng of happy young wealth-producers, he is entranced, and longs to get through school so that he can take part, for a few hours each day, with the young people, under such delightful conditions. He can't understand how any one ever thought of not wishing to work. All this because science has been used to take away every possible disagreeable phase of all necessary labor.

There are many things that are now done that will not be necessary under the new conditions. And with shortness of hours there is nothing that the worker with his knowledge of sciences cannot make it a pleasure to do. Things that we now consider very disagreeable with their long hours and bad sanitary conditions can be changed and made pleasant. Men don't at present have to be driven to do their own work, even under the most disagreeable circumstances, then why will they not do their own work, in the Cooperative Commonwealth, under these pleasant conditions, when educated and brought up for the purpose? When chattel slavery prevailed, as we said, men thought that labor must continue to be always what it was then, and that because the slave sought to escape he wouldn't work for wages. So now the capitalist, and those who believe in capitalism, think that labor must continue always to be just what it is now; and as some people don't like to work now under these terrible conditions, they won't work under the new and better conditions.

It is a wonder to me that men are so willing to work as they are under the present conditions. The fact is, the mind of the child is such that it accepts what it is taught now, and will do the same then.

The boy that was born a slave thought that it was natural for him to be one, and the young master took it for granted that he was intended to be master. But the boy that is born free, never thinks that anyone ought to own him; nor does the youngster born at the same time with him think that he ought to own him. But instead, they both go to school, often in the same class. They at once accept the conditions under which they were born. No, my friend, there is no danger of the children not at once accepting the new conditions under Socialism, and we have proved there will be so little loss through idlers, even in the first generation of old folks, that it will not be found worth bothering about. And as the old and infirm should of necessity be looked after with the best of everything from the very beginning, it will be found when the time comes that the thing to do will be to let everyone work and be sure that we have abundance of everything for all, and then let everybody help themselves, wherever they may be, to what we have on hand, as we do with what the public now owns. Indeed, they can be better trusted then than now, with all fear of the future banished forever.

But I must close this letter, as what I am now saying is but calling your attention to what I have already said. I promise you to consider the transition period, about which you seem to be anxious, in my next letter.

From your old friend,
G.W. WOODBEY

Letter IX

San Diego, California

Mr. J. Jones.

Dear Friend: I now proceed to fulfill my promise, to write you my thoughts about the transition period, by which is meant the period that must elapse between the time the Socialists go into power and the putting of the industries to work under the collective system.

From the time the people vote the Socialists into power, thus telling them to prepare the document to be known as the Cooperative Commonwealth, and submit it to them for adoption, a period, long or short, must elapse. And you wish to know what the people are to do during that time, and the rancher in particular. How are they to live? Will the industries be taken all at once? Or will they be taken one at a time?

From the election of the Socialists to the time when the majority have passed upon the new document, private business must go on just as it did before. Like the adoption of a new constitution for a state, the instrument itself will set a day for going into effect. And on that day all the industries that have not already been taken will pass into the hands of the people at once, and the new system will take the place of the old. Just as the old colonial system of government governed the people until the articles of confederation took its place, and the articles of confederation governed, until they were replaced by the constitution, so the constitution under which we now have private ownership of the industries, will continue until the people adopt the cooperative system, with collective ownership.

The new government will no doubt take over the goods in the stores and warehouses of capitalists, as they belong as much to the producers as do the buildings of a factory and its machinery, or a railroad and its rolling stock. The justice of taking the land is founded upon the fact that God intended it for the common use of all. The industries will be taken because they are the common product of the workers, for which they could not have been paid, because they had to produce their pay over and above what went into the plants of industry. The goods in stock should be taken for the common use of the people, as they are the remaining product of their labor, over and above their wages. So the people, including the farmer, will continue to live (or exist), as they now do under the capitalist system during the transition period.

But you want to know what we can do if the owners of everything shut down all work with the intention of starving us out, when they see that they have been outvoted. The result would be that the majority would walk in and help themselves to what was on hand, and go on running the industries. Such a majority would be in no mood to be played with in that way. And that would be the best thing that could happen, to shorten the period of transition, as the new system would then be rushed through at once.

Now as to the probable length of time this transition period will take. It took four months to draw up the constitution of the United States ready for submission to the states. It may take that length of time for the Socialist Congress to prepare the new system and listen to the discussion of the minority before submitting it to the people. That it will go to the people there is no doubt, just as a Socialist party constitution now goes to a referendum. And more than this, the document would be voted upon by the whole people of the United States.

As the matter would be urgent, the first president elected as a Socialist, with a Congress behind him, would doubtless call an extra session and the work would be done as speedily as possible consistent with its magnitude. It would seem but reasonable that the document when completed should include the whole of the industries, so that the vote of the people would settle the matter. This document called the Cooperative Commonwealth, would not be simply an amendment to the present constitution of the United States, any more than the constitution was an amendment of the articles of confederation. So in that case we would not have to follow the methods laid down to govern amendments to the constitution.

My friend, I want to call your attention to one other instance in this country's history to show how speedily things can be done. The South voted herself out of the Union, adopted the constitution of the Southern Confederacy and elected the officers under it, besides raising an immense army, all between the first of November and the fourth of March.

Say the change from capitalism to Socialism was made under the next administration, the same men would do the work under the new system that are doing it now, and we would find the industries all in a process of organization, with the possible exception of the farming industry. And as to that there is information enough lodged in the archives at Washington as to the production of crops to enable those who are now doing the farming to proceed on a large scale, with the best machinery furnished from the shops of the nation, to produce all the whole people need from that source. If the rancher wanted to, he could continue to live in the country where he is now. Or, if he wanted anything different, he could live where he pleased, and still work in the agricultural department of the nation. And so with the workers of every other department. You understand we could not have Socialism with each man producing on his own account, but each department would be a part of the whole, like the wheels of a clock. I started in the first place to write to you about the distribution of wealth, but have been induced to write this letter because you seem to fear that even after the Socialists get in power there might be a long period of transition, during which time there would be nothing to distribute. We are now in the transitional or evolutionary period of this movement, and it will go on until the Socialists go into power, and then all that remains will be taken at once.

But before I am done I suppose I will have to answer your apparent fear of Communism, especially as you seem to think there is a great difference between it and Socialism. I might add here in closing this letter, that in case of a war over the seating of a Socialist president, the same process in the formation and operation of the Cooperative Commonwealth would be necessary when the strife was over, and the right of the majority to govern was acknowledged. The war of the rebellion didn't change the laws governing slavery, but only made those who oppose emancipation keep quiet until the laws could be changed. So it must be again in case of strife.

Yours in the cause,
G.W. WOODBEY

Letter X

San Diego, California

Mr. J. Jones.

My Dear Friend: I promised to write you regarding the difference you seem to think exists between Socialism and Communism. But before doing so I see in your letter just received you have some doubts as to whether factories and other places of work will be made as beautiful as I think. It seems to me that we see, in our many splendid public buildings, only an inkling of what will be done when the people own and control everything. I was over at Washington, D.C., a few months ago, and visited the White House, the war and navy departments, the Capitol building, the public library and other places. Now these buildings, the best in the nation, are made pleasant to work in, although not so much so as I imagine they would be under Socialism. A lesson for the future may also be gotten from our state buildings and schools. Many of these buildings belonging to the people are only public workshops. The people of the future will have learned that it is just as easy to have all places where they work pleasant as it is the few they now have. They will learn also that it is just as feasible to have a public building department, whose business it will be to beautifully and substantially house all of the people, as it is now to build executive mansions, universities and common schools.

As to the inequalities of the wage system which now prevails under capitalism in all of our public departments being transferred into the Cooperative Commonwealth, in place of the plan I seem to favor, you need have no fear of that, for the following reasons: All such questions will under Socialism have to be settled by the vote of the majority. I know that after doing your best at work in some of the departments of collective industry, you would never vote for anything less than an equal show at the public crib with all the rest, neither would any other worker.

The wage system as it now prevails in public departments, is a part of the capitalist system, and will pass away with it. The old idea, that each person might be allotted his share of the wealth produced at the close of each year and receive the same and care for it himself, now seems to me absurd, because all products, until the persons want to use them, can be better cared for in the public warehouses. And if we produce all that can be used, which can easily be done, no one need have anything allotted to him, so long as he can get all he wants anywhere. Your sons don't need to have any of the wealth allotted to them which has been produced by the common labor of all on the farm.

Let us now come to the question you raise about the apparent difference between Socialism and Communism. Socialism, you say, means that every one in the new commonwealth shall fare according to his deeds, while Communism means that every one shall fare according to his needs. The main objections, then, that you raise to Communism is that while all men have needs, some might want to live without doing any deeds. This question as to whether every one can be relied upon to do his duty under

The Distribution of Wealth 237

Socialism has been too fully discussed in my previous letters to devote any further time to that matter here. Hoping that you have not thrown my letters in the waste basket, I will ask you to read them over.

The same thing that you speak of is often stated in another way. Under Socialism it will be possible to secure to every man the full product of his labor. And it is further said that if one man is more industrious than another he will get more than another. This is doubtless said to satisfy those who cannot get over the idea of laying up a fortune. But it becomes more and more plain to me that as production with machinery becomes more complicated, the single individual, as in a shoe factory, for example, where he can only do a certain portion and can work only as fast as the slowest person, cannot produce any more than the rest. And where this is not the case, as in unskilled labor, it would not be possible to estimate how many more pounds one lifted than another, for example. A man could not work just when he pleased, and quit when he pleased, any more then than now, without crippling the efficiency of the plant. So those who operate the plants of industry for the whole people will have to come to some conclusion as to hours and regulations among themselves and live up to them. These regulations will doubtless be based upon a knowledge of the number of people to be supplied along that particular line. The community might lay up in store a superabundance to meet the needs of the people, and thus each individual would have his relative interest in the collective store. Even if one man did produce more than another, he might also consume more and that would be a fair stand-off. It has been erroneously supposed by some, that Communism would allow every one to help himself, regardless of whether he worked or not. Historical research has shown that communism of some sort was in existence centuries before Christ. But it will hardly be denied that the best form of it was that set up by Christ and practiced by the early Christians for three hundred years, beginning at Jerusalem. It began with the Master and the twelve Apostles, who had a common purse. These early churches had no control of the Roman state, but they sold their possessions, put them into a common stock and every one was served as he had need, and no one said that aught that he had was his own. This common stock could not have been kept up without those who belonged to this organization continuing to put their earnings into it. And it is well known that it continued for three hundred years, or at least until the days of Constantine, who made the first successful attack upon it. It was an essential part of the early church creeds. And when you hear the church of today repeat the Apostles' Creed, and come to that part, "I believe in the communion of saints," perhaps not one out of a thousand knows that it refers to the common stock arrangement of the early churches, from which the churches of today have departed.

This rule governing the common stock was the one mentioned by Paul: "If any will not work neither should he eat." If men would not contribute to the support of the common stock of the church they were not to be allowed to help to consume it. Just as every one will be expected to do their duty under Socialism, so that in that respect the two are exactly alike. No other method could have kept the institution alive for centuries, in the midst of the Roman Empire, with its competition on every side. Nor did each one put into this ancient commonwealth just as much as another, but each one did his best, just as we will be expected to do under Socialism.

It was this cooperative feature that brought down upon the early church the persecution of the rich rulers of the Roman Empire, and it was the departure of the church from this plan of distributing wealth that opened the door for the entry of the rich, with all their robbery of the poor, into the organization. This accounts for why the church is not now persecuted as of old. When rich people entered the ancient church they were required to put their belongings into the common stock. So Socialism will require that the rich, who have in their possession the goods produced by the poor, shall put them into the common stock of the nation, to be distributed to all, themselves included. "The spoils of the poor are in your house," said the prophet.

The fact is the term "Communism" is simply the older name

applied to the idea of cooperation among men. Socialism being the more modern name applied to the same thing. The use of the term "Socialism" is only a little over fifty years old. So up to the time when this term "Socialism" came into use, "Communism" was the one used to designate this same movement. And the objection to Communism arises from the misunderstanding that some one is to get something for nothing, which was no more true of the ancient Communism of the early Christians than it is of modern Socialism. Whatever one took out of the common stock for his own use was that moment his own property, to be used by him, the rest being supplied from the same source. The real difference between the two is that under Socialism we are to work together collectively, which, so far as I know, the early Christians did not do.

Hoping that I have been able to make it clear to you that under Socialism it will be possible to equitably distribute the products of industry and that you and your family will at once join the movement, I will close this somewhat lengthy correspondence by saying that I would be pleased to hear from you soon.

Yours in the cause of the revolution,
G.W. WOODBEY

If the reader thinks that this book will do anything to help the cause please do your best to circulate it.

SEND ALL ORDERS TO
G. W. WOODBEY, 3780 N ST.
San Diego, Cal.

SINGLE COPY 10 CENTS
100 COPIES AND UPWARD 5 CENTS.

Woodbey's Arrest in Long Beach

Common Sense, Los Angeles, October 8, 1904

Editor *Common Sense:* We arrived in Long Beach on the 23rd to speak under the direction of the State Committee, and were promptly arrested at the close of our meeting by the police, under the charge of violating the city law by selling books without a license. As we had been there before and sold books without any, we did not think of getting into any trouble. This however is not our first arrest by the powers that be. We are selling only our own books, *What to Do and How to Do It* and *The Bible and Socialism.* When they told us to stop we did so and went to the store of one of the comrades, and there sold a few more books, and it was in his store we were arrested.

The arrest was made at the instance of a good republican, who according to his story, freed the Negro, and now has a mortgage on him for all time to come. On asking a number of foolish questions and being laughed at by the crowd, he became very angry, but was noticed to come to the store, buy a book and go at once and return with the marshal, and when the officer was noticed to hesitate, he was heard to say, "Take him, take him."

When we arrived at the court room, with a number of citizens trooping after us into that public building, they were promptly told by their Master, the policeman, to get out; they had not business there, and they scattered like whipped curs. Of course, on arrival at the station we were promptly searched. When to their great delight, they found we had a small revolver in our pocket, which had been bought by us after the loss of some $75.00 worth of property. We are not in the habit of carrying it, but on packing our baggage it was left out and we had placed it in our pocket. Thus we were in for two charges. You see it was very unfortunate for us that we were not a member of the Citizens' Alliance,[9] so we might have been a walking arsenal without any fear of arrest. You know it is a very grave offense to violate the laws made by capitalists, unless they do it themselves. The locals everywhere should look up just what their city laws are, so far as they bear on our work; so that the speaker will not have to go to consult the officers.

Comrade Volk promptly went our bail.

Lovejoy, John Brown, Phillips, Garrison and Fred Douglass were law violators. And there was a time in our lives when if we had run off ourselves we would have been a criminal in the meaning of the law. That time is past and so will the crime breeding system of capitalism under which we now live.

It is needless to say we were promptly fined $15. Some of the comrades have been prompt in helping us out of the difficulty financially, and will do more; for all of which they have our thanks.

G.W. WOODBEY

Remarks of Rev. Woodbey at the 1908 Socialist Party Convention

Now, what I say I am going to say very calmly and dispassionately. There is a question before us as to whether this convention should adopt any immediate demands. I believe that we should, and I believe it for this reason: In my judgment, the time is coming when the Socialist party will go into power in some large city and in some of the states of the union, and they will do that long before they get in power in the nation. Let us suppose that in the last election in the city of Chicago the Socialists had carried the city and got the entire administration. Now, I am going to ask you whether the Socialist party in the city of Chicago would have felt itself under obligations to do anything to relieve the workers in the city of Chicago. If they did, it would have to be done on the plan of immediate demands. (Applause.) Let us suppose that the Socialist party got control of the State of Illinois, and they may do that in many of the states of the union long before they get control in the United States. It is true in Germany; it is true in some of the European countries where they have had control in some parts of the country for years. Now, then, suppose they get control, will they attempt to use the state machinery so far as capitalism will allow them to use it for the benefit of the workers? Would the workers in the city of Chicago, in power in the city of Chicago, attempt to operate any of the municipal franchises? Would they? Or would they say with you gentlemen who are waiting for the setting up of the Cooperative Commonwealth, "No, we will not do a single thing. We will run the city of Chicago just as it is now being run until we can reach out and get it all." I tell you that I believe this is the line that we will have to take upon this question of government ownership. No Hearst party,[10] Republican party, or any other party is going to declare in favor of government ownership without paying for the franchises. I am for the Socialist party declaring in favor, as fast as they can get in possession in any locality, of taking everything without a cent of compensation, and forcing the issue as to whether there is to be compensation or not. (Applause.) I take the ground that you have already paid for these franchises—already paid more than they are worth, and we are simply proposing to take possession of what we have already paid for. Well, you say the courts will defeat us. All right, let them defeat us if they will. We will throw the responsibility for the defeat on the capitalist parties that defeat the thing. Another thing; I don't know a great deal about what is being done over in Wisconsin, but my notion of it is that in Wisconsin they are doing things, understand.[11] I believe in insisting on taking everything in sight, understand, as fast as we can get it. Another thing: I don't know a European nation, including Germany, France, England, Holland, Denmark, Norway, Sweden, and all the rest of the countries, but what has a municipal program. They go farther than that; they even start cooperative institutions under the direction of the Socialist party. Listen, we can't afford to wait for the alleviation of the suffering of the people. We must do it as fast as we can get in charge.

* * *

It is generally supposed that the western people, those living on the Pacific slope, are almost as a unit opposed to Oriental immigration. I am not saying that those living on the western slope oppose them, but where Oriental immigration comes to the western coast it is supposed that the people of the west are in favor of their exclusion. I am in favor of throwing the entire world open to the inhabitants of the world. (Applause.) There are no foreigners, and cannot be, unless some person came down from Mars, or Jupiter, or some place. I stand on the declaration of Thomas Paine when he said "The world is my country."[12] (Applause.) It would be a curious state of affairs for immigrants or the descendants of immigrants from Europe themselves to get control of affairs in this country, and then say to the Oriental immigrants that they should not come here. So far as making this a mere matter of race, I disagree decidedly with the committee, that we need any kind of a committee to decide this matter from a scientific standpoint.[13] We know what we think upon the question of race now as well as we would know two years from now or any other time.

And so far as reducing the standard of living is concerned, the standard of living will be reduced anyhow. You know as well as I do that either the laborer will be brought to the job or the job will be taken to the laborer. Understand? We will either have to produce things as cheap as they can be produced upon foreign soil or the means of production will be carried to the Orient and there the thing will be done. The natural tendency of capitalism is to reduce the standard of living; the standard of living will be reduced anyhow.

Now, listen: It seems to me if we take any stand opposed to any sort of immigration that we are simply playing the old pettifogging trick of the Democrats and Republicans, and will gain nothing by it. (Applause.) I believe it is opposed, as I understand, to the principles of international Socialism. I do not pretend to say that the international Socialist organization takes square ground as to what we should say on the question, but to me Socialism is based, if anything, upon the Brotherhood of Man. This stand that we take in opposition to any sort of immigration is opposed to the very spirit of the Brotherhood of Man. I hope, therefore, that all that part of the committee's report which imposes a restriction on immigration will be stricken out by the convention. It ought to be done; in good faith it ought to be done, because, in the first place, the Socialists are organized in Japan; they are getting organized in China; they will soon be operating in every civilized nation on earth. And are the Socialists of this country to say to the Socialists of Germany, or the Socialists of Sweden, Norway, Japan, China, or any other country, that they are not to go anywhere on the face of the earth? It seems to me absurd to take that position. Therefore, I hope and move that any sort of restriction of immigration will be stricken out of the committee's resolution. (Applause.)

Proceedings, National Convention of the Socialist Party, Held at Chicago, Illinois, May 10–17, 1908, Chicago, 1908, pp. 208-09, p. 106.

Socialism has steadily grown, until almost all legislative bodies of the world have their Socialist members and the question can no longer be ignored. While in some nations Socialism promises to become dominant at no distant day, the most significant thing in the Socialist movement is to be found in the substantial agreement of Socialists throughout the world.

The first thing the capitalist parties of this country have done is to ignore the movement. But that day has about passed, and when they have to meet the Socialist agitation the growth of Socialism will be much more rapid.

The attention given Socialist speakers and the demand for literature is significant.

Socialism is an attempt to organize the working class into a political party to take control of the powers of government, and set up the cooperative commonwealth, thus doing away with all classes.

Because the Socialists recognize the existence of a class struggle they are some times accused of stirring up class hatred. But, instead, they simply recognize the fact that capitalism, by its unequal distribution of wealth, has forced on us a class struggle, which the Socialists are organizing to put down and bring on the long talked of period of universal brotherhood.

Socialist Agitation

Chicago Daily Socialist, January 3, 1909

The first step toward bringing about Socialism is agitation, which is the only means by which the public can be educated. It may be done through the press, the pulpit, the rostrum and private conversation. Socialism is now passing through this period of agitation and thousands are anxiously listening to the glad tidings.

It has been well said that the cooperative commonwealth must first be builded in the minds of the people before it can be put into actual practice. This work of building the new commonwealth is now going on night and day in all parts of the world. Socialism, when once intelligently understood, is a fire in the bones of its converts and must flash out; so when you have made one intelligent Socialist he makes another one, and so on indefinitely.

The Socialist press throughout the world is now a great power, amounting to many hundred publications, from monthly magazines to great dailies, and these in the languages of all the civilized nations. Vast book concerns are running night and day, sending out tons of literature, in all cases the agitators of new ideas—in religion, science, or government—have created a new literature adapted to their purpose, just as the Socialists are now doing.

We are not contending that a thing is necessarily right because it has its agitators and its literature; the claims of a question at issue to be right rest upon a different ground.

In the beginning of the movement many persons were imprisoned and otherwise mistreated in all countries, but economic equality.

This work of the fathers was not the work of a day, but required hard work and bitter agitation, which caused the revolutionary agitator of that time to be hated, then as now, as a common enemy of society.

Many of the revolutionists of a hundred years ago were born aristocrats, having little or no sympathy with the poor workers; but they could not accomplish their purpose without them so that now what they said and did will help us in our work.

The present exploiter of the working people can see the sacredness of the revolution of a hundred years ago, but like their Tory ancestry they hang, shoot and imprison the revolutionist of today, who would go on to complete the work begun in the past.

But after all we know that with few exceptions the owners of everything in all ages have stood on the side where they thought their material interest lay.

But in spite of those who would block the wheels of progress the agitator of a right cause is bound to succeed in the end.

We have progressed from an autocracy or government of one man to one that limits the power vested in that one man, by lodging it in the hands of the people. This representative form of government might just as well be called a limited monarchy as a republic, and both of them are open to the danger of being turned into a plutocracy or government of the rich, such as we now have in this country, leaving us only the shadow of a government representing the people. Thus it has come about that the men now in Congress represent the holding of the rich rather than the masses of the people. What else is meant by a business administration such as Taft is expected to give us? How much business has the working man?

But so long as we recognize the right of the individual to own what the public must use, he must control government in order to protect his holdings.

The next great revolutionary document was Lincoln's Emancipation Proclamation, issued September 23, 1862, to take effect

The New Emancipation

Chicago Daily Socialist, January 18, 1909

In 1776 the work of the agitators of this country culminated in the issuing of that revolutionary document, known as the Declaration of Independence, declaring their emancipation from Great Britain, and sounding the final death knell of the so-called divine right of kings, and declared that "All just governments derive their power from the consent of the governed."

The idea then expressed was not that the people might govern themselves, but only that no one should assume to do it without their consent. But, nevertheless, it had in it the seeds of further revolution. Among English-speaking people the idea may be traced back to the days of King John in 1215, when the barons forced from him the Magna Charta. While this was not the work of the masses of poor, yet it served in after ages to put hope into them for better things, as the work of forcing the king could not be done without the aid of the poor class who served these same barons.

Jefferson never dreamed of the broad construction that we Socialists are now putting upon his declaration. "All men are born equal, and are endowed by their Creator with certain inalienable rights, among which is life, liberty and the pursuit of happiness." This notion of equality, while it may at times have been a drawback, by satisfying the individual citizen with poor conditions, yet on the other hand it may be now turned to good account as the working man is waking up to the fact that a great deal of the boasted rights he thought he was secure in have either gone glimmering or else he never really possessed what belongs to him. So the average Socialist sees in it not only political but

January 1, 1863. This proclamation, like that of the Declaration of Independence, was the culmination of a fierce agitation, which raged for more than a half century, and has not inaptly been styled "the romance of American history."

In this case the slaveholders, like the capitalist, were compelled to control the powers of government in order to protect what they deemed their rights, and slavery died when they could no longer do that.

The slave power, like that of the capitalist, was a gradual growth on the western hemisphere, from the time when the Spanish landed the first slaves from Africa in 1517 down to the time when the abolition agitation overturned the whole thing. It would be useless to recount the many horrors through which the Negro slaves passed in their capture on the slave coast, in their passage to this country—the bullwhip, the slave pen and the auction block—because it is too much like the policeman's club, the lockout and the bullpens from which white and black workers are now suffering. This, however, together with the feudal system, shows that the Negro was not enslaved because he was a Negro, but because it was supposed that more profit could be made out of his labor. For attempting to overthrow the slave system Lincoln and Lovejoy were shot, John Brown was hung, while Garrison, Phillips and Fred Douglass were mobbed.

But the workers of all colors now find themselves in need of another emancipation, from a condition of wage slavery which as completely robs them of the hundreds of millions of wealth produced by their labor as did chattel slavery. The agitation is now going for the new emancipation, and the agitators are equally hated and despised.

Many of the Negroes who are just now beginning to wake up to the fact that there is something wrong, are yet under the impression that the accumulation of wealth in the hands of a few Negroes will solve this problem, and that, too, notwithstanding the fact that a few white men have all the wealth and the rest of their brothers are getting poorer every day.

Give the Negro along with others the full product of his labor by wrenching the industries out of the hands of the capitalist and putting them into the hands of the workers and what is known as the race problem will be settled forever. Socialism is only another one of those great world movements which is coming to bless mankind. The Socialist Party is simply the instrument for bringing it about, and the Negro and all other races, regardless of former conditions, are invited into its fold.

Why the Negro Should Vote the Socialist Ticket

When the Rev. Mr. Johnson, Pastor of the African Baptist Church, openly declared his intention to vote the Socialist ticket at the coming election, it created so much commotion that he decided to call a meeting at his church for the purposes of stating his reasons for becoming a Socialist and to advise all the members of his church to do likewise.

When the pastor appeared at the meeting place, he found a crowded church and every eye was fastened upon him when he arose and said:

Brethren—I am not here to make you a political speech as such speeches are usually made, nor has anyone paid me for what I am about to say. Since it has become known that I am a Socialist there has been a great deal of comment and some criticism from my members.

I feel that I ought to meet this criticism and tell you why I am going to vote the Socialist ticket and also why I think the Negro voter wherever he is permitted to to do so should do the same.

It is the purpose of the Socialist movement to get the working people into a party of their own so that through this party, they may look after the interests of all who work regardless of race or color. All who do anything useful for the good of all men or society are considered workers. Most of those who work, and nearly all of our race, are wage workers, and when we talk about the working class, we mean those who work for wages, though of course there are workers who do not work for wages, such as the farmers, for example. There are also doctors and preachers, who, though they do not work with their hands, yet belong to what we call the working class.

Very few of the working class own anything of any value.

The workers do all the work, produce all the things to eat, build all the houses, create all the good things, but do not have very many of these good things themselves. The Socialist Party proposes to change this state of affairs and to fix things so that the workers will have the wealth that they produce.

But before the Negro or any other working man votes the Socialist ticket, he will have to have some knowledge of what Socialism is. This I have found out and that is the reason why I am going to vote the Socialist ticket and why I came here tonight to explain it to you.

Socialism means the collective ownership of the land, mines, factories, shops, railroads, etc. It means that the people who use these shops and work in them shall own them collectively and that the purpose in so owning them will be to see that enough of everything is produced to satisfy the needs of all.

By collective ownership we mean the kind of ownership we have in the streets, schools, public libraries and all other things owned by the public. You know that whatever belongs to the public belongs by right to all of us. When you work for the public or in some one of the public departments, you will have a public job like the mail carrier, the school teacher, etc. As we will then not have to divide what we produce with the capitalist, we will all have the means of getting every thing that we need.

Some of you want to know what we Socialists mean by capitalism? Look at the street car system, running here in front of the church. Well, then, look at its roadbed, rails, ties, depots, car barns, electrical machinery and all else used to operate the road. Now all the things in that street car system was made by labor.

But the laborers when they were building this road did not get all they earned. They do not get what they earn now in running the cars. A part of what labor earns is always kept by the capitalist. This part is called profit. The profit which is taken from labor in time becomes capital and the man who owns capital is called a capitalist.

Under Socialism, when we build a railroad, it will belong not to some Vanderbilt or Gould,[14] but to the people. And when we ride on that railroad, or use it, we will not have to pay a profit to the capitalist. And when the public owns all of the mines, shops, factories, railroads, etc., and when we all have an equal voice in their management, there will be a job for everybody, both black and white.

The Negro should vote the Socialist ticket so that all the workplaces which the public does not now own, may be made public property.

Of course the present owners won't like to have these things go over to the public any more than the slave holders wanted to give up the slaves. But the working people are in the great majority and when they all join together and vote the Socialist ticket, the capitalist will have to give up.

All other parties have abandoned the Negro, and if he wants an equal chance with everyone else, he can get it in no other way than by voting the Socialist ticket.

The Socialist Party, composed as it is of the working class, is opposed to the disfranchisement of the workers, either white or black, because it will require all of the workers to get Socialism. The working people must therefore lay aside their prejudices and get together for their common good. We poor whites and blacks have fought each other long enough, and while we have fought, the capitalists have been taking everything from both of us.

The Negro should vote the Socialist ticket because when Socialism is established, he being a part of the public, will have an equal ownership in all that the public owns, and this will entitle him to an equal part in all the good things produced by the nation.

It is not necessary that I should mention all these things. Just look around you and think of the many things you see and want but cannot get. These things will still be produced under Socialism by your labor and that of others, the difference being that under Socialism, you will have a chance to get them and not have to worry about how you will live any more than you need to worry now whether you can walk on the street from this meeting.

When you and your family raise a crop on your farm, you all

help yourselves to the good things to eat. So when the nation works together like the family, doing everything that you now see going on in the nation, each member of the great commonwealth will get all he needs of anything produced—each one getting all that his labor entitles him to. And we could not lose our property, for the title to the shops, mines, factories, railroads, etc., would be in no one person's name but in that of the public. We cannot lose or sell our interest in what the public owns. Nor can our children run through with it after we are gone. No one has to buy an interest in what the public owns. It was ours as soon as we were born and so will be with our children.

The Socialist Party stands for taking away poverty just as Lincoln and the Republican Party took away slavery. Neither the Republican Party nor any other party outside of the Socialist now stands for taking away poverty.

But of course, you want to know how we Socialists expect to do all of this. It is so different from what you are used to that it is hard for you to understand just how there is to be a change. It is simple enough. Just as the people now own the post office and the public school publicly—so under Socialism they will all own and operate the railroads, the mines, and all great industries. Every one under Socialism will work in some one of the vast public enterprises. The public will be concerned in seeing that enough is produced so that as near as can be there will be no lack of anything.

The men who own the places where we work now stop us as soon as they cannot sell all they we have produced, regardless of how badly we need a job. Under Socialism whenever we are producing too much we will cut down the hours of work and thus have more leisure time. Everybody would have to work under Socialism at something useful. Some would be overseers and managers, but they would not be our bosses as now, and if we did not like them, we would elect others in their places.

You know what the Bible says: "They shall build houses and inhabit them; they shall plant vineyards and eat of the fruit thereof, and they shall not build and another inhabit, and they shall not plant and another eat the fruit thereof."

We are now building fine houses for others to live in and producing all kinds of things and letting others who do nothing, use them. The only way to stop it, as the Bible tells us to do, is by voting the Socialist ticket.

One reason why this meeting is called here tonight is because I know that you have been told that Socialism will interfere with your religion.

This is not true. On the contrary, Socialism will enable you to quit fighting each other and to treat each other as brothers. Having enough to eat is not going to make you lose your religion or your belief in God.

For my part as a preacher, I know that we would all be far better off if we had Socialism. The Bible says: "Your Heavenly Father knoweth that you have need of all these things." Meaning by that, food, clothing and houses. But God has put the things that you need here on the earth and the capitalist class has gobbled them up and you must by your votes change the condition.

I have said this much to you only to get you started to reading Socialist books and papers as you do other papers and books. In this way, you will soon learn more than I can tell you in a speech.

I want you to think for yourselves and then act. The Socialist movement is a part of a great world movement which includes all races and both sexes and has for its motto: "Workers of the world unite. You have nothing to lose but your chains; you have a world to gain!"

This was the text of a leaflet, available at the Tamiment Institute Library of New York University; and in the Socialist Party papers, Duke University Library.

What the Socialists Want

The Christian Socialist, February, 1915

Just as George Stephenson, the Negro mail carrier, walked out in front of the beautiful new post office on the way home from his work he heard some one say, "Hello, there! Are you ready to give me your subscription for *The Christian Socialist* yet?"

"See here, John Parker; I believe you are as persistent as the unjust judge of which Christ spoke. And, besides, you have the aid of my wife. So I suppose I will have to capitulate."

"I am not much of a Bible student, but, my friend, I think you have your Bible allusions a little twisted. It was a woman whose persistence brought the judge to time. But I hope you are not comparing yourself to the judge."

"Well, really, to tell you the truth, I have paid but little attention to the Socialist movement, because, as a Negro, I didn't think that it concerned me very much, as we always get the worst of it. But I am in earnest now, Parker. Please tell, in short, and the simplest way possible, just what it is you Socialists are trying to get at, any way. I have listened to some Socialist speakers use a lot of highsounding phrases which I didn't understand."

Standing there with his dinner pail in hand, all covered with coal dust of the mine until you could hardly tell that he was a white man, Parker smiled complacently as he said: "You want to know what we Socialists are after. Well, that is dead easy, it seems to me. Now listen, and I will leave off all scientific terms, and come down to the plane of bread and butter. You and I are both working men trying to make a living. When we come to work, we find that a few men own the land, the factories, the railroads, the mines, in fact, all capital, so that we cannot work unless they say so. And when they do let us work, they keep the largest portion of what we produce. I suppose, however, some exceptions might be made in your case, as you are working for the public. Now, don't forget that our labor created all this capital, or tools with which we work. For, to be plain about it, stripped of all its trappings, that is all there is to capital. And then, in turn, these tools or capital which we, the workers, furnish, are used by the capitalist to fleece us with.

"Do you see George, nothing can be done without labor. A capitalist then, of course, is simply the owner of capital and not being a producer, he cannot furnish any capital, or pay us, the workers, for furnishing it. Instead, the capital is furnished out of that portion of the worker's product which the capitalist didn't let him take for wages. If labor had got all it produced, it would have owned all the capital, as well as the surplus product now taken by the capitalist."

"All well enough, Friend Parker, so far as the present situation is concerned. But, in the language of Boss Tweed,[15] if you Socialists don't like it, what are you going to do about it?" asked Stephenson.

"So far so good, then. We Socialists would turn this whole plant of industry over to the entire people just as they now own the streets, schoolhouses, and public buildings, like the post office which you are working in, and have them operated under different departments, for the benefit of the people in place of having them now owned by a few capitalists and operated by the workers for the benefit of these private owners. I mean by this that we will take over all that the public must now use, leaving in the hands of private individuals such things as each uses privately. These factories, lands, railroads and mines we will then use under public departments, with a view to creating and transporting all that the people need, so that there will be no lack of anything. And there need not be, with our modern machinery. The post office department handles all the people's mail, and the departments yet to be taken over can do the same in their line. We Socialists think it is about as easy for the people to do all the farming, manufacturing, transporting and other things for themselves as to do what they are already doing in the way of public enterprise. And when all the industries belong to the people, of course grafting will stop, because people don't steal what they are free to help themselves to. You see, the men in the post office who stole several millions could put their loot into their private industries. But there will be no private enterprises under Socialism, recollect."

"But how will you get possession? Take these things away from the present owners?"

"Why, certainly. Don't they of right belong to the worker? And will not the present owners, who produced nothing, get as much public benefit out of them as anyone else, if he will do his share of the work?"

"But how can you make this confiscation harmonize with the Bible, which you Christian Socialists claim to believe in?"

"Well, let's see about that. It tells us of a time to come when 'They shall build houses and live in them, and they shall plant vineyards, and eat of them. And they shall not plant, and another eat, and they shall not build and another inhabit.' Don't you see that is just what we are doing now, and that the change is coming? 'The spoils of the poor are in your houses, what mean you that you break my people to pieces and grind the faces of the poor? said the Lord of hosts.' The capital and other things now in the hands of the rich are but the spoils of the poor.

"What, according to the Bible, will be done about it? Listen. 'He shall judge the poor of the people. He shall save the children of the needy and shall break to pieces their oppressors.' The children of the needy can only be saved, in the sense here referred to, by breaking up this oppression and returning to them the product of their labor. Under the law God gave the Jews, the thief had to restore fourfold. But we will just take what the thief has his hand on at the time."

"Well, I reckon there is little use contending with you Socialists. There seems to be no answer. So, good-bye."

"Hold on a minute, we would solve the race problem of this

and all other countries, by establishing the brotherhood of man which Christ taught," shouted Parker after the mail carrier, as he took his departure.

Why the Socialists Must Reach the Churches with Their Message

The Christian Socialist, February, 1915

The first reason is, that the Socialists cannot win without reaching the millions of working people who belong to the various churches of the country. The only question is how best to reach them. I have found that there are a large number of our comrades, who seem to think that the way to do it is to attack the Christian religion as such. Or in other words that it is necessary to make atheists, infidels or agnostics of the professed Christian before you can make a Socialist out of him. It is useless to deny that there are a large number of our so-called standard works, whose authors seem to have written more to teach anti-religion than Socialism. These books fill our propaganda tables everywhere, and we hand them out to the professed Christian who wishes to study Socialism.

I find that so long as that is done, it will not avail us to say that the other political parties have the same class of men in them. Because an all sufficient reply to that is that while the Republican party, for example, had Robert G. Ingersoll[16] in its ranks, yet that party never circulated his works on religion, as Republican campaign documents. I submit that if they had, they would have made themselves in a measure responsible for what he taught on religion. I have not only been told by this class of comrades, but have read from the pens of others that man cannot be a Christian and a Socialist. Because our party circulates these opinions and declares them from the soap box, occasionally, I find myself compelled to keep on explaining when I speak to church people.

Socialists Must Reach the Churches   261

It seems to me that the only way to successfully reach the church people is to show the church member that the economic teaching of the Bible and of Socialism are the same, and that for that reason he must accept Socialism in order to stand consistently by the teaching of his own religion. I make it a practice to criticize the church members and the ministry very heavily for not following the teachings of the Bible on economics. As I view it, the Socialist speaker, when speaking to the Christian upon Socialism from the Biblical standpoint, should confine himself strictly to its economic teachings. I hold that I might just well write books on baptism, and in it mix some references to Socialism, and have the Socialist circulate it, as for a Socialist to write a book on atheism or agnosticism, and mix in a little Socialism and ask the Socialist party to circulate it.

It is my experience, that when you show the church member how the Bible, in every line of it, is with the poor as against their oppressors, and that it is only because we have not been following out its teaching, that professed Christians have been found among the worst oppressors of the poor and that no man is entitled to be called a Christian who does not measure up to the teaching of the Bible, you have made the first step toward converting him to the idea that it cannot be done in its entirety without the collective ownership and operation of the industries. The church members must be taught that charity is only a temporary relief, designed to relieve the intensity of the suffering, while this system continues. I have known Socialists to make the mistake of denouncing all of the charitable efforts of the churches indiscriminately, forgetting that we ourselves are continually raising funds to help strikers and other sufferers.

What we Socialists need to do is to point out that the Bible itself does not recommend charity as the final solution of the problem of poverty. Another mistake is that we Socialists in talking with Christians ofttimes denounce the teaching, "Servants, obey your masters," when at the same time on the very street in which we are speaking, we are doing our best to observe the laws passed by our capitalist masters.

We social democrats claim to believe in majority rule, and if we preach against obeying the laws made by our masters while we are in the minority it is a suggestion to them to disobey as soon as we become the majority. The Christian religion with its golden rule, and other precepts, has taught a doctrine that has been all of this time gradually undermining the gigantic system of oppression, but did not seek to put the thing down until the people are made ready for it.

Not long ago I had a debate with a preacher who pointed out from our books a great mass of these attacks upon the Christian religion, Christ, God and everything sacred. I simply admitted that his quotations were correct, as indeed they were. Some of these quotations went on to show that the adoption of Socialism would result in the overthrow of not only the church but of Christianity itself. In reply, I proceeded to give a definition of Socialism and then insisted upon him answering whether in his judgment that would be the results, and made him admit that he did not think that would. I then told him that I was willing to admit that the Socialists as a party in my judgment are making a mistake in circulating that kind of teaching. But I contended that no mistake of the Socialist could relieve him from the responsibility of advocating what he must admit is a good thing, any more than which in his judgment the church made a mistake, in the advocacy of some false doctrine.

I am not attempting to go into the merits of these questions but trying only to set forth some of the difficulties I find in reaching church people and how to deal with them. When once we have succeeded in showing the church people and the pastors of small churches, that if they are to follow the teachings of the Bible, they must be with us in advocating the overthrow of the capitalist system, we will have made the greatest step yet made in the cause of Socialism. It will not do to send those who do not understand the Christian people, to carry this message, for the reason that they are sure to say something that will spoil the whole thing.

NOTES TO PART 1

1. Karl Marx (1818-1883), the founder of "scientific socialism," was one of the most influential thinkers of all time.

2. Herbert Spencer (1820-1903) was the formulator of Social Darwinism, an effort to apply Darwinism to Anglo-Saxon civilization as a superior development out of previous civilizations.

3. The problem of how Marx's Jewish origin may have influenced the content of his analysis of society has been explored by many writers. *See,* in this connection, the article "One of the Most Gifted Sons of the Jewish People," published in *The Vokshod Weekly Chronicle,* St. Petersburg, at the time of Marx's death in March, 1883, and reprinted in English in Philip S. Foner, editor, *Karl Marx Remembered: Comments at the Time of His Death* (San Francisco: Synthesis Publications, 1983), pp. 180-83; Louis Harap, "The Meaning of Marx's Essay 'On the Jewish Question,'" *Journal of Ethnic Studies* 7 (November, 1979); pp. 120-38; Murray Wolfson, *Marx: Economist, Philosopher, Jew, Steps in the Development of a Doctrine* (New York: St. Martin's Press, 1982).

4. Frederick Engels (1820-1895) was the famous collaborator of Karl Marx; with Marx he prepared *The Communist Manifesto* (1848). Author of many important works, including *Socialism: Utopian and Scientific.*

5. John D. Rockefeller, Sr. (1839-1937), symbol of the "Robber Barons," founder of the Standard Oil Trust, who became one of the wealthiest capitalists in the United States. His career as a philanthropist, involving such institutions as the University of Chicago and the Rockefeller Foundation, was cleverly exploited to cover his activities as a monopolist and "Robber Baron."

The Standard Oil Company became the major example of monopoly in the late nineteenth century, and was brilliantly exposed in Henry Demarest Lloyd's *Wealth Against Commonwealth* (1894) and Ida M. Tarbell's *The History of the Standard Oil Company* (1904).

6. Sir Thomas More's *Utopia,* published in 1516, described an ideal commonwealth.

7. Elijah P. Lovejoy (1802-1837) was an Abolitionist editor killed by a pro-slavery mob in 1837 in Alton, Illinois. William Lloyd Garrison (1805-1879) was the famous founder of the anti-slavery weekly *The Liberator* (1831) and the American Anti-Slavery Society (1833), and propounder of the doctrine of immediate emancipation. Wendell Phillips

(1811-1884), an orator and reformer, was one of the greatest of the Garrisonian Abolitionists. Frederick Douglass (1817-1895), born a slave in Maryland, escaped from slavery in 1838, and went on to become the most famous of the black Abolitionists. He was one of the greatest orators in American history. John Brown (1800-1859) was the great Abolitionist fighter who attacked Harpers Ferry in 1859 with a band of black and white abolitionists in an effort to end slavery. He was captured, tried for treason, and hanged.

8. *What to Do and How to Do It* was actually published in 1903.

9. The Citizens' Alliance represented open-shop, anti-labor groups who usually practiced vigilante tactics against progressive and labor forces.

10. William Randolph Hearst (1863-1951), one of the leading "Yellow Journalists," publisher of newspapers which he manipulated for his own gain and who boasted he had helped bring on the Spanish-American War, championed a number of progressive causes including Municipal Ownership. Hearst ran for Mayor of New York City in 1905 on a Municipal Ownership ticket with wide labor support, and was also the candidate for Governor of New York in 1906 on a public ownership platform.

11. The reform movement in Wisconsin (known as the "Wisconsin idea"), under the leadership of Republican Governor Robert M. La Follette, placed major emphasis on the direct primary, reform in the method of railroad taxation, reduction of railroad rates, regulation of public utilities, a Corrupt Practices Act to make it difficult to use large sums of money to influence nominations and elections, an anti-lobby measure to limit the power of lobbyists, an inheritance tax, and a graduated income tax.

12. Thomas Paine (1737-1809), one of the greatest champions of freedom and foes of autocracy and aristocracy, came to the American colonies from England in 1774 where he contributed immensely to the success of the American Revolution with such publications as *Common Sense* (1776) in which he called for a struggle for independence from Great Britain and not merely the redress of grievances, and his *Crisis* papers during the War for Independence. In 1789, while in England, he rallied to the support of the French Revolution, and published the immensely popular and influential *Rights of Man* (1791-92). Faced with prosecution, he fled to Paris, where he was made a French citizen and elected to the Convention. In *The Age of Reason* Paine presented his deistic views, and in *Agrarian Justice* his opposition to land monopoly and belief in equal distribution of land among the mass of the people. He returned to the United States in 1802 to face a barrage of conservative attacks, but he continued to be hailed and revered by popular, especially working-class, circles.

13. Woodbey is referring to the fact that the resolutions committee at the 1908 Socialist convention declared itself unable to express a definite opinion on the subject of racial differences as a basis of exclusion of certain immigrants, and recommended the appointment of an investigating committee to study the subject and report to the next convention. (*Proceedings, National Convention of the Socialist Party, Held at Chicago, Illinois, May 10 to 17, 1908*, Chicago, 1908, p. 105.)

14. Cornelius Vanderbilt (1794-1877) and Jay Gould (1836-1892) were two of the leading "Robber Barons" after the Civil War. They exercised control over railroads which they operated at the expense of the public welfare.

15. "Boss" Tweed ruled the Tweed Ring, a corrupt political organization in New York City, from 1860 to 1871, operating through Tammany Hall.

16. Robert Green Ingersoll (1833-1899), lawyer and orator, was known as "the great agnostic," famous as an agnostic lecturer.

PART 2

Writings of Woodbey's Predecessors

Socialism from the Biblical Point of View

by Rt. Rev. James Theodore Holly, D.D., LL.D.

AME Church Review; IX, 1892-93

Socialism is the subject now uppermost in all minds, almost to the exclusion of every other thought, in this closing decade of the nineteenth century.

It has been variously treated by all classes and orders of men, from the Roman Pontiff of the seven-hilled city to the obscure country preacher; from the German Emperor to the ward politician; from Herbert Spencer to the anonymous writer of penny-a-line sophisms in the daily journals.

Thus theologians, politicians and philosophers have boldly entered into the arena to discuss the solution to be given to this all-absorbing social problem. But as yet no practical solution has been arrived at, by which the question can be disposed of in a satisfactory manner; meanwhile society, shaken to its very foundations in all its ramifications, approaches, with the celerity of the lightning's flash, one of the most terrible crises that have ever afflicted humanity.

It may be (indeed it seems now to be) too late to ward off the fatal collapse. Perhaps the Rubicon is passed in the down grade of social destruction, by which the present framework of society must be swept by the board. It may be that Christendom has committed that much-dreaded unpardonable blasphemy against the Holy Ghost; and therefore the irrevocable decree has gone forth from on high, crying: "Babylon is fallen; Babylon is fallen."

Such an impending crisis should not astonish any Bible student conversant with the prophecies concerning these last days of the seven times of the Gentiles, now about expiring. Nevertheless, as the friends around the bedside of a man dying of an incurable disease, should not object to have a reliable diagnosis of his disease; so, though the social malady of Christendom, as at present constituted, be also incurable, no one should object to have a reliable diagnosis of the deadly complaint.

Where, then, can we hope to obtain a clue to those morbific symptoms by which we may be able to understand this cause? Ah! there is but one book, the infallible repertory of the Creator, the Redeemer and the Sanctifier of the human race, which can give us the desired clue. That book is the Holy Bible!

The question of socialism will forever remain an insoluble enigma, unless we study it from the Biblical point of view.

We proceed therefore to this study from that point of view. There is one verse in the Gospel which gathers up in one focus, under one head, all the teachings of the Bible from Genesis to Revelation. They are the words of Jesus, the Great Physician of Souls. They are contained in His memorable Sermon on the Mount. They express the whole of God's designs towards man; and therefore they contain, as in a nut-shell, the complete diagnosis of socialism.

Let him who has ears to hear, listen to these inspired words, fraught with divine wisdom:

"Seek ye first the Kingdom of God, and his righteousness, and all these things shall be added unto you." (St. Matt. 6:33.)

By analyzing those words, we will discover three great divisions of the social question.

(1) The kingdom of God to be sought brings before our thoughts theology and Church administration.

(2) The righteousness to be sought brings into prominence philanthropy, or the law of justice and equity between man and man, and State administration.

(3) The things promised in addition (see preceding verses, viz., food, raiment and shelter) bring to the front industry and the various means of carrying it on to supply man's necessities. Hence, under the first head we have dogmatics; under the sec-

ond, politics; under the third, economics. These three things, from the Bible point of view, include the whole framework of socialism in its application to man on earth.

The task given to the human race at its creation was that of working out that application, as God's vice-gerents, over the lower kingdoms and elements of nature. To equip man for the task, God endowed him with three lofty faculties, viz., free will, reason and inspiration. Those three faculties, in the order that I have named them, were to be successively brought to bear on the three social divisions, as I have also named them, to work out their development and application—viz., in religion, or dogmatic theology; in government, or political jurisprudence; in industry, or economical distribution.

By the application of free will to dogmatics, mankind, in the most advanced countries, has worked out liberty of conscience in matters of religion. By its application to political jurisprudence, the most advanced communities have reached the right of suffrage or the elective franchise, on the part of the governed, in choosing their governors. By nowhere yet has the application of free will to economics achieved the much-desired liberty of labor.

It is, therefore, this third and last point, developed in our analysis, which forms the part of the social problem now at the order of the day; seeking a solution which, if it does not or cannot come by fair means, must come through the foul disorders with which the gospel dispensation is to close; to be followed by the inauguration of the reign of righteousness, by the returning Prince of Peace.

Hence, our social diagnosis, from the Bible point of view, is narrowed down to the teachings and examples given in the inspired book of God, on the question of industrial economics. But before going into this examination, a word will be added in reference to the two other faculties with which man is to work. Reason, the second faculty, comes after long experience by diverse essays on the part of man, in the exercise of his free will, enabling him to choose the good and refuse the evil methods of procedure. Inspiration, the third faculty with which man is to work, is a direct communication from God, to help man out of otherwise inextricable difficulties, when he is at his wit's end, both as to his free will and his reason.

The Bible is the authentic and general depository of this guiding inspiration from God to man. We have seen that free will has achieved solid results in the religious and political development of the most advanced portions of the race, but not yet anything tangible in economics to insure the liberty of labor. But reason and inspiration, that follow respectively after the essays of free will, have as yet done little or nothing to put religion, jurisprudence and industry upon a solid, all-enduring basis. After sixty centuries man is still in the first experiments in the exercise of free will. His reason is not yet mature, nor his inspiration clear in the task before him, to work out a satisfactory solution of the social problem, committed to him at his creation by the Creator.

We go back, therefore, to the creation to study this problem on the economical or industrial side, as set forth in the Bible. The point now up for solution, and to which we wish to arrive, is that of the liberty of labor in our economical relations, as we have already reached liberty of conscience in religion, and liberty of suffrage in politics, by the force of man's free will. What, then, are the Bible conditions by which the liberty of the laborer is to be guaranteed?

I answer, that at the very dawn of the creation of man, the basis of social economics was laid by God, according to the Scriptures, inseparable from the family, the family homestead and the personal supply of the indispensable necessities of daily sustenance. Adam and Eve were united in holy marriage, with a nuptial benediction containing a command to raise up a household of children; and Eden was the family homestead, prepared for them, ready furnished with the supply of all the necessaries of life. This being done, and they being placed beyond the want of any good thing, and above penurious misery, were henceforth to engage in the industrial occupation of dressing and keeping the garden. These preliminary conditions being secured to them, they were thereby assured the liberty of labor. They were not driven to work by the dire necessity of hunger and other physical wants.

This arrangement was not an exceptional one, incident on the very beginning of the human race. More than 3,000 years afterwards, when God interfered actively again in the social affairs of humanity, in calling a special people to be the model of all other peoples, and the medium of their benediction, He established the same conditions in favor of that chosen people, by His commandment given to their leaders, Moses and Joshua. A land, already planted and cultivated, from which a rebel and apostate race was expelled, was given to the elect nation which was settled there, and a homestead, forever inalienable, secured by the law of jubilees, was given to each family. Moreover, the slavish drudgery of unremitting labor was provided against by its being limited between sunrise and sunset (Ps. 104:23.), thus securing each night for repose, to which was added, for the same purpose, the whole of the seventh day in each week, and the whole of each succeeding seventh year, after their entrance into the possession of Canaan. Thus did God give us a practical example of His intention that every man should sit under his own vine and under his own fig-tree, "with none to molest him" or make him afraid. (Micah 4:4.)

Examples speak louder than words. The acts of God toward the human race are not of less importance than His precepts spoken to them. "The powers that be," in this world, are bound in their administration to conform themselves to these divine examples, or reap the fatal consequences of their refusal to do so. A stupid casuistry, more culpable than that of the Jesuits, has led theologians to tell us that the ten commandments spoken on Sinai are binding on Christian people; but that Divine economical administration, executed by Almighty God Himself, for the social regulation of His chosen people, is not binding on Christian nations! It is this miserable theology that has brought Christendom to the very edge of the frightful social abyss now yawning beneath the feet of every so-called Christian nation.

The masses of the population in each nation are without family homesteads as an inalienable heritage; labor is prolonged to the late hours of the night; the day of weekly rest is encroached upon by drudging occupations or entirely ignored;

unprincipled land monopolists are grabbing up the land by millions of acres, aided in their thievery by political administrators, who are accessory to the theft of God's domain, given by Him as a heritage to the whole human race, so that each family might have a home thereon; marketable commodities, including the necessaries of life, are kept at the highest prices by infamous speculators, stock jobbers and trust combines. Such are the audacious inequities practiced in so-called Christian countries in the nineteenth century of the grace of Jesus Christ! And such is the organized brigandage that goes under the name of lawful government!

The poor millions have not where to stand or lay their heads without paying a tax in the shape of rent to some law-shielded thief, for this God-given privilege and right to have such a standing ground is wrested from them under this miserable caricature of government. The very sight of such organized injustice makes the blood of an honest man boil in his veins, and makes him feel the necessity of excusing Proudhon,[1] when, in the excess of his indignation, he exclaimed, *"La propriété, c'est le vol!"*

Marriage, the inalienable right and duty of every normally constituted man and woman, is thereby rendered a grievous burden for the toiling millions, and the pleasures of home life are absolutely cut off from them. They have no vine and fig-tree under which they can sit, with none to molest them or make them afraid. Gaunt hunger and the rack renters, as in Ireland, drive them from their miserable straw pallets in death-breathing, overcrowded rooms, to labor late and early for the mere bread to keep soul and body together from day to day.

But I am asked if the Bible does not recognize the possibility of unequal conditions of material wealth among men? Yes, I respond; and the Gospel teaches us how the rich capitalists should, in times of distress, act toward the poor laboring man. This lesson is given in the parable of the householder, who hired laborers in his vineyards. (St. Matt. 20.) Take notice that he is called a householder, that is, a father of a family, and who therefore could or should feel for other fathers of families less happily situated than himself. He does not, in a time of distress among poor people, wait for laborers to come to him seeking work. Still less does he turn his workmen out of doors by a "lock-out," as a soulless man did at Homestead, in Pennsylvania.[2] No; the householder of the Gospel parable was not a heartless, wanton wretch, bent on his own avaricious gains. On the contrary, as a Christian altruist, he rather thought of the unemployed poor in the time of their distress; and he went out into the public streets hour after hour, and hired men there standing idle, to go into his vineyard and work. He agreed with the first laborers hired for the price of that day's labor. At the end of the day he gave the same wages to all, even those who had only worked one hour. All doubtlessly would have worked the whole day if they had been employed. All, perhaps, had families to support, and the price of that day's labor would likely be only sufficient to support the family for another day. Hence, the father-heart of that householder led him, in his noble generosity, to pay to his last workmen even more than they had earned, that their families might also enjoy the same benefit as those of the earlier workmen. If he had been anxious about large profits, or to make a million of dollars from his dividends, as did a stockholder at Homestead, the householder would never have acted with such generosity toward his poor workmen. When hard times came he would have locked them out! This is heathenism of the worst kind in the midst of Christendom, and is every whit as abominable before God as the cannabalism of the savage South Sea islanders. There is no Gospel morality in our organized modern industry, and therefore offerings from such ill-gotten riches are made as if God could be bribed by the mammon of iniquity. But such gifts, amassed by grinding the face of the necessitous poor, and heartlessly wrung out of the blood and sweat of careworn toilers, are already smitten with the curse of Heaven in answer to the sighs and groans of the oppressed laborers that mount up thither, crying for vengeance on the avaricious oppressors; and thereby those offerings are an abomination in the sight of the Almighty, for He cannot and will not behold with pleasure iniquity, injustice and oppression.

It may now be thought by the timid and time-serving that

this is an extremely radical application of the principles of Biblical socialism; that they are pushed to too rigorous consequences, and that their open annunciation is fraught with tremendous peril in the present state of society. My answer to this objection is that the peril thus dreaded has already announced itself; the deadly conflict of the industrial forces of society is already upon us; the social crisis is now at abnormal fever heat; the patient, *i.e.,* the present order of society, is in its last agony; the death rattles are in its throat! I have simply, as to the causes of the disease, anticipated a *post-mortem* examination of the remains, and rendered a further autopsy of the cadaver useless, by a Biblical diagnosis of the social malady under which Christendom suffers. It is evident, in the light of this *ante-mortem* examination, that Christendom has brought this dangerous disease, now *in extremis,* upon itself, by ignoring, during the last fifteen centuries of the Church's domination in Europe, since the conversion of Constantine, with the most inexcusable pig-headedness, the fundamental social principles revealed in the Bible, and practically illustrated by the Holy Ghost in the fraternal community of the first converts to the Gospel. (Acts 4:32-37.)

The time has been, when, almost at the last hour marked on the dial-plate of our new dispensation, the awful social abyss into which the Church and the world, mutually locked in each other's embrace, are now about plunging, might have been avoided; for the menaces of God, as to evils ahead, like His promises of blessing to be bestowed, are always conditional. As the promised blessings may be forfeited by failing to fulfill the conditions of obedience, so the threatened evils may also be avoided by ceasing to do evil, and by returning to a right course of action. But a limit, called "to-day" in Scripture, is put to the time wherein such a return is possible. That limit passed, by men hardening their hearts, like Pharaoh of old, there is nothing further to hope for; and the willful sinner has only left to him "a certain fearful looking for a judgment and fiery indignation."

The last hour struck to give the Church and the world warning, if haply they would seize the last offer of repentance, when the French Revolution broke out at the end of last century; while he who was its infuriated and devil-possessed genius, carried fire and sword throughout Europe into Asia and Africa; tracking his pathway across three continents with human gore. The warning being thus given, and the momentary peril over, the world and the Church were put on trial again. What was the result? Did they begin to amend their ways? On the contrary, the diplomacy of Europe began its new lease of life, by the tomfoolery of the hypocritical "holy alliance," so called; and the subsequent policy of its governments was directed toward restoring and consolidating all the ancient social privileges and abuses that had prevailed previous to that terrible upheaval in France. So much for the world after its warning. The Church hardly showed itself so wise as those children of the world in their generation. It has wasted its precious opportunities in tithing the mint of doctrine, the anise of ritual and the cumin of discipline (which they ought to have done); but it omitted the weightier matters of the law: judgment, mercy and faith (which it ought not to have left undone).

That there might be no excuse on the score of ignorance of the import of that terrible warning, in the Providence of God, a man was raised up in the very midst of the revolutionary effervescence in Paris, at the end of last century, who, during forty years, devoted himself to the grand and sublime study of the social destiny of man, and the solution of the problem of the terrestrial well-being of humanity; in a word, the realization of the descent of the New Jerusalem from heaven to earth, when the tabernacle of God shall be among men. Those who have studied the works which he published during those forty years, recognize the self-evident proof that he demonstrated the solution of the social problem of humanity with the most inexorable mathematical vigor. That man was Charles Fourier;[3] a man whom many persons, otherwise intelligent, commit the stupidity of classing in the same category with the many mere social enthusiasts who displayed none of the profound, reverent and patient science of Fourier, in studying God, man and the universe. Of all the men of public reputation, I do not hesitate to declare my most solemn conviction that Charles Fourier was the most Christ-hearted man that has trodden our planet since the days of Jesus and His Apostles!

Forty years of study in elaborating the grandest problem given by God to the heart and intellect of man to solve; a few years of patient waiting, during a few hours each day, after the solution was found, in childish faith, sublime angelic hope and Christ-like love, expecting that some of the world's or the Church's great men would call on him and put at his disposal the means of practically realizing the solved social problem— by these circumstances, I say, the last dread warning was given to Christendom; and his work was done! Then, while the dignitaries of Church and State heedlessly mixed with the giddy, bustling crowd of Paris, rolling beneath him as a living sea, through its streets, one morning the faithful woman-servant of this lone man, in going to his attic chamber, when the usual hour for his appearance below had passed, found him by his bedside, dead, and on his bended knees! The soul had gone to God who gave it; and that great heart, which had beat so high with love of God and man, and had thrilled through every nerve of his frame, a sympathetic response to every human woe and grief, now lay still and cold in the icy embrace of death.

The second great French revolution, that of 1848, followed in about twelve years from the taking away from our midst of this great ignored social prophet and messenger of the nineteenth century. From that onward until to-day, everything in Church and State has pursued a downward, anti-social career. This downward impetus is now so great that there is no return possible upon one's steps. On, on, society must go, until it precipitates itself into the yawning gulf beneath.

When Judaism had reached a similar fearful declivity, such as that now just ahead of Christendom, the tender-hearted Christ wept bitter tears of sorrow over Jerusalem. Judaism, great as was its culpability, had only committed the sin against the Son of man. But there will be no such Divine sorrowing over the fall of Christendom, as the mystical Babylon of the Apocalyse; for it will have committed the blasphemy against the Holy Ghost, the unpardonable sin of the ages, for which all the past eternity has waited to witness its accomplishment!

The voice of the strong Lord God Almighty, who judgeth her, will be heard from the heavens in the day of her calamity: "Reward her even as she rewarded you, and double unto her double according to her works; in the cup which she hath filled, fill to her double." And down will go the whole Babylonish fabric of Christendom, ecclesiastical, political and financial, in one general crash, as that great millstone cast by the angel into the sea, saying: "Thus with violence shall that great city, Babylon, be thrown down, and shall be found no more at all."

The only tears that shall be shed at the fall of mystic Babylon, or anti-social Christendom, will be purely human and self-interested tears: the cry of the miserable kings of the earth, whose abused power will have ceased; the howl of the avaricious merchant princes, whose usurious gains will have been swept away; and the clamor of the traffickers in ships, for their occupation which will have been taken away! (Rev. 18.)

The incurableness of this chronic malady of Christendom, in consequence of its persistent anti-socialism, is now made apparent in its last stage by the *gangrene* of mortification taking place at this moment.

This plague-spot has shown itself in, around and about Africa. The so-called Christian and civilized powers of Europe, assembled in a den of thieves which they styled an international conference, have deliberately parceled out Africa among themselves. The tens of millions of the masses in each country of Europe have been reduced down to mere animal fare; the hundreds of millions of India have had their life's blood sucked out of them; opium poison has been injected into the veins of the hundred millions of China, at the point of the bayonet; and all this to fill the bottomless coffers of avaricious *millionaires*. England, up to the present time, has had the monopoly of this highway robbery. Henceforth this general thievery is to be carried on by a company—a trust combine—of so-called civilized and Christian nations. The hypocritical pretext is put forward that this occupation of Africa is to protect the natives from the ravages of the slave-trade, to civilize and Christianize them! As a matter of fact, the poor African, like the Divine Master, is being crucified between two thieves! The Semitic Arabs steal their bodies and the Japhetic nations of Europe are stealing the lands and homes of these poor sons of Ham! The Babylonish confusion of rum, gunpowder, Bibles, missionaries, traffickers and political agents is being poured pell-mell into Africa, with all the bitter rivalries, animosities and jealousies of sects and nationalities. This has lighted up civil war among the natives brought under their heterogeneous influence at Uganda, as has hitherto been the case elsewhere, notably in Tahiti and Madagascar.

The anathemas of Christ, pronounced against apostate Judaism, are now applicable to apostate Christendom. In view of the internecine conflict stirred up among the native Christian converts in Africa, under the very eyes and by the instigation of their foreign preachers and teachers, one may well exclaim in the burning words of our Lord: "Woe unto you Scribes and Pharisees, hypocrites! For ye compass sea and land to make one proselyte, and when he is made, ye make him twofold more the child of hell than yourselves. . . . Ye serpents, ye generation of vipers, how can ye escape the damnation of hell!" (St. Matt. 23:15, 33.)

This is a terrible point to reach in the downward course in which Christendom is now tending, because of long-organized social injustice. But this awful lake of fire yawning before us, is that the last word the Bible has to say on God's socialistic purposes with humanity? Ah! thank God, I can answer with a *thousand* no's, indicating the glorious period of the coming millennial reign of Christ.

Look up, and see the Prince of Peace descending to take possession of all the nations of the earth. "He shall judge the poor of the people; He shall save the children of the needy, and He shall break in pieces the oppressor. . . . Yea, all kings shall fall down before Him; all nations shall serve Him." (Ps. 72:4, 11.) Then shall the social destiny of man, religiously, politically and economically, be accomplished. Then, will, reason and inspiration shall have fully accomplished in man their highest and noblest triumphs, and reached their perfect accord; for then, indeed, will the kingdom of God have come, and His will shall thenceforth be done on earth even as it is now done among the good angels in heaven. Amen! Even so, Lord Jesus, come! Come, wearing Thy thousand crowns, and take to Thyself Thy great power, and reign over the humanity that Thou hast redeemed, and the earth which Thou hast purchased with Thy most precious blood!

Port-au-Prince, Haiti.

The Negro and Socialism
By Rev. R.C. Ransom

AME Church Review XIII, 1896-97

The substantial wealth of man consists in the earth he cultivates, with its pleasant or serviceable animals and plants, and in the rightly produced work of his own hands. The material wealth of any country is the portion of its possession which feeds and educates good men and women in it. In fact, it may be discovered that the true veins of wealth are purple—and not in rock, but in flesh—perhaps that even the final outcome and consummation of all wealth is the producing as many as possible full-breathed, bright-eyed and happy-hearted human creatures.—*Ruskin*.[4]

That the closing years of the Nineteenth Century are pregnant of great changes must be apparent even to the least observant. The minds of men are moving toward new goals; new battle cries are upon their lips. Men have come to regard the close of a century as the end of an epoch, and the beginning of a century as the commencement of a new era. The last century was an epoch of revolt against political despotism. The message of the Eighteenth Century to man was, "Thou shalt cease to be the slave of nobles and despots who oppress thee; thou art free and sovereign." The dawn of the Nineteenth Century opened an epoch of human progress unexampled in the history of the world. Universal education, universal suffrage and the freedom of the slave are included in the long catalogue of splendid achievements. Since the beginning of the century applied science has transformed the world. The industrial revolution has given man such large dominion over the realm of nature, through the application of steam and electricity on an immense scale to machinery, that we stand literally in the midst of a new heaven and a new earth. With the acquisition of political power and the splendid conquests of science in the domain of nature, a larger self-consciousness has come to the masses.

"Since the middle of the century there has sprung up and spread will nigh throughout Christendom a deep discontent on the part of workingmen. To give to the poor like tastes with the rich is to create an inevitable demand for substantial equality of condition and to stimulate discontent until such equality is secured." One of the clearest and profoundest writers on social and industrial questions has recently stated with what feelings the wage-earning class regard the immense conquests and progress of the century.

"What avails it that the waste places of the earth have been turned into highways of commerce, if the many still work and want, and only the few have leisure and grow rich? What does it profit the worker that knowledge grows, if all the appliances of science are not to lighten his labor? Wealth may accumulate, and public and private magnificence may have reached a point never before attained in the history of the world: but wherein is society better, if the Nemesis of poverty still sits like a hollow-eyed spectre at the feast?"

Professor Huxley[5] thus expresses his dissatisfaction with the existing state of things: "If it is true that the increase of knowledge, the winning of a greater domain over nature which is its consequence, and the wealth which follows upon that domain are to make no difference in the extent and the intensity of want with its concomitant physical and moral degeneration amongst the masses of the people, I should hail the advent of some kindly comet which would sweep the whole affair away as a desirable consummation." To the opinions of these thinkers, each one of whom is regarded as an authority in his department of inquiry, we have to add that standing over against huge monopolies and aggregations of capital are also gigantic labor organizations—"trades unions," "federations," while the "captains of industry" and "money kings" are confronted by labor leaders, "agitators" and "grand master workmen." Out of these conditions modern socialism has been born. This new movement has stirred the heart and touched the brain of every civilized land. Its presence is recognized by men of every school. Its powerful effect upon modern thought can be seen in politics, theology, philosophy and literature. Socialism aims to bring about a readjustment of the relations between man and his brother man, and thus presents to the opening hours of the twentieth century problems surpassing in magnitude any with which civilization has had to deal. "It has ceased to be a theory," says Mr. Kidd[6] "it has begun to be a kind of religion." There is much vagueness of definition and misapprehension in regard to the true meaning of socialism.

It has been attempted to make it cover every scheme of social, political or industrial reform. Socialism in a broad and general sense rejects the doctrine of selfishness which rules the present social order and affirms that altruism is a principle sufficient to govern the relations of men in the sense it is opposed to individualism and does not regard society as composed of an army of warring atoms, but believes that social system to be the best in which the interests of the individual are made subordinate to the interests of society, while allowing freedom for the highest development of his own personality. Dr. Westcott, bishop of Durham, distinguishes individualism from socialism in the following words: "Individualism regards humanity as made up of disconnected or warring atoms. Socialism regards it as an organic whole. The aim of socialism is the fulfillment of service; the aim of individualism the attainment of some personal advantage— riches, place, or fame. Socialism seeks such an organization of life as shall secure every one the most complete development of his powers; individualism seeks primarily, the satisfaction of the particular wants of each one, in the hope that the pursuit of private interests will, in the end, secure public welfare." Socialism is not a form of anarchy; on the other hand it is its bitter foe. Socialists believe in a republican form of government—a democratic state. They do not believe in the abolition of government, the destruction of the state. They are, however, opposed to the centralization of government or political power. They seek not the overthrow of government, but to gain their ends through existing governments. Socialism is not a scheme of plunder. It aims not at an equal division of all property and wealth. Professor Richard T. Ely,[7] who is a profound student of sociological science and social reform defines socialism as follows: "Socialism is that contemplated system of industrial society which proposes the abolition of private property in the great material instruments of production and the substitution therefore of collective management of production, together with the distribution of social income by society and private property in the larger proportion of this social income."

By the material instruments of production is meant the land, the forests, the mines, the tools. By gaining control of the instruments of production, it is proposed to put an end to the struggle for existence, by permitting all the people to hold, manage and distribute the surplus wealth which is now held and distributed by the few. In his great work on Social Evolution, Mr. Benjamin Kidd says: "True socialism has always one definite object in view, up to which all its proposals directly or indirectly lead. This is the final suspension of that personal struggle for existence which has been waged, not from the beginning of society, but, in one form or another, from the beginning of life."

We have gone as far as the limitations of a magazine article will permit, in attempting to show the interpretation, which leading exponents of sociology and social reform, place upon the spirit of unrest which pervades almost every avenue of life and is the distinguishing mark of the present age. The present social order with its poverty and vast reserve army of unemployed, cannot be accepted as final, as the ultimate goal for which the ages have been in travail. If man is the child of God, the present social order is not divine. God, who does not withhold from men their eternal heritage, nor condemn them to an eternity of misery without giving to each an equal chance, has never sanctioned as by divine right, a social order into which the vast majority must be born only to find, "no trespass," posted upon every portion of the domain of nature, which is their heritage, and to lead a life of privation and suffering in a struggle to maintain an existence, which the bounteous storehouse of nature is able to sustain in comfort at the touch of toil and skill.

> The proudest now is but my peer,
> The highest not more high;
> To-day of all the weary years,
> A king of men am I.

Socialism places its chief value upon man. Socialism, like the inspired Carpenter of Nazareth, places more value upon man than it does upon riches. It believes that the rights of man are more sacred than the rights of property, believes indeed, that the only sacred thing on earth is a human being. Socialism would bring all the people to participate in the rivalry of life upon a footing of equality, allowing to each individual the widest possible range for the development of his powers and personality, with freedom to follow wherever his abilities may lead him.

Socialism and industrial reform is not a question of race: it is not confined to the boundaries of any nation or continent; it is the question of man. The claims of society upon each individual, the bond of union and dependence of nation upon nation and man upon man, are becoming so strong as to sound forever the death knell of the domination of one race over another. The days of race domination are ended, the solidarity of the human race is coming to be admitted by all. It cannot but transpire, because of his past and present situation, that the programme of socialism, will in time, powerfully appeal to the American Negro. The American Negro belongs almost wholly to the proletarian or industrial class. He constitutes a large and important factor in the development of this country and the production of its wealth. No question affecting our social and industrial future can be considered settled until he has rendered his judgment and cast his vote. The Negro by his valor assisted in establishing the American nation and he was present at its birth. By his patriotism and courage he helped to save the Union from destruction. During the days of slavery the effect of his unpaid labor was to debauch or reduce to serfdom the poor whites of the South, while it bound fetters upon the free toilers of the North.

Since emancipation the Negro has been busy fighting for the recognition of his manhood, his political and social rights, and slaking his age-long thirst at the fountains of knowledge. But a generation ago, penniless, homeless, ignorant, and despised, he could have little thought beyond securing for himself the most elementary condition of civilized life. He has had little time either for reflection, or for grappling with the deep questions that concern the destiny of nations or the welfare of mankind. But a new generation has been born under new conditions. A generation little influenced by the traditions of the past; a generation whose political faith will neither be a heritage nor a sentiment; a generation who will play an active part in every phase of the nation's life; a generation, who, struggling from the depths of poverty and oppression, will not lend unwilling ears to a scheme which proposes such a readjustment of the social and industrial relations among men, as to permit all to stand upon an equal plane and each to have an equal chance in the race of life. The great army of toilers who have been crying out against our present social and industrial conditions, have steadily refused to recognize the cause of the Negro workmen as one with theirs. This penniless freedman has had to contend against the frown and active opposition of organized labor for a chance to win his bread. In the great hives of industial activity, the Negro finds almost every door leading to the skilled trades closed against him. In the South, where Negro labor is the main dependence, both their wages and the consideration with which they are treated is vastly inferior to that bestowed upon white laborers doing similar work.

It has been attempted to proscribe the Negro's sphere in the realm of industry, and to feel that it is an impertinence when he aspires beyond the limitations which have been set for him. The sphere of a Negro is not to be a barber, waiter, or a porter, any more than that of a Chinaman is to keep a laundry, or that of an Italian is to be a vender of fruit, or that of a Jew to be a peddler. The great "labor unions" and "brotherhoods" of this country have, by introducing the word "white" into their constitutions, excluded the Negro from membership. Of course there are exceptions; many of the unions admit colored men. The Federation of Labor draws no color line[8] and the American Railway Union has submitted the question of striking the word "white" from their constitutions to a vote in all of its branches.[9] But when the Negro is admitted to membership in a labor union it is difficult to obtain work, and if he is successful in obtaining employment, it is by no means an infrequent occurrence for white laborers to refuse to work with him. This refusal is based not upon the ground of the Negro's inferiority as a workman, but upon the ground of color. If, then, the Negro has little sympathy with, and takes little interest in, the cause of organized labor, his attitude is easily explained. It thus transpires, that in the uprising and unrest against present social, economic and industrial conditions, the Negro has been mostly a silent spectator. He has felt that it was not his fight. Indeed the disasters and defeats which organized labor has suffered while battling for what it believed to be its rights, have mostly accrued to the Negro's material benefit. They have been the lever which has opened the doors of factories, mills, and mines, which organized labor had barred against his entrance. When once the strikers' places have been filled by Negroes, if they are permitted to return to work, they are compelled to take their places at the Negro's side.

There are more than a million Negro toilers in this land; they are citizens; they are here to stay. Their destiny is bound up with the destiny of the Republic, with the destiny of man. The Negro will not continue silent; even now there are signs that he is growing articulate. He will be a conspicuous figure on the stage of the twentieth century, in those days when social reform will be the burning question of the hour. In these days the old political parties are crying—"Rally! Rally!" but the people are demanding—"To what cry?" The old rallying cries no longer stir men's hearts. The forces that impelled men to action in the past, are mostly spent forces. New issues have arisen, new causes stir men's hearts, among which socialism is the mightiest. The old relations of men, intrenched behind centuries of custom, will not be able to beat back the rising tide. The battles of socialism are not to be fought by white men, for the benefit of white men. It is not, as we have said, a question of race, it is the question of man. So far as America is concerned, this question cannot be settled without the Negro's aid. The cause of labor, of the industrial army, is one. Our present social condition, which is organized, not upon a basis of equal cooperation, but of selfishness, will not give way, until this army can present an organized, united and unbroken front. While one class of toilers is outraged and oppressed, no man is free. When millions of toilers are degraded, labor is degraded, man is degraded. That the Negro will enthusiastically espouse the cause of socialism we cannot doubt. Social and industrial oppression have been his portion for centuries. When he comes to realize that socialism offers him freedom of opportunity to cooperate with all men upon terms of equality in every avenue of life, he will not be slow to accept his social emancipation. The day is not far distant, when with clearer eyes, through the smoke of battle, we shall see the steeples of a new civilization rising. A civilization which shall neither be Anglo-Saxon, Asiatic nor African; but one which, recognizing the unity of the race and the brotherhood of man, will accord to each individual the full reward which the free exercise of his powers has won, and the right to stand upon an equal plane and share all of the blessings of our common heritage.

NOTES TO PART 2

1. Pierre Joseph Proudhon (1809-1865), philosophical "Father of Anarchism," published *Philosophy of Poverty* in 1846. This was criticized by Marx in *The Poverty of Philosophy*.

2. The reference is to the lockout of the members of the Amalgamated Association of Iron and Steel Workers, employed at the Carnegie, Phipps and Company plant in Homestead, Pennsylvania, June 29, 1892. The anti-union action was taken by Henry Clay Frick, manager of the steel company, but it was fully supported by Andrew Carnegie, its owner. The lockout led to the great Homestead strike of 1892 which ended in a defeat for the steel workers.

3. François Marie Charles Fourier (1772-1837), a French utopian socialist whose basic concept was the Phalanx, had many influential followers in the United States, Horace Greeley among them.

4. John Ruskin (1819-1900), son of a wealthy British wine merchant, became a critic of the degrading features of capitalism and a prolific author of books on art and more beauty in life.

5. Thomas Henry Huxley (1825-1895), British biologist and humanist, and advocate of Darwinism and education reform.

6. Benjamin Kidd (1858-1916), English social philosopher whose theories had a considerable vogue at the turn of the century, especially among laymen who wished to reconcile religion and evolution.

7. Richard T. Ely (1854-1943), professor and Christian Socialist, author of *The Labor Movement in America* (1886).

8. For evidence that this evaluation of the racial policies of the American Federation of Labor is not accurate since it ignores outright exclusionist practices against black workers, *see* Philip S. Foner, *Organized Labor and the Black Worker, 1619-1981* (New York: International Publishers, 1982), pp. 71-81.

9. Despite an effort of Eugene V. Debs, its founder and first president, to prevent it, the American Railway Union limited its membership to whites when it was organized in 1893. The ban against black membership was reaffirmed at the national convention in June, 1894, by a vote of 112 to 100.

PART 3

Articles of Reverend George W. Slater, Jr.

Introduction

We know little about Reverend George W. Slater, Jr., before he became a socialist. The *Chicago Daily Socialist* engaged him to write a series of articles for the paper under the general heading "Negroes Becoming Socialists," but it did not bother to introduce him to its readers with any biographical sketch. However, in the first article of this series, "How and Why I Became a Socialist," Reverend Slater reveals that during the winter of 1907-1908, a period of rising unemployment and economic distress resulting from the Panic of 1907 and the ensuing business recession, he had tried to alleviate the sufferings of his black parishioners by organizing a cooperative enterprise through which they might purchase goods at savings of between 25 and 30 percent. The giant manufacturers frowned upon the venture, however, and he was unable to purchase supplies. The salesmen for the companies told him frankly that any dealer furnishing him with supplies would be driven out of business by the manufacturers.

This experience opened his eyes to the futility of trying to alleviate the sufferings of poor blacks under the existing economic system. When he heard Woodbey's analysis of how only socialism could help abolish poverty, he was immediately converted and joined the Socialist Party. Once converted, Slater eagerly assumed the task of recruiting blacks for the party. This he did by means of weekly sermons in his church, Zion Tabernacle in Chicago, by the distribution of his pamphlet, *Blackmen, Strike for Liberty* (no copy of which exists), and especially through the articles he published in the *Chicago Daily Socialist,* beginning with the issue of September 8, 1908, and ending with that of March 27, 1909. Although they appeared only for a limited time, Slater's articles marked the first time in American history that a socialist organ carried writings by a black American on a regular basis.

Although he stopped contributing to the *Chicago Daily Socialist* after March, 1909, Slater did not cease work for the Socialist Party. When Local New York attempted to win black votes in the municipal campaign of the fall of 1911, it called upon Slater for aid. He furnished it with a pamphlet, "The Colored Man's Case as Socialism Sees It," which was widely distributed in Negro circles.[1] (All copies of the pamphlet, along with other pamphlets by Slater, have disappeared.) From 1912 to 1919, Reverend Slater is listed in the city directory of Clinton, Iowa, as pastor of the Bethel African Church.[2] From that city, he distributed a pro-socialist monthly, *Western Evangel,* no copies of which are in existence. In addition, in the fall of 1912, the *Cleveland Citizen* reported that Slater had formed a "Negro Socialist Literature and Lecture Bureau," and was sponsoring a national conference of colored men in Chicago "to create a nationwide interest in socialism."[3] It is doubtful that the conference ever took place, since there is no report of it in the Chicago press, including the *Chicago Daily Socialist.*

In 1913, Slater was appointed secretary of the Colored Race for the Christian Socialist Fellowship. In that capacity, he published several articles in *The Christian Socialist.* In his last article for that journal, he took issue with R.R. Wright, the editor of *The Christian Recorder,* who contended that while socialism had much about it that was praiseworthy, it could not replace the social service of the church in meeting the needs of the poorer classes. In the manner made familiar by Reverend Woodbey, Slater pointed out that "Scientific Socialism is the only systematic expression of the social message of Jesus." Social service dealt merely with symptoms, while socialism addressed itself to the abolition of wage slavery, "the main root of our social misery." Since the doctrines of socialism were the logical fulfillment of what the prophets, Jesus, and the Apostles had sought, "should not Christians, the Church, and its social service element say Amen?" he asked.[4]

P.S.F.

NOTES

1. Foner, *American Socialism and Black Americans,* p. 178.
2. Ibid.
3. *Cleveland Citizen* (Sept. 14, 1912).
4. Rev. George W. Slater, Jr., "Socialism and Social Service," *The Christian Socialist* (February, 1915).

How and Why I Became a Socialist

Chicago Daily Socialist, September 8, 1908

Having been asked to write an article each week for the *Chicago Daily Socialist* pertaining to the subject of "Socialism and the Negro Race," and as I have espoused the principles of Socialism just lately, I think it will be both interesting and profitable that in my first article I should relate "How and why I became a Socialist."

Now, it is obvious to me that the reason why I had not espoused the Socialist cause heretofore was due on the one hand to ignorance of its principles, purposes and methods, and also due on the other hand to prejudice which had been engendered by cunning innuendoes and prevalent falsehood disseminated by its detractors. It is all so plain to me now. What a lesson I have learned. How consistent and wise it is to "prove all things" before passing judgment.

Now, for my experience which prepared me for Socialism. Last winter when my parishioners had little work and little money, and the prices of food were exorbitant, I contrived a cooperative scheme whereby I could furnish them food very near the wholesale price.

Before a salesman for a certain wholesale house in this city I laid my plans. He told me that my plans were feasible and that I could get the goods. He also said that I could save the people at least 25 or 30 percent on their gross purchases.

At once, I put a young man to soliciting orders. After I had sent in my order I got a letter from the salesman asking me to call immediately. I complied, whereupon he said that he was sorry to inform me that the management of the firm had refused to permit him to fill my order because I was not a bona fide retail dealer, that I was not buying to sell again at a profit. He said that I must have a store and sell over a counter.

I admitted that I was not seeking a profit, but that I was endeavoring to help a large number of poor consumers, and that my plan calculated to get the goods to the people as directly as possible from the wholesale houses or the producers, thus cutting out the middleman's profit, and the added expense of rehandling. Upon these grounds I insisted that he should sell me the goods. Then I was plainly told the wholesale people had an understanding with the retail dealers that would make such a business transaction with me a direct violation of that agreement. And further, I was told that if they sold me the goods for the purpose for which I wanted them that the retail dealers would boycott them.

To this I replied, "Is it true that there is an understanding between the wholesale and retail dealers, whereby the poor consumer is compelled to pay more than is necessary for the necessities of life?" The salesman replied by saying, "Mr. Slater, if I had my way I would sell them to you, but I am under orders."

Chagrined and indignant, I returned and told my people of the turn of affairs. But I said in my heart and also before the public that such a situation and such agreements were unjust and in the face of such hard times, positively wicked, and that I would find a way out and break up such a situation.

To carry out my determination, I began to inquire about President Roosevelt's "trust busters," as they are called; but I soon found out that the trusts were busting the busters.

Several other plans were suggested to me, but I found that they were inadequate. The more I studied the more I saw the direful condition of the poor people.

About four weeks ago I saw, at the corner of Thirtieth and State streets, a colored man speaking to a very attentive audience. When I drew near I learned that it was Mr. G. Woodbey, a national Socialist organizer, whom I had chanced to meet on a northbound Halsted streetcar one Monday morning last May, during a Socialist national presidential convention.

To Mr. Woodbey I listened very attentively. Two or three times afterwards I made it convenient to hear him. I bought several books on the subject of Socialism and read them eagerly. The more I read the more I was entranced with the purity, simplicity and justice of the principles, purposes and methods of Socialism. I saw that tenets of Socialism were the solution of our problem; the ethics of Jesus in economic action; the solution of the poverty question with its attendant evils; the making possible of a practical brotherhood; the solution of the more serious phases of the so-called race problem.

When the facts were made plain to me I at once espoused its cause, brought it before my people, and threw open my church for a Socialist meeting every Tuesday night at 2900 Dearborn Street.

Negroes Becoming Socialists

Chicago Daily Socialist, September 15, 1908

Fellow Colored Citizens: We are at a crisis in our race variety history. Therefore an error just now on the part of our influential race leaders will result in most serious consequences to all thus retarding the wheels of our progress.

In the *Guardian,* a weekly journal of Boston, Mass., with a wide circulation throughout the United States, Colonel Waterson,[1] a noted white Democratic leader is quoted as putting his stamp of approval upon the endeavors of Bishop Walters in attempting to deliver the Negro votes this fall to the Democratic Party.

It is not necessary to, nor is there any apparent evidence to warrant the impugning the good motives of the bishop in order to take decided issue with him on this proposition. The fact that Bishop Walters is the most influential minister in the second largest organization of color in the world, and also the further fact that an error, however honestly made by one in such an influential position at so critical a time, will be direful in its results. Those two facts alone are sufficient reasons for discussing the falsity of the bishop's position with avidity.

There is no disguising the fact that the majority of the intelligent Negroes are not enthusiastic over the success of the Republican Party this fall. And they are looking for something better. Although admitting the fact that they are very dissatisfied with the Republican Party, yet it does not by any means follow that the Democratic Party will prove any more satisfactory, while there is a very strong probability that the success of the Democratic party may prove even more unsatisfactory to them.

What are the reasons set forth by Bishop Walters for the colored voters bolting the Republican and supporting the Democratic Party?

They are as follows:

1. The Republican Party has not done all it might have done for the colored people—practically neglecting their welfare.

2. As the Democrats are in the majority in the South that it is wise to make overtures to them and thus gain their friendship, by which they would both punish the Republicans for their dereliction and also make it easier to solve the race problem. These two, I believe, sum up all the reasons.

Now the question to be decided is: If the Negro forsakes the Republican Party and supports the Democratic Party will that solve or even tend to solve his problems? Before we can answer this question we must ascertain the cause of the problems. Mr. Ray Stannard Baker, in the September number of the *American Magazine,* rightfully reduces the causes of the race prejudice to two main causes.[2] He says it is race prejudice which is due on the one hand to our national dislikes of unlikes, and on the other hand to the political and industrial competition.

The prejudice that is due to the dislikes of unlikes in this age is not the cause of the most serious phase of the question; contact and education soon removes that. But the political and industrial competition is the fundamental cause thereof today. And therefore this problem cannot be solved by any political jugglery. The cause being fundamental, the remedy must be the same.

The change of political allegiance may conciliate the professional politician, but it would not by any means eradicate the prejudice due to industrial competition which is the source of the intense hatred. This industrial competition is one of life and death struggle between the poor whites and poor blacks for the bread of existence. And as "self preservation is the first law of nature," this law has defined every political situation.

What, then, is the conclusion?

Since the most serious phase of the race problem has its seat in the industrial situation, which situation is due to the ill-born capitalistic competitive system, whereby white men are made to hate even other white men, both also of the same political faith with the most intense hatred, it is most foolish and illogical to conclude that a change of political allegiance on the part of the colored man will, under the present industrial system, help his condition materially. A few leading Negroes may get a few political appointments and a little money, but the masses will remain as before.

The fact is patent to any thoughtful mind that neither the Republican nor the Democratic Party can solve the problem. Neither can education, industrial training nor the recognition of the dignity of service do it. This is evident from the fact that these have not solved even the white man's industrial problem, as seen in the death struggle between the union and non-union laborers, and the 5,000,000 unemployed men in the United States today.[3]

The only solution for this problem is the destruction of the capitalist competitive system whereby a large part of the working class of people being unemployed get not much more than a mere existence, while at the same time a very small part of the people (rich) who produce nothing get at least 85 percent of all that is produced.

This competitive system must give way to the Socialistic or collective system, whereby the government guarantees to every man, white, black, yellow, brown or red, equal justice and opportunity, and also, the enjoyment of all that he produces instead of only 15 percent of what he produces, as the Republican and Democratic parties practically stand for.

The poor whites and blacks hate each other because they are fighting for each others' little morsel of bread instead of working together to produce more bread.

If every Negro voter in the United States would vote the Socialist ticket, with Debs and Hanford as the presidential candidates, the worst phases of the race problem would be practically settled in less than six months.

Booker T. Washington's Error

Chicago Daily Socialist, September 22, 1908

In this generation, doubtless, there is no one colored man, who, among all classes and race varieties, has the same influence as Mr. Washington, the principal of the Tuskegee Industrial Institute of Alabama. The source of Mr. Washington's great influence is in the fact that he has built up a magnificent institution for the industrial training of the colored youth, which industrial training he has been successful in making a large portion of the world believe is calculated to solve the vexatious race problem.

Notwithstanding the vehement desire of every good man to have the problem solved, yet he must ask and honestly answer the question, whether any proposed solution tends to solve or tends to aggravate the problem.

In my article of last week it was made plain that the cause of that degree of prejudice that produces the worst phase of the race problem is the industrial competition wherein the poor whites and blacks are in a death struggle for mere existence. If this is true the industrial training of the colored man, if it would solve the problem, must remove the cause (industrial competition) of this prejudice.

The question is: Will industrial training do it? Emphatically, I answer, No! And deliberately I make the further statement that the industrial training of the Negro instead of tending to diminish rather tends to increase the race antagonism.

Competition always engenders more or less ill-feeling between the competitors, and the degree of that animosity is commensurate with the value of the prize and skill of the competitors.

If the prize is life, liberty and the pursuit of happiness, and the skill of the competitors is equal, the hatred is the most intense conceivable. All must admit this deduction.

To every intelligent observer it is plain that the industrial training of the colored man instead of taking him out of the labor market rather fits him as a keen competitor in every industrial activity, thus enabling him to successfully compete for the best jobs the market affords. And because of this fact it is becoming more and more so that when the poor white asks for more pay he is confronted with the alternative of either being content with what he is getting or of being discharged, with a colored man taking his place—a man, because of his training and mode of life, is capable of holding the place satisfactorily at a lower wage. And in many instances the black man experiences the same from the white man.

In the southern states there are many industrial schools (two and three to the state) that annually are graduating colored youths as skilled mechanics. The capitalist of the South, on the whole, prefers the colored man as a laborer for at least three reasons as follows: The capitalist of the South is used to the Negro laborers; the Negro laborer is not so apt to go on a strike, and is usually satisfied with less wages than the white man.[4]

Train as much as he may, the whites find an equal and sometimes a superior competitor in the black man.

On the other hand, the white man sees his family suffering for the necessities of life due to the fact that the colored man has the job that he might have had. On the other hand, the skilled colored man sees the same thing happening to his dear ones—thus the natural dislikes of unlikes because of the fierce, ungodly struggle for a mean existence, instead of being removed by education and contact, this dislike of unlikes is heated to the most intense hatred.

The intense hatred for the Negro is not found among the rich class, for the simple reason that they do not fear him as a competitor—he is no menace to their welfare. But such hatred is widespread among the poor whites for reasons given above.

Now, the seriousness of this situation is in the fact that the poor whites are in the majority—they make up at least 80 percent of the population. With this vast majority the Negro comes into contact every day. The poor white man, being in the majority, controls the ballot, and, therefore, their hatred for the black man, who is threatening his very existence, is reflected in the dereliction of duty on the part of politicians and the adverse legislation, court decisions and public sentiment.

If the industrial training of the Negro only tends to intensify the race prejudice, what, then shall be done? Shall the Negro and those who are interested in his welfare refrain from educating and training him? To this question there is but one answer, and that is, No! For that would be setting the hands of progress back. What, then, shall be done? The only logical and just thing to do is to remove from the realm of competition the exertions of men in the full life, liberty and the pursuit of happiness, and the right to earn an honest and adequate livelihood for themselves, and loved ones, and to place such endeavors in the realm of collective cooperation wherein the government guarantees every man equal justice and opportunity.

This is the aim of the Socialist Party. It stands for the collective ownership of the land and means of production by all the people for the good of all the people, thus giving every man an opportunity to work every working day of the year, receiving therefore all he produces, which will average $7 per day.

Under this system no man will be rich, but every man will have all he needs of the best things of life.

The Cat's Out

Chicago Daily Socialist, September 29, 1908

This article is intended primarily for the colored people in the United States. Every comrade will help me to reach them by giving his paper after he has read it, or another one, to some colored person.

For years I have felt that there was something wrong with our government. A few weeks ago I heard Comrade Woodbey, a colored national organizer of the Socialist Party, speaking on the streets in Chicago. He showed me plainly the trouble and the remedy. From that time I have been an ardent supporter of the Socialist cause. You, I know, will be the same if you read my article thoroughly which as a fellow sufferer, I beg you to do.

The colored man is the worst off of all the working class of people. This is because he gets less wages, less protection, less education, pays more for food, clothing, house rent, etc.

Why is this so? It is because this government is so run that the necessities of life, such as food, clothing, houses, etc., are produced more for the purpose of permitting a very few men to make profit out of them rather than to use them for the benefit of all the people. That is, that in order for the rich men to make money you must work for him for much less than you produce for him. Therefore, the colored man, being the weakest and least-protected, is at the greatest disadvantage, hence he is the most ill-treated . . . .[5]

The government statistics show that in the United States the workingmen produce on an average $2,451 a year, $204 a month, $6.80 a day, 65 cents an hour. But they receive on the average only $437 a year, $36.42 a month, $1.20 a day, 15 cents an hour.[6]

You see that the laborer produces $2,614 more than he gets. That is a great difference, isn't it?

When you produce $6.80 a day you get only $1.20. Well, who gets the remainder—$5.60—of the money which you have earned? Why, the rich men of the country. Is this just? It has been estimated that it costs the average family $3 a day to live in any way honestly decent. Now, if you receive only $1.20 a day, don't you see that you are getting poorer all the time while the rich are constantly getting richer?

It is reported that Mr. Rockefeller's income each year is over a hundred million dollars. There are eighty millions of men, women and children in the United States. By this you see that Mr. Rockefeller alone received each year over a million dollars for every man, woman and child.

I want you to note well the following important facts.

There are in the United States between ten and twelve millions of people on the very verge of starvation; six million and five hundred thousand people looking for work and can't get it, those who are working are not getting enough to live decently on, old men, women and children suffering for the comforts of life and the sick uncared for.

Now the bad thing about this is that these poor people can't do any better—they must work for just that which the rich see fit to pay and can work only when they want them. Is this right? No.

Perhaps you ask how is it that these rich men have so much power. I will tell you. It is because the rich own principally all the land and all the machinery by which all the food, clothing, houses, etc., are made. Therefore, you cannot buy nor work the land nor the machines, nor even make more machines, unless the rich man wants you to, and also, if you buy or use it it must be at their own price—which price is so much that the poor can't pay for it. In other words, you are their slaves—to work only when they want you to and to receive only that pay which they are pleased to give, and to make you pay for the necessities of life what they choose.

I know you proud Americans in the "land of the free and

the home of the brave" don't like the word, "slave," but that's what you are. For you know that if you don't do what pleases the rich you lose your job and are blacklisted, and that means that you must either beg, steal or starve.

In last Sunday's Chicago *Record-Herald,* F.H. Griswold, editor of the real estate department, quoting a *Wall Street Journal,* said that the farm products alone of America for 1908 will amount to $8,500,000,000. Now, this would amount to about $106.25 for each person, or $532.50 for each family in America. I know that you are asking yourself the question. Why, then, is it that so many millions are starving when America produces so much food? It is because the rich take it that they may become richer.

Mr. Griswold also said that the farms alone in the United States represent an investment of $25,000,000,000. This amounts of $312.50 for each person, or $1,563.50 for each family. Who gets the benefit of all this wealth? Not the poor, but the already multimillionaires.

There is enough land and wealth in the United States to give every family at least three acres of land, a good house, a team, implements and an automobile, and the government thereby instead of being bankrupt, would be many times wealthier.

Why is it not done? It is because the rich won't permit it. They control the government. They want you to remain their slaves. They want the nation themselves.

Well, I am sure, you say, I see it all now. But what can we poor working people do to help ourselves? What is the remedy for the great wrong? Well, now, I will tell you.

A few days ago Lincoln Steffens,[7] a newspaper man, asked President Roosevelt and the Hon. Mr. Taft and Bryan[8] this question, "What is the matter with America and what can be done about it?" Neither of these men answered the question. Think of it, will you—three great men, who are bidding for the support of the millions of workless, starving men—three men, either too ignorant or too selfish to answer the most important economic question before the people today.

A few weeks ago the Hon. Mr. Taft was asked the following

question. "What is the poor man to do when he is starving, out of work, and can't get it?" To this query Mr. Taft's only answer was, "God knows." What a shame! An insult to the American intelligence.

But these questions were answered. They were answered by Eugene V. Debs,[9] candidate for the presidency on the Socialist Party ticket, and the poor workingmen's friend. He said the trouble with America was due to the competitive system, whereby the rich men rob the poor men every day out of nearly all they produce. And Debs' remedy for this trouble is to so organize the government that all the people together will own the land and the machinery; that every able-bodied man must work, giving him the full value of what he produces which is at least $6.80 a day; that all the old and decrepit be liberally provided for by the public; that all men be given an opportunity to work every work day of the year, and that each man, woman and child be guaranteed equal justice and equal opportunity.

As I see it, the Socialist Party today is, in spirit, the old abolitionist party of chattel slavery days—and is destined to free all wage-slaves—white, black, yellow and brown.

Let me urge upon you to get a Socialist party platform and read it very carefully, and then vote for your own interests as poor people—for your wife and children—by voting the Socialist ticket straight.

Abraham Lincoln a Socialist

Chicago Daily Socialist, October 6, 1908

Let me again kindly ask the comrades to help me reach my people by giving this article to some colored person.

A white comrade of the South, after reading my article of Sept. 16 in which I answered Bishop Walters of the A.M.E. Zion Church who is now advocating the election of the Hon. Mr. Bryan this fall for the presidency, wrote me a long letter wherein he related the following horrible and almost inconceivable incident:

"What do you suppose your brother (Bishop Walters) would say should he witness a scene that I have in mind, that happened in the good old solid Democratic state of Mississippi last fall in cotton picking time when a poor woman fell short of her task and a big brutal Democratic warden in the presence of his wife had her beaten, the unfortunate woman's child being born while she was being beaten.

"The woman he then had hauled up to Vicksburg, where, I was told, she died. The monster's wife, who witnessed this horror, immediately left him on account of it and still refuses to return to him, and these things are happening all over the South as near as I can find out."

Another heartrending and almost inconceivable fact was reported in some detail in the Chicago *Record-Herald* Friday, October 2, wherein it is declared that:

"Five thousand Chicago children frequently are sent to school breakfastless.

"Five thousand other school children habitually are hungry as the result of receiving insufficient nourishing food.

"Lack of a 'square deal and a square meal' is the principal reason why so many boys become truants and delinquents."[10]

These deplorable conditions such as this suffering woman and these school children exist among the poor laboring class of people, whose brawn and brain—both black and white people—have created all the well nigh incalculable wealth of this country.

The little ones of the working class pass along the streets and see the stores laden with the good things which God and the labor of the parents have so richly produced—they see these good things, yet they starve, become imbeciles, sicken and die.

The poor working class in this country are vastly in the majority—at least 80 percent of the total population. With them the necessities of life—food, clothing, house and independency—are the most important considerations. Since this is true, for their interest alone should the government be exercised, for their interest alone should political parties exist.

But the contrary do we find. Our government, which is controlled by the rich, utterly disregards the vital interest of the poor workingman. Since the Republican party was first organized it has been in power almost continually, and the condition of the poor has grown steadily worse. And when the Democrats were in power they were no help to the poor man, and in the states where they now control the poor are robbed, killed and outlawed.

The only party today that stands for the interest of the workingman, black and white, is the Socialist Party with Eugene V. Debs as the presidential candidate. The Socialist Party stands for amending the constitution and reorganizing the whole government fabric thus making of first moment the interest of the toilers. This plan of the Socialists is in perfect harmony with the American ideals; as you will see by reading the following preamble to the Declaration of Independence:

> We hold these truths to be self-evident. That all men are created equal, with certain inalienable rights; that among these are life, liberty and the pursuit of happiness; that to secure these rights governments are instituted among men, deriving the just

powers from the consent of the governed; that whenever any form of government becomes destructive of these rights it is the right of the people to alter or to abolish it and institute a new government, laying its foundation on such principles and organizing its powers in such form as may seem most to effect their safety and happiness.

Now, if you will read carefully the following excerpt of Lincoln's speech in 1865 in New York to a body of laboring men, you can see that Lincoln was at heart a Socialist.

President Lincoln said:

"It is assured that labor is available only in connection with capital; that nobody labors unless somebody else owning capital, somehow by the use of it, induces him to labor. Labor is prior to and independent of capital. Capital is only the fruit of labor, and could not have existed if labor had not first existed. Labor is the superior of capital and deserves higher consideration.[11] I bid the laboring people; beware of surrendering the power which they possess and which, if surrendered, will surely be used to shut the door of advancement for such as they, and fix new disabilities and burdens upon them until all of liberty shall be lost.

"In the early days of our race the Almighty said to the first of mankind: 'In the sweat of the face shall thou eat bread,' and since then, if we except the light and air of heaven, no good thing has been or can be enjoyed by us without first having cost labor. And inasmuch as most things have been produced by labor, it follows that all such things belong of right to those whose labor has produced them. But it has happened in all ages of the world that some have labored and others have without labor enjoyed a large portion of the fruits. This is wrong and should not continue.

"To secure to each laborer the whole product of his labor, as nearly as possible, is a worthy object of any government.

"It seems strange that any man should dare to ask a just God's assistance in wringing bread from the sweat of other men's faces."

Taft, the Republican Party, and the Negro

Chicago Daily Socialist, October 13, 1908

The subject, "Taft, the Republican Party and the Negro," is chosen for the reason that the Hon. Mr. Taft is the chief exponent of the Republican party claiming to be the party of Lincoln with the Negroes as a political asset. Because of this attitude of the Republican party toward you, my colored brother, your patient consideration is asked for this article.

A short time ago, Mr. Taft was asked the following question: "What is a poor man to do, when he is starving, out of work and can't get it?" To this question his only reply was: "God knows." A few days ago Lincoln Steffens asked him together with President Roosevelt and the Hon. Mr. Bryan the following question: "What is the matter with America and what can be done about it?" To this question he nor the other prominent public characters ventured a reply.

In a recent speech he said concerning the Negro: "It will be greatly easier for the Negro to obtain his civic and political rights when he becomes useful to the community and a source of profit to many members of it. Prejudice against the race fades away most rapidly when there are pecuniary reasons for its disappearance."

This answer of "God knows," this silence to Lincoln Steffens' proper query to our so-called public servants, and this paragraph from a recent speech in this age of our boasted civilization should be to the American people the cause both of a blush of shame and also of an insult to their intelligence. And because of Mr. Taft's representative character such stamps him, him and also the party that gave him birth as unfit to guide the destinies of these millions of human beings cursed with a system of wage-slavery.

These expressions are significant. They serve to show on the part of Mr. Taft either gross ignorance, selfishness, or indifference—either one of which ought to be reason sufficient to preclude his possibility of being president of the United States.

As to his ignorance. The vast majority of the people today are crying out to the man who wishes to be their president, for a solution to their economic difficulties and he turns them away by saying virtually, I don't know. To the solution of the Negro problem he says, in substance, there will be no solution until many persons of the community in which you live can make a profit out of you—that is, when you become like the horse or the ox, or the ass, or like you or your parents were of chattel slavery days, a mere thing to come, go, and do for the only purpose of making others rich off your unrequited toil—then and not until then will you get your civil and political rights.

Now, is it true that Mr. Taft is ignorant of the fact that the source of both the poor black and white man's problems today is resident in the industrial competitive system whereby poor men fight and destroy each other for crumbs under the rich man's table—which system is fostered by the capitalist?

If you excuse Mr. Taft by saying he does not know these things, then, how can you reconcile such ignorance on his part with his claim that he answers this direct question; but on the other hand makes only a clumsy evasion. I ask you again, can you reconcile this selfishness for personal gain with that necessary exalted, unselfish character of an incumbent of the nation's presidency? The times call for men who would "rather be right than president."

As to his indifference. If Mr. Taft can be indifferent to the welfare of thirty millons of toilers, six millions of whom are out of work, ten millions on the verge of starvation, when they demand an alleviation of their painful burdens—if he can be indifferent when knowing these facts and when the truth spoken from him at this very time would wake up the voters to a sense of their duty this fall—I say that such indifference stamps him not only as unfit for the presidency, but also stamps him as the possessor of a personality impossible of intelligent moral respect.

In that historic speech of Abraham Lincoln in 1865 in New York to a body of laboring men, he says: "Labor is superior to capital and deserves higher consideration. . . . And inasmuch as most things have been produced by labor it follows that all such things belong of right to those whose labor has produced them. . . . To secure to each laborer the whole product of his labor as nearly as possible, is a worthy object of any government." In these propositions was Abraham Lincoln right? You must answer, yes. Does the Republican party stand for them today? You must answer, no.

Now, I ask you, if the object of the government that shall be maintained by either of these two parties does not honestly and in fact espouse the inalienable rights of life, liberty and the full 'enjoyment' of the full product of your toil, I ask you, can you consistently support such a party? However much it may go against your prejudices you must say, no, I cannot.

If you will read carefully the Socialist Party platform you will see that they stand squarely upon the principles of equal justice and opportunity to all, regardless of race or color, and squarely upon the destruction of this capitalist competitive system whereby the rich oppress the poor.

The Hell of War

Chicago Daily Socialist, October 28, 1908

Lately I have been ruminating on war. I have been thinking of its character, cause, effect, and results. Recently, by the demagogues, much has been made of the black man's prowess on bloody battlefields, thereby playing upon his imagination, emotions, and vanities, thus inciting him to the support of certain men and political issues.

The cities, villages and country roads are placarded with excellently designed lithographs containing smooth, tempting phrases that are calculated to entice the thrifty, intelligent, strong, yet jobless young men to forsake the training and activities of civil life for that of killing other men.

I have been comparing the impression which these glowing panegyrics and beautiful lithographs make with the impressions which are made by the real experiences as related by history, and I find that the facts of experience contradict that impression which is made by the politician and the lithographs.

The actual experience cries: "War is hell!" I have asked myself the question: "Why is there war anyway?" The world answers my question by saying that war is to defend the honor of the country; to protect its weak; to maintain great and good principles. To this answer of my query, the facts reply: "Tis a lie."

If the verdict of facts is to be final, then why is there war? To this further interrogation history sends down the answer: "War is to satisfy the pride of bigots; to increase the already bulging coffers of greed—a commercial conquest with bullets and bayonets." Some one has said that "war is a rich man's game." It is. War is a game of checkers—the player is the rich class; the checkers are the poor class. It is a game wherein, for the player (the rich) to win, about half of the checkers (the poor) must be removed; the poor soldiers must suffer excruciating pain, and die like fools.

Let lies cease! Let the truth be known. Dear reader, the interests of the rich alone are advanced by war, while the sons, brothers and husbands of the poor are either weakened, maimed for life or killed, leaving sisters, daughters, wives and mothers, orphans and widows unprotected and inadequately provided for, even by that government for which they thought they were giving their lives. Because of this slaughter game, these women folks, who are just as good as any that ever breathed, are poorly quartered and compelled to become the scrub and washer women and victims of the lusts of these glutted war checker players. Isn't this Hell?

The 1,000,000 call:

Comrades, during this year, Nov. 1, 1908, to Nov. 1, 1909, I have set myself the task of reaching 1,000,000 colored people with the great message of Socialism. Each comrade who reads this call, I humbly ask to help me to reach my people.

I have prepared a personal letter and pamphlet entitled *Blackmen, Strike for Liberty,* which I wish the colored people to read. I can send these to all the colored people whose names and addresses you send me at the following rates:

All postpaid—Single copies 2¢; 12 copies 10¢; 25 copies, 25¢; 50 copies, 50¢; 100 copies, $1.00; 500 copies, $5.00; 1,000 copies, $10.00.

Address Rev. Geo. W. Slater, Jr., 3009 La Salle Street.

Reaching the 1,000,000

Chicago Daily Socialist, November 4, 1908

The campaign of 1908 is over, the one of 1912 is on; already the firing is effectual. Several thousand of my pamphlets entitled, *Blackmen, Strike for Liberty,* have been sent out, and a good start in reaching my desired 1,000,000 colored people this year is begun as you can see from the following letter from a minister of the Second Baptist church in Ottumwa, Iowa:

> My Dear Brother. Someone sent me one of your leaflets, entitled, *Blackmen, Strike for Liberty.* I read it carefully; it converted me to Socialism. I most heartily congratulate you, and very much appreciate the bold and active stand you have taken. I believe you are going to accomplish great good.
>
> I will be in Chicago some time this month on business, at which time I hope to call upon you, since you have caused my conversion to Socialism, and get some more information and inspiration, and go out and help you. The colored man needs to join some new party that will assist him in having a chance in life, thereby gaining for himself a political identity and becoming a factor in governmental matters of this country. Push on, you are making things go. I hope to see you soon, you have my sympathy and best wishes for success. You have one more to help you in me. After I come up and meet you, hope to be able to arrange with you to have you come here and speak. Let me hear from you soon.
>
> S.W. Batchlor

Comrades, if we can reach the preachers and teachers in any considerable numbers with similar results as with this good pastor, the 1,000,000 mark will be an easy task.

Last Wednesday night Mrs. Slater and myself were walking

with an acquaintance who was relating the hard times she and her husband were having to provide for themselves and several children. I gave her one of my pamphlets, asking her to read it well. Thursday evening when I was starting for the street car her husband came running after me and wanted some more of the pamphlets, as they described, so he said, his experiences and he wanted to give them to others. He said he wished that all the colored ministers and churches would do as I am doing and help the poor people to get free, for the poor colored people had given largely of their means to support them for years.

Mine Eyes Have Seen It

Chicago Daily Socialist, November 9, 1908

What have my eyes seen? I will tell you. Now, think as you read. Last Thursday night, in the office of the *Daily Socialist,* with these eyes and heart of mine, I witnessed the bridging of the great river of commercial strife, of the imaginary difference of professional and manual labor, of the so-called natural dislike of unlikes, and of race variety prejudice. Yes, I saw, not simply bridged, but more exactly speaking, I saw that river dried and filled up, with the beginning effort of men to save other unfortunate beings—all refugees.

Let me tell you, I actually saw Jew and gentile, professional and manual laborer, man and woman, theist and atheist, believer and unbeliever, men of the occident and orient, white and black—all forgetful of their individual opinion in one heart-tied determination to save from the bloodstained hands of despotism the persons of humble citizens whose only offense is their activity for priceless liberty.

While in the meeting a prominent Jewish merchant came to me—a gentile and Christian minister—and said: "Comrade, isn't this great? Isn't it soul inspiring? Don't you find a bond of true brotherhood here?" And I said, emphatically, "Yes." Then I felt a thrill go through me. It seemed that my whole being was one of intense emotion. When this comrade had passed out there came to me an attorney, a bright, keen-eyed, intellectual young man, who had taken active, observant interest in the whole proceedings. He looked me squarely in the face and grasped my hand like a vise. I said, "Here is a bundle of nerves with a heart as big as the world."

When I got home I did not sleep for some time. I thought over it all. I thought of what I had read of the meetings of the grand old abolitionists, who had held just such meetings years ago to plan for the freedom and protection of the black chattel slaves and refugees. In spirit this was the same kind of a meeting—the only difference being that instead of white Americans working to free and protect the black slave and refugee—all men were represented here in protecting all men the world over. What a movement! Has the world ever seen such before?

Comrades, my people, to a man, ought to be in this movement. If they knew the movement they would be in it. For they have hearts large with sympathy for the oppressed, for they are alike sufferers.

Comrades, amidst the snows of the north, the vines of the west, the factory-coped plateaus of the east, the bloom, cotton-fields, chain-gangs and peonage system of the south, comrades in these regions, tell my people that the day dawns, the sun is rising, the mist is dispelling, darkness is receding, the shout of universal brotherhood begins to rend the earth.

Beneath that skin of ebony, though much warped by maltreatment, there is a heart of pent-up enthusiasm, affectionate, underlying devotion, of potential, worldwide humanitarianism that is susceptible to the inspiring touch of this great movement—a heart, when once opened to grasp the meaning of our cause, will know no ceasing in heartfelt devotion till liberty, like the giant colossus, strikes the earth. Help me tell them the story.

Know the Truth

Chicago Daily Socialist, November 17, 1908

Error is entangling and destructive. Truth is extricating and constructive.

The following quotation is a part of an address given to the public at Houston, Texas, by the colored "Texas Law and Order League." In referring to the misdeeds of the colored people it says:

"As the criminal element does not come within the reach of the schools and the churches, we emphasize that steps be taken to break up idleness and the adulterous practice by invoking the strong arm of the law.

"Each local league should bring to the attention of the peace officers and the grand juries the existence of these hot beds of crime.

"No feverish or spasmodic effort will reach the evil, but a steady, determined and persistent effort will accomplish much.

"We are not unmindful that this work of saving the good name of the race from disgrace has many unpleasant and ugly sides, but to reclaim the fair name of the race, when a black face was a guarantee of protection for home and womanhood, will more than repay for all the sacrifice. Asking the favor of the Almighty in all we have done."[12]

The objection to the remedy here proposed by this league for the elimination of this criminal element—the objection is that the remedy, like that of most reformers, aims only at an effect while slighting the cause of the evil. The cause of a phenomenon must be removed first before you can completely destroy the effect.

The league calls for "invoking the strong arm of the law to break up idleness and the adulterous practice." This sounds good. But it takes more than sound to destroy evil. Is it not true that the strong arm of the law has been ever invoked in vain against such practices?

Civic federations everywhere even now do this very thing with no appreciable diminution of these evils. Your prisons and chain gangs are quite full of men, women and children, and the authorities are planning to establish more. Why don't the strong arm of the law produce wholesome results in these cases?

I will tell you why it does not. The cause of the evil has not been reached. The cause of idleness and adulterous practices are in most cases resident in our competitive industrial system.

Most men are idle not because they are too lazy to work. They cannot get work; the conditions of labor are so degrading; the wages are too meager to provide a comfortable living although they work most slavishly. During the periods of greatest prosperity, only one out of every four can get work. Out of 30,000,000 workers, 6,000,000 are in enforced idleness all of the time. Those who do work receive in wages on an average only $487 per year, or $1.20 per day, when, at the same time, it costs him more than twice that much to live comfortably. It is further interesting to know that they produce over five times as much wealth as they receive in pay, i.e., they provide $2,541 in wealth per year, $6.80 per day. By this you will see that they produce for each worker $2,014 per year, $6.60 per day more than they get. Who gets this over production? The capitalist who does comparatively nothing while the poor who produced it suffer for the necessities of life.

You doubtless will ask, "Why is this so?" I will tell you. It is because the "strong arm of the law" supports a competitive industrial system which is one primarily for profit alone and not for the laudable purpose of housing, clothing and feeding well all the people. Hence the greed of the money captains spurs them on to take advantage of the ignorance and weakness of the poor, honest laborer, white and black alike, and compel him to perform the most irksome tasks for a mere pittance. This is the fruitful source of the vast amount of idleness—there is no encouragement in it for the worker. Human nature is such that such industrial conditions inevitably drive men to prefer a life of comparative so-called idleness.

As to the adulterous practice. The colored people have inherited a very keen susceptibility to such a practice through the kind of life that was forced upon them during chattel slavery days. They were confronted constantly with the very damaging spectacle and influence on the part of many masters who were the fathers of many mulatto children. They see the same thing going on today. The majority of the 2,500,000 mulattos today know that in their veins is the blood of the bourbon aristocracy of chattel slavery days and also of the present day—mark you this practice was and is not among the poor whites and blacks of the South, but among too large a portion of the rich white men and poor colored women of the South. It is the same old practice of chattel slavery carried on in wage slavery. This practice is not carried on with the connivance of the colored fathers, brothers, and even husbands; but in spite of their protests.

Again, for the poor colored man and woman to marry, and provide a comfortable home for themselves and children is impossible. They fare better, industrially, apart. This condition inevitably produces adulterous practices.

The league bewails the fact that now a "black face is not a guarantee of protection for home and womanhood." During chattel slavery days, a black face was such a guarantee,[13] but the conditions of life and the evil examples of the ruling classes then and now have not been such as are calculated to perpetuate that high moral regard in the colored man, or even in the white man for all of that.

The league invokes the aid of the Almighty in all they have done. This is a vain plea. For the Almighty cannot make effective for good the strong arm of the law in this matter. This whole competitive industrial system must be changed to the Cooperative Commonwealth. This exploitation of the poor, these rents, interests and increase are clearly against the teaching of the Almighty whose blessing they wish to invoke

Idleness and adulterous practices will appreciably diminish with their attendant evils when our political and industrial fabric is so organized as to conserve the interest of all the people instead of just a very few.

Roosevelt and the Race Problem

Chicago Daily Socialist, December 1, 1908

On last Thanksgiving day, in Washington, D.C., at the cornerstone laying of a colored Y.M.C.A. building, President Roosevelt, in his speech, said in part the following:

"What is known as the race problem is one of the most difficult; and it exists in the North as well as in the South. But of one thing we can rest assured, and that is that the only way in which to bring nearer the time when there shall be even an approximately fair solution of the problem is to treat each man on his merits as a man. He should not be treated badly because he happens to be of a given color, nor should he receive immunity for misconduct because he happens to be of a given color. Let us all strike, according to our ability and as far as the conditions will permit, to secure to the man of one color who behaves uprightly and honestly, with thrift and with foresight, the same opportunity for reward and for living his life under the protection of the law and without molestation by outsiders, that would be his if he were of another color.

"No words of advice and encouragement on my part can count in any way compared to what has actually been done by those colored men who have shown by their own success in life how a colored man can raise high his standard of good citizenship. It is the colored man himself, and no outsider, who can do most for the colored race."

It is reported that the president also pointed out that it was to the great interest of the white people that all possible educational facilities be given the colored population, and to prove that the Negro would make good if given a fair chance, he gave as an example the thriving colored town of Mound Bayou, Miss., of 2,000 people, with a surrounding prosperous population of 4,000.

You will notice that the solution which the president proposes for the race problem is the "same opportunity" and justice, and all possible educational facilities.

It is evident that the president recognizes that the race problem is very largely an economic one. In the main this is true. But the president fails to show how the Negro is to obtain the "same opportunity" and justice, and the use of all possible educational facilities.

I am sure it will pay us to look at a picture of the economic situation of the Negro today. The colored man finds his worst trouble with his own class (working class) with whom he daily comes in competition with his labor and skill. There being not enough work for all at a living wage, the competition is most keen. The Negro, being the weaker competitor, is worsted in the struggle.

The bitter competition engenders more or less of nothing but hatred one for the other, and the colored man being the victim develops the greater animus. While this latter clause is not so true of the old Negro of slavery days, yet it is obviously true of the younger one. And the more intelligent he becomes, the more sensitive he is to the discriminations and injustices which he wrongfully suffers, therefore he increasingly becomes hateful and resentful, which passion on his part aggravates the problem. The poor, white laborer, being vastly in the majority, retaliates through adverse legislation and court decisions.

Now it is plain that for the colored man to get his rights under these conditions he must first become superior to the white competitor—he must not only equal him, he must surpass him. For, in competition, equals negate each other—neither gets a price, and if the contest is sufficiently prolonged they ruin each other.

Is it possible for the Negro with all of his disadvantages, educationally, politically and financially, to surpass the white man? And, if it were possible would that solve the problem?

Would you not still have a race problem, with the only difference that the two competitors have simply changed places. For the Negro to surpass the white man either the colored man must possess greater capacity of potentialities, or the white man must reach his limit of development and retrograde. We have no sufficient data to warrant us in using either of these propositions as a basis of reckoning.

Again, if the colored people should somehow be given just now their equal justice and opportunity, are they as a mass able to maintain themselves under much severe competition? You cannot say that as a mass they would. Whether this is true or not is not the great economic question for the Negro today. The fact is that he has not got equal justice and opportunity. The question is, if these things are desirable how shall he get them? And also, how and under what conditions shall these rights be exercised so as to tend largely to solve his problems. These questions the president failed to answer. Just as he has failed, just so has the government, though professing to be able, failed to present and work a solution of the race problem.

The heart of the colored people for a long time was turned toward President Roosevelt as their Moses.[14] But he can't even get them out of Egypt. And because he hasn't succeeded, many are saying hard things. But his acts have been quite consistent with his capitalistic position. And no man nor congress can do any better until the industrial and political fabric of our government is changed to the collective commonwealth.

Just as the old system of chattel slavery had to be destroyed before the colored man became freedmen, just so must wage slavery and industrial competition be destroyed before the race problem will ever approximate an appreciable solution.

If every local would send for a bundle of my *Black Men, Strike for Liberty,* and distribute them among the colored people it would not be long before a million colored people would have gotten the message of Socialism.

Emancipation

Chicago Daily Socialist, December 10, 1908

The word "emancipation" is from a Latin word which means to deliver out of the hand of. It was the custom that when one purchased a thing, he put his hand on it, by which act he signified the possession of the object. To take it out of or to take his hand off of by another either by force or purchase would be to emancipate the object.

New Year's day is held in sacred remembrance by the colored people throughout the United States, for on Jan. 1, 1863, Lincoln, of blessed memory, issued the Emancipation Proclamation which made them freedmen—free from chattel slavery, for they had been abject slaves, victims of a system maintained by a people who were constantly singing the "land of the free and the home of the brave."

This was a happy day to them as my parents have often told me—their ecstasy knew no bounds. They have told me of how the colored people shouted, sang, praised God, rolled and tumbled. It meant so much to them.

For a long time a note of solemn gladness and extollation of the virtues of the government was evident in their celebrations. And as long as the older people who had suffered the evils of chattel slavery, and were then enjoying such liberties—as long as this class controlled these assemblies their present burdens and oppressions seemed very light.

But this note is changed now. The celebrations are held by the younger men and women, who from training, reading and reflection have ambitions of which their fathers never dreamed. Because of which they have problems different from those of chattel slavery days; but their condition is about as burdensome to them because of their more highly cultivated tastes and broader outlook on life.

While these younger people may sing America in these assemblies, yet it is a more perfunctory performance—they know that they are singing a lie. Some eloquent man or woman may deliver a panegyric on the life of Lincoln which will bring forth hearty applause, and yet there may be even in his speech a deprecation of the dereliction of Lincoln's political descendants, and some may even dare to denounce the whole governmental regime and call the stars and stripes a "dirty rag," as has been done more than once. Whether this is well in the younger people is not the question. It is a fact and signifies a dissatisfaction and daring that must be wisely reckoned with.

Some will eulogize the brave black soldiers of the American wars, while others will say that every black man who took part in the nation's wars was a fool. For they could point to the old soldiers and their widows and orphans who are neglected, and to the further fact that the very black mob who suffered from the country's protection, they and their loved ones are unprotected beneath the folds of the stars and stripes. They know that under such conditions they could not say hurrah for Old Glory without stultifying their consciences.

In fact, they recognize that they are oppressed—that they are still slaves—wage slaves—that the vast majority of them can make only a precarious living that some one else has the say-so whether they work, eat, or live; that this some one else who is not immediately responsible for their obligations has the say-so as to how much they may receive as wages, or whether they shall beg, steal or starve.

They know that there is something very wrong; but just how to remedy it they do not know. They do not know that the politicians which they are supporting are responsible for these conditions. They do not know that many of their own race politicians know the remedy, but that they fear to make it known; that these politicians are in the business for the profits only, caring nothing for their welfare.

If these assemblies could be imbued with the economic wholesomeness of the Socialist theory of giving to each man all that he produces, "enough for all men, all the time," a worldwide brotherhood, what light and hope will come to them.

From every section of the country, we are receiving news of the fact that we are reaching my people with the message. My pamphlet entitled *Blackmen, Strike for Liberty,* seems to strike the right tune. Emancipation day would be an excellent time to distribute my pamphlet among the colored people....

Pullman Porter Pity

Chicago Daily Socialist, December 22, 1908

The *Chicago Tribune* of December 17 (1908), in reporting the investigation of the Pullman Sleeping Car company before Commissioner Lane, points in part to the tell-tale testimony of General Manager Dean in reference to the colored porter's miserably small pay for the most physically destroying labor, as follows:

"A tip is entirely voluntary," said Mr. Dean, "because it is usually not paid until after the service is performed and the porter knows he has to treat the passenger properly or he will not get it. The tipping system is largely a matter of selfishness, anyway, and was brought about by the desire of some persons to get better service than some one else. We pay our porters $25 per month, which is about as much as the average Negro earns in other lines of work, and in addition we give porters and conductors an extra month's pay for good service for a year. This payment amounted to $165,000 last year. Besides that, if a man is disabled we give him a pension amounting to half his salary."[15]

Let me call your attention to the three things in this testimony which ought to open the eyes at least of every Pullman porter and family, if not every colored wage worker, as to his real economic condition, and ought to enlist the sympathy of every person, white or black who has left in him any love for the laboring class of people. These three things are: First, $25 per month salary; second, only voluntary tips; third, $12.50 per month disability pension.

1. To be a Pullman porter, one must be an able-bodied man, for the work is hard and nerve-racking. You will see that the only

salary that these strong men get is $25 per month, $6.25 per week, 89 2/7 cents per day. Think of it that these men, many of them with families, do this hard work out of which the Pullman company realizes a profit of at least of 15 to 20 percent for 89 2/7 cents per day! This miserable day's pay is all that this company obligates itself to pay the porters. No man can live comfortably on this small pay. In order to be in easy access to the trains these porters must live largely in those cities where the cost of living and enjoying life is high. If you reckon on the expenses of an unmarried man, it is plain that the porter's salary is miserably small. To live will cost him per week about the following: Meals, $3.15; room, $1.50; laundry, 60 cents; shaves and haircut, 55 cents; car fares, 30 cents—making a total of $6.10, leaving only 15 cents for a little pleasure, self improvement, provision for a "rainy day" or old age. Now anybody with good common sense knows that it is impossible for any man to live in anyway like a human being on such a salary, unless he supplements it through begging or stealing.

2. But, perhaps, some one will say that I have forgotten to reckon tips. No, I have not forgotten them. I just could not reckon with them, because the tips are a purely voluntary matter on the part of the patrons of the sleeper. The porter may get them and he may not. The patron can require the porter to wait on him and do the most menial acts without giving him a penny for it, if he chooses. If the porter refuses and the patron reports him, his job is in jeopardy. This tipping system puts the porter in the position of a beggar—the system is a begging one wherein the slave porter does the most menial work and bears the insults of many an inhuman being, depending for his pay upon the mere whim alone of the one for whom he works. The company does not guarantee him any tips, nor does the one for whom he does the menial service.

In other words, the Pullman porter is nothing more than a slave, working when and where they want him to work and getting for his labor only what they see fit to give him—little, large or nothing. The fact is that some of the porters, recognizing the situation and making the best of it, have become adept at playing the poodle-dog and sycophancy and together being fortunate enough to secure a good run, make good tips, while the majority of them have poor runs, and although they do their work well, find it impossible for them to be footballs for some of these unreasonable traveling babies; hence to live they shoot craps, or play the races—either of which soon lands them where they are branded as criminals. They are branded as criminals by the very company patrons and public who have robbed them of the hire of their labor. This extra month's pay at the end of the year is contingent upon what the company may term good service. The porter can't count on it, and, if he could, it would raise his salary only a little over $2 per month, which is not enough to take into account, for the conditions remain practically the same. The extra month's salary is nothing but a little scheme to keep the porter digging and humble—a good slave—for twelve months.

3. The pension of one-half the salary when disabled. That would be but $12.50 per month. How much good will that do a disabled man? He can't live on that and the company knows it. When disabled and off the road he can't make any tips or anything else, for who wants a disabled man? This pension scheme is a little scheme of some sharp capitalist to still the rising dissatisfaction among the porters and their friends, and to encourage them to greater endeavors, application and continuance in service by means of which the company can make more off their unrequited toil.

White men would not stand for any such treatment and the company knows it. These white men would organize and force a better system of wages for this work.

If any set of men should have a sympathy for the Socialist cause it should be the Pullman porters. For under Socialism there would be no 15 or 20 per cent profits given to a lot of men who never do a lick of work on the Pullman cars, but the profits would go to pay the men who do the actual work. These porters then would get at least from $80 to $100 per month regular salary and even more.

Wake up, Pullman porters! You can help save yourself.

The New Abolitionists

Chicago Daily Socialist, January 4, 1909

The word abolitionist should solicit the attention of every colored man. The old abolitionists were at the bottom of the movement that brought to them their freedom this day, January 1, forty-three years ago, when Abraham Lincoln of blessed memory issued that noble emancipation proclamation.

I have read with interest the great and good work of the abolitionists of antebellum days, and because of their sacrifices for the liberation of my poor ancestors I have loved them. When a boy I could not understand clearly why these grand men were so hated and ruthlessly persecuted for trying to help such suffering people as colored slaves. But it is all very plain to me now, as I see how the members of the new abolition movement (the Socialists) are treated the very same way. Well, this is a strange old world—so contradictory.

Society will applaud to the echo finely composed essays, orations and sermons on the loftiest ideas, of human brotherhood, improvement, purity, protection and liberty, and then whirl on its heels to persecute, disgrace and destroy the men who will dare to urge society to put into practice the very sublime sentiments and principles which they just had applauded.

In antebellum days preachers preached love, freedom, human brotherhood and that God was no respector of persons, but as soon as the abolitionists proclaimed, that the day was at hand that this preachment should eventuate into real life acts, at least in respect to the colored slave, these grand men and women were subjected to innumerable indignities, sufferings and sometimes death—for this Lincoln was assassinated.

The old abolitionists stood for the overthrow of chattel slavery and the essential manhood rights of the colored man; but the new abolitionists, while in spirit kind no more noble, yet in magnitude are far greater. They stand for the overthrow of wage slavery and for the maintenance of manhood rights not of any race variety or in any particular country alone, but for the establishment of a practical human brotherhood and cooperation throughout the entire world.

Through experience and reasoning from every walk of life men are beginning to learn that the only true, safe and therefore happy way to live is through industrial cooperation wherein every man will be protected from the cunning and vicious ones and guaranteed his rightful enjoyment of all the good things that the world affords. They know that it is right for all men to be well fed, housed and clothed. They know that there is enough wealth in the world to easily do it, if men were free to enjoy whole production of their labor. They know that while, on the one hand, the rich are becoming richer and enjoying more of the world's best things, the poor are, comparatively, becoming poorer, while they work harder or have no work at all.

They also know that all forms of existing government have most ingloriously failed to conserve the best interest of the largest portion of the people; hence they believe in a Cooperative Commonwealth, the only object of which is to protect equally every man.

The Colored Man Welcome

Chicago Daily Socialist, January 4, 1909

As seen from excerpts of letters written to Rev. Slater by white comrades:[16]

Rev. George W. Slater, Jr., is doing an excellent work in educating the black men and women of the country and showing them that their proper place is in the Socialist movement. Comrade Slater is himself a fine example of the educated, wide-awake teacher, of his race, whose whole heart is in the work and who ought to be encouraged in every possible way to spread the light among the masses.

EUGENE V. DEBS.

Permit me to congratulate you on the splendid work you are doing. I find the colored man, once he breaks away from the Republican party, is very susceptible to the Socialist philosophy. Your effort to reach these people should be encouraged in a substantial way by all those who are working for industrial freedom.

F.D. WARREN.
Editor Appeal to Reason.

I have been reading some of your valuable articles in the *Chicago Daily Socialist.*

A few days ago, when I read your account of the meeting at which the Jew clasped your hand and exclaimed: "Isn't this great?" I said "yes, that is great, that a Jew could clasp hands in so righteous a cause with the black man."

I extend to you, dear comrade, my hand clasp across the long miles and thank you for your good work for the greatest of all causes—Socialism. Your work is a grand one. Few of us realize what an influence for our cause you are putting into being.

I hope you will receive the inspiration, strength and help necessary for you to do what you have planned. I believe your plans, carried out, will see an entirely new million "white" voters cast by "black" men in 1912. I am rated with the Caucasian race, but I don't think my heart or hopes are whiter than yours. I know my work can never be as grand as yours promises to be.

F.E. ASHBURN.

I've been reading your ideas as printed in the *Daily Socialist* for some time and am much in harmony with your principles. Though my ancestors were all slave owners and I am of southern birth, I have always considered chattel slavery the darkest blot on American history.

I realize that it depends on men of your type, thinkers of your race, to lead your brothers from the land of bondage.

I sincerely hope you will receive the hearty cooperation of all right thinking white men and women in your efforts to spread the light. With best wishes for your success, I beg to remain, your humble comrade.

J.H. GRIGSBY.

Your articles in the *Chicago Daily Socialist* have aroused me to the task of organizing a local composed of colored comrades. While I am of a fairer race as regards the complexion of the skin yet my heart beats in unison with the down trodden toiler of whatever race, color or creed. I have a number of acquaintances and personal friends among the colored people of South Bend of which River Park, where I reside, is a residence suburb.

I am but a poor white carpenter, facing a winter of unemployment, hence I cannot give freely of funds but such as I have I give you without hope of personal gain, but in order to establish the Cooperative Commonwealth.

W.F. MILLER,
River Park, Ind.

I do not know the name or address of a single Negro but will enclose a quarter to send the good news to a few you perhaps have on your list.

Make Socialists of them, and when one stops to think what greater service could one render a person regardless of color?

When one becomes a Socialist he is in a position to help himself.

I expect my grandfather who was a democrat and slave owner would be restless in his long sleep could he see his grandson tonight. But why?

What a grand movement this is of ours anyway.

A.N.

It does me good to see what you have to say in defense of the poor misused and down trodden people, both white and black. I left Europe in 1892, or rather left Denmark. I will never forget the feelings that came to me when sailing into New York harbor, and seeing the statue of liberty holding up the much boasted torch of liberty. My heart was practically beating in the top of my head. I stopped in Pennsylvania and New Jersey at first, but liberty and equality of opportunity was not to be found there. I went west one state at a time thinking to catch up with them; but they are not here. I am now about as far west as I can get without going to Siberia or Russia.

Capitalism and the panic broke up my home in the east in 1895. I spend the following winter in Chicago, using the floors of many police stations for my bed.

CHRISTIAN ANDERSON,
Puget Ronte
Olympia, Wash.

The Colored Strike Breaker

Chicago Daily Socialist, January 14, 1909

In the struggle between labor and capital the former is the under factor, and therefore suffers. Labor revolts against capital because it cannot and also because it is not well for it to be satisfied with less than the full product of its toil. This position of labor is a just one.

Compulsory education has increased intelligence among the laborers. Because of this increase in education, higher has become his general taste and greater his demands. To satisfy that higher taste and to supply the greater demand, he needs comparatively greater returns from his toil. Hence he asks for higher wages. The capitalist's greed for gain causes him to raise higher the price of food.

When the laborers' demand for higher wages is acceded to by the capitalist, the capitalist in turn raises still higher the prices of goods for the purpose of preserving his profits. This raising of prices continues until it has reached the limit of the ability and willingness of the consumer to purchase. When the capitalist reaches the consumer's limit he finds that the laborer is still demanding more, which more wages encroaches perceptibly upon his profits. At this the capitalist balks. Then the laborer in one way or another protests, which protest usually takes the form of a strike.

In order to break the strike the capitalist is forced to find two agencies, as follows:

1) He must find other laborers who are willing to work for a less wage than that demanded by the contending laborers.

2) He must find other poor laborers, who as detectives,

police, or soldiers, are willing to protect the strike breakers until the strikers are starved into submission.

The colored laborer, more and more, is becoming a factor, one way or another, in labor disputes. Frequently he is used as a strike breaker. For this purpose it appears from certain indications that the capitalist will attempt to use the colored man more and more. It is certain that the business, industrial and agricultural schools are fast qualifying the colored man so that he can do the capitalist's work satisfactorily. (By the way, you know that he is being educated in capitalist schools.) Because of this increasing preparation, the doubt as to his ability for such an agent in the hands of the capitalist, supported by capitalist owned and controlled police and army, is fast disappearing.

Under the existing economic conditions there can be found white men who will readily serve as strike breakers, for the temptation for a hungry, freezing, clotheless and houseless man to work for a half loaf when he hasn't any under these conditions, the temptation is too strong, especially at this time of his little information and class consciousness. Also the colored man has the same strong temptation confronting him. Also it is true that the colored man has as much right to take the place of a striker as a white man.

While it must be admitted that the colored laborer has as much right as a white man to be a strike breaker, yet the question is patent whether it is wise for the colored man to be recognized by the poor white laborer as a menace to his laudable aims.

To my mind it is very unwise, for the following reasons:

1) The good that the strike breaker receives is but temporary, because soon he is reduced to the same necessity to protest against low wages or to starve. The new position which he holds is not because the capitalist thinks any more of him or desires to give him good wages. He has the new position because he is willing to work for a lower wage than the other, thus the capitalist can make out of him more profits. From press, pulpit, platform and school rostrum, practically, the people have been taught that the great desideratum is the "almighty dollar," the

"Rule of Gold," instead of the "Golden Rule." Therefore it is inwrought in his very make-up that the more dollars he has, the more respectable he is on earth (which is no lie), and also in heaven (which is a lie).

Profits are the outcome of exploiting the weak. The selfishness, greed and cunning which is necessary to produce profits is still with the capitalist, and he continues to systematically exploit the strike breaker just as he had done the striker.

2) It is unwise, because by becoming recognized as a strike breaker he is intensifying the already dislike of a strong foe—organized labor—a foe which is strong because it is intelligent, large numerically, well organized and its members enjoy the elective franchise throughout the country, which unique qualifications this body uses against whatever and whoever it considers a menace to its aims. The poor white laborers of this country are large in the majority in every walk of life, and through the influence of organized labor they are becoming more and more conscious of their position and power, and therefore are becoming more assertive. Even if it was desirable, it is not probable that the colored man could succeed ultimately against such odds. In a final struggle, which is inevitable, the poor white policemen, detectives and soldiers will take the part of their fathers, mothers, brothers and sisters, as they usually do even now, thereby leaving the colored man unprotected against the vengeance of his poor white neighbor.

3) God, of one blood, made all nations to dwell upon the face of the earth in peace—not in strife. Strife between men of a common destiny is subortive of their best interests. The capitalist knows that strife among them is against the financial interests, hence the trust. The laboring people must and are learning the same, though slowly, but surely, hence the inevitableness of economic Socialism.

Tillman vs. Till-Men

Chicago Daily Socialist, January 30, 1909

Senator Tillman's[17] attempted land deal to me is a very significant development. Its significance is in the fact that the senator's attitude in this matter is not an uncommon one in the congressmen of our country. His attitude is a fair sample of our congressmen's utter disregard for the welfare of their constituency.

The congressmen are supposed to be the servants of the people not their lords. For the purpose of public service they are elected, honored, given large liberties of discretion, initiative, procedure and conservation, and for such services they are paid by the people, the majority of whom are very poor. They are given these great powers and thus paid not to enhance their own personal welfare, only as the enhancement of the general interest increases proportionately their own. Their position with its consequent power and influence was never intended to be used to take advantage of the weakness, ignorance, and confidence of all already very burdened people to exploit them further. And the congressman who does take such advantages betrays his trust wilfully.

This is the very thing which Mr. Tillman did. He saw a chance to get control of about $70,000 worth of land in the West for the paltry sum of $147 for himself, family and relatives. But, before he could get adequate possession, it was necessary for congress to act. So pretending that he was interested, in the public welfare, he consumes the people's time, the people's money, and the people's energy, in an attempt to have certain things done, the only ultimate purpose or motive being to rob the people of $70,000 worth of valuable land while thousands of his supporters in South Carolina at that very time had neither comfortable homes, sufficient food, or decent clothing.

Presenting a chivalrous attitude once I heard him declare that if any one harmed an old Negro servant which he had, he would kill the offender. With the same attitude he has gone through South Carolina making the poor whites of his state believe that they were in great danger of Negro domination and that he was their only savior, posing as a statesman and a patriot, declaring that if given their confidence that he would unselfishly look after their interests, lead and defend them. But in the presence of this $70,000 land deal where is his boasted Southern chivalry and patriotism? It is gone as the dark precedes before the light.

If he had had their interest at heart and was their true servant, he would have apprised at least his poor white supporters of the great chance in the West and would have organized them so as to get a good home for them where they could more readily make a living. At any rate he could have organized 100 families which would have contributed $1.47 each and for them bought that land, which transaction would have given these poor people, each family, control of $700 worth of valuable property—land which would mean much to his poor till-men in South Carolina. But he did not. What do the till-men of his state think of it? We will wait and see.

If Senator Tillman had been in the employment of some mercantile establishment and had taken its time, money, influence and power to enhance his own coffers, he would have been discharged at once in disgrace.

Do not the people in South Carolina white and black alike need Socialism? Under Socialism Senator Tillman could never have done such a thing. It would never have even entered his mind. For the land would be owned collectively by all the people so that he nor no one else could exploit another. He would have known that the people had the power to recall and would have impeached him in short order.

Race Problem's Socialist Cure

Chicago Daily Socialist, March 27, 1909

The Guardian of Boston, Mass., one of the most widely read colored newspapers among the intelligent Negroes,[18] published the following comments on the speech delivered by Rev. Geo. W. Slater at the Labor Lyceum of Rochester, New York.

"The solution of the race problem lies in Socialism, and the only hope for the worker, black or white, is in the adoption of Socialistic principles by the government. Such are the ideas preached by Rev. Geo. W. Slater, pastor of Zion Tabernacle, Chicago, before the Labor Lyceum, Sunday, on 'The Race Problem.'

"'The problem is not one of natural dislikes of unlikes,' said the speaker. 'Race animosity is not found in communities where there are few colored people; it is where the colored people are present in numbers sufficient to be a factor in competition for the necessities of life that race hatred is engendered.'

"The speaker ridiculed the theory of political competition and the fear of Negro domination, and said that for ten millions of people, most of whom have little education to dominate seventy millions is absurd.

"The Negroes are not organized and do not work as a unit or with any purpose. Negroes vote the Republican ticket blindly and instinctively, regardless of whose name appears on it.

"The speaker denied emphatically that the Negroes are trying to secure social equality with the whites. The white men of the South are the men who are forcing social equality. As evidence he gave the large number of mulattos. He said that the idea of colonization was impracticable.[19] The solution of amalgamation was fantastic and absurd, and then he proceeded to destroy the theory which Booker T. Washington preaches and has put into practice at Tuskegee.

"The idea of Mr. Washington that industrial training of the Negro will solve the problem is wrong. Under the present industrial system this training rather will aggravate it, simply making of the Negro a keener competitor, and the struggle between the races more bitter.

"As long as the Negro can be used as a weapon of the capitalist to strike the labor unionists, so long will we have a race problem. The solution is the taking out of the realm of competition the energies of men used for securing the necessaries of life. Instead of competition, we must have cooperation. Instead of capitalism, brotherhood. The Socialist party, which teaches these things in its program, is the party which will solve the problems of the black man, as well as those of his white brother."

The Negro and Socialism

The Christian Socialist, July 1, 1913

Both as Secretary to the Colored Race for the Christian Socialist Fellowship[20] and also as a lecturer for the party, I have worked not a little among my people. There obtains among them in regards to Socialism three things: 1. They are very much prejudiced against the word Socialism; 2. Their past experience and present condition make them quite susceptible to the doctrines of the Cooperative Commonwealth; 3. The colored people readily take an interest, when once they fully understand its tenets.

The colored people almost to a man are of the working class. There are fully 12,000,000 under the stars and stripes. Comrades, what a field for propaganda work during the next four years. This field has been woefully neglected. They can be won and are being won to our cause.

Quite frequently colored newspapers, preachers, and teachers, and assemblies are reported in the collegiate press recommending the study and encouragement of Socialism. Recently in Florida a colored Baptist convention spent a whole day in discussing Socialism, and ended up by endorsing its teachings. One of the leading Negro journals accepts articles from me on Socialism. These are straws.

At this stage of propaganda work among my people, the best method is to supply them with simple literature on the subject written by some colored man. The fact that some colored person wrote it will get their attention and they will read it through carefully—this will be good seed sown.

For this kind of propaganda I have just the literature which the centers, locals and individual comrades can order very reasonable in bundles, or if they send me name and addresses, with four cents for each name, I will mail the literature to each person sealed. In some localities this is the better plan for obvious reasons.

I have on hand the following literature:
1) *Blackmen Strike for Liberty* by Geo. W. Slater. 5¢ each.
2) *The Advantages Socialism Offers the Negro* by Dr. J.T. Whitson. 5¢ each.

Lincoln and the Laborer

The Christian Socialist, February, 1915

Three-quarters of a century after the Revolution, Lincoln trembled at the return of despotism, seeing its coming in our competitive industrial wage system.

In a speech before an audience of workingmen he said: "In my present position, I could scarcely be justified were I to omit raising a warning voice against this approach of returning despotism." he characterizes the "returning despotism" as follows: "It is the effort to place capital on an equal footing, if not above labor, in the structure of government. It is assumed that labor is available only in connection with capital; that nobody labors unless somebody else, owning capital, somehow by the use of it induces him to labor."

It is important for all working people to digest this further statement of Lincoln's: "Labor is prior to and independent of capital. Capital is only the fruit of labor, and could never have existed if labor had not first existed. Labor is the superior of capital and deserves much higher consideration."

The Socialist stands for giving to labor the much higher consideration. Isn't this simple justice?

In 1863 Lincoln said: "I see in the near future a crisis approaching that unnerves me, and causes me to tremble for the safety of my country. As a result of the war corporations have been enthroned, and an era of corruption in high places will follow, and the Money Power of the country will endeavor to prolong its reign by working up the prejudices of the people until all the wealth is aggregated in a few hands, and the republic is destroyed."

To show that Lincoln was no mean prophet, let me quote you a Wall Street circular of March, 1892, reading as follows:

"We must proceed with caution and guard well every move made, for the lower orders of the people (the working classes) are already showing signs of restless commotion. Prudence, therefore, will dictate a policy of apparently yielding to the popular will until all of our plans are so far consummated that we can declare our designs without any fear of organized resistance. The Farmers Alliance and Knights of Labor organizations in the United States should be carefully watched by our trusted men, and we must take immediate steps to control these organizations in our interest and disrupt them. At the coming Omaha Convention, to be held July 4th, our men must attend and direct its movements, or else there will be set on foot such antagonizing to our designs as may require FORCE to overcome. This at the present time would be premature. We are not yet ready for such a crisis. Capital must protect itself in every possible manner, through combination and legislation. The Courts must be called to our aid, debts must be collected, bonds and mortgages foreclosed as rapidly as possible. When through a process of law the common people have lost their HOMES (think of it), they will be more tractable and easily governed (better slaves) through the influence of the strong arm of government applied by a central power of imperial wealth under the control of leading financiers. A people without homes will not quarrel with their rulers. History repeats itself in regular cycles. This truth is well known among our principal men now engaged in forming an imperialism of capital to govern the world. While they are doing this, the people must be kept in a condition of political antagonism. The question of tariff reform must be urged through the organization known as the Democratic party and the question of protection and reciprocity must be forced to view through the Republican party. By thus dividing the voters, we can get them to expend their energies in fighting over questions of no importance to us except as tethers to lead the common herd. Thus by discreet action, we can secure all that has been so generously planned, and thus far successfully accomplished."

In 1864, "The world," said Lincoln, "has never had a good definition of the word liberty, and the American people are just now in want of one."

There can be no real liberty until the competitive wage system is abolished, the laborers have free access to the soil, the machinery of production, and the full product of their labor—yea, until the laborers who are the majority in brain, brawn, integrity, and numbers, rule the world.

Socialism and Social Service

The Christian Socialist, February, 1915

In an editorial in *The Christian Recorder,* an influential Negro church journal, R.R. Wright, the editor, made the following remarks on "Socialism and Social Service."

> Social Service in its relation to the church has nothing to do with Socialism. Many people confuse the two. The social servant attempts to prevent social diseases and to cure the same, i.e., to solve social problems, by working in harmony with the most advanced social laws handed down by sociology. Socialism says that there is one cure for all these ills, and that is for the means of production, the machinery of society, to be the property of the whole. Socialism is essentially economic, and believes that our ills are all on account of an improper distribution of wealth. When the state owns all the property (except wages, food, clothing, homes and fuel), directs all the industries so that the profits may go to society, just as the post office is now conducted by the government, and the water works, electric and gas, lights are furnished by the city. We should solve our problems, say the Socialists. To do this Socialism endeavors to get hold of the government and enters politics.
>
> Socialism is to Social Service as Christian Science is to the practice of medicine. The social worker tries to work in accordance with the best advance in social science, just as the enlightened physician tries to work in harmony with the best results or related medical sciences. But the Socialist has one cure—collective ownership—for all social ills, just as the Christian Scientist has one cure—prayer and faith—for all physical ills. While much in Christian Science may be used in medicine, no physician will agree that Christian Science shall take the place of medicine; so while Socialism has much of truth in it and can teach the social worker much, yet Socialism is not identical with Social Service, which covers a much greater field.

Then the motive of Social Service in relation to the church differs from that of Socialism. Socialism's motive is economic betterment. That of Social Service is spiritual and moral betterment. Socialism is the cry of men who would appeal to individual selfishness largely; while social work appeals to the idea of brotherhood. Its roots are spiritual. The two are not the same.

Slater's Reply

My Dear Friend Wright:

On your editorial in the issue of *The Christian Recorder* for July 16, 1914, entitled "Social Service and Socialism" I submit a few observations:

1) You say, "Social Service in its relation to the church has nothing to do with Socialism." Granting that, consciously, Social Service has nothing to do with Socialism yet it is a fact that unconsciously it has, and, furthermore, consciously, it certainly ought to and even if unconsciously, it must have. Scientific Socialism is the only systematic expression of the social message of Jesus. It would express in the political and industrial life of the people of the world the spirit of the Gospel. Socialism addresses itself to the task of the abolition of wage-slavery with all of its attendant and resultant evils. Wage-slavery is the main root of our social misery. Our wage system is the cause. Socialism aims directly at the cause. Social Service expends itself too much on mere effects. Just as the church was derelict in coming to do with the abolition movement in the matter of chattel slavery, so the same is true of the Social Service movement in the church to-day. Finally, the church had to espouse the abolition movement. Socialists believe that Socialism is the next step in the evolution of the ages, and that Social Service, therefore, is a more conscious awakening of the church to its economic privileges and duties, which awakening will lead it to espouse the cause of Socialism.

2) Another criticism that you make on Socialism is, "Socialism is essentially economic and endeavors to get hold of the government and enter politics." This criticism cannot be a serious one, for it stands to reason that even Social Service, before

it ever will be of any permanent benefit to society must, just as the prophets, Jesus, and the Apostles did, become largely economic in its teachings, enter politics, and form the governments of the world after justice. "The kingdoms of this world shall become the kingdoms of our Lord and His Christ" a kingdom of justice—justice in economics, food, shelter, clothing, etc. The Socialist party, as any other party, takes no account of religions, but if the Socialists do from reasoning, scientific research, and philosophy what is contained in economic teachings of the Bible, should not Christians, the church, and its social service element say Amen? The Socialist's position is that economic justice must be maintained first before any large measure of the kingdom of God on earth exists. Hence, the Christian Socialist.

3) I am sure that you do not mean to infer, although you seem to, that the Socialists do not take into account the most advanced social laws handed down by sociology. The leading Socialists are acknowledged sociologists, and some of the best in the higher institutions of learning and open fields of endeavor are ardent Socialists.

4) You say, "Socialism is the cry of men who would appeal to individual selfishness largely; while social work appeals to the idea of brotherhood." Your criticism here says entirely too much—it needs qualification. There is a "selfishness" and a "selfishness." If your latter clause means that Socialism does not appeal to the idea of brotherhood, you err egregiously, for Socialism has always made its appeals upon the fact of the universal brotherhood of man, and from this fact has deduced its economic tenets. The Socialist appeal to individual selfishness (if you call it selfishness) is the same in kind as the Christian's, only the Socialist party narrows down to the economic field. They teach that the individual will find his largest good in the larger good of the whole. The Socialist teaches that the present competitive industrial system is an exploitation of the real producers of the necessities of life—food, shelter and clothing— the things we all struggle for, and of which nature is so bounteous

a source. They teach that if the producers will form a cooperative industrial government, democratically operating the means and democratically producing and distributing the products of production, wherein society as a social whole receives more, that the individual will receive for his toil very much more of the good things of life. This is a commendable selfishness.

NOTES TO PART 3

1. Henry Watterson (1840-1921) was the editor of the Louisville *Courier-Journal* in Kentucky and a leading advocate of white supremacy in the South.
2. Ray Stannard Baker (1870-1946) was one of a group of reform journalists of the pre-World War I period. His articles in the *American Magazine* on the Negro were later published as a book *Following the Color Line* (1908).
3. The depression of 1907-08, following the panic in October, 1907, hit the working class severely. "There are 184,000 men out of work in New York City alone," a labor paper estimated in the spring of 1908. "There are at least 75,000 out of work in Chicago. There are 30,000 out of work in St. Louis. There must be more than 500,000 unemployed in the whole country on the most conservative estimate." (*Solidarity*, May 15, 1908). While unemployment increased in the following months, it never reached the figure stated by Reverend Slater.
4. This was the standard socialist position. In socialist literature, blacks trained in the industrial schools and "brainwashed" by Booker T. Washington to avoid unions and strikes were said to be preferred by capitalists and to be displacing white workers. In real life, however, the blacks with such industrial training found that, owing to the racist policies and practices of employers and unions alike, they could not obtain employment at the trades for which they had been trained. (*See* Philip S. Foner, *Organized Labor and the Black Worker, 1619-1981*, pp. 78-82, 122-24.) Even Slater himself had a glimpse of this position, for in his article "Pullman Porter Pity," he seemed to understand that a job as a Pullman porter was often the only work an educated, trained black could obtain.
5. At this point Slater reprinted the answer given by Walter Thomas Mills to a black woman who had asked him in Oklahoma what the Socialists would do for the Negro. The main tenor of the reply was that they would do nothing except give the Negro the same opportunities as those enjoyed by whites.
6. Socialist Congressman Victor L. Berger declared in August, 1911, in supporting his old-age pension plan in Congress, that American workers had an average income of not over $400 annually.
7. Lincoln Steffens (1886-1936), journalist and reformer, was one of the most famous of the muckrakers who wrote for *McClure's Magazine.*

Author of the famous work, *The Shame of the Cities* (1904).

8. William Howard Taft was the Republican candidate and William Jennings Bryan the Democratic candidate in the presidential election of 1908.

9. Eugene Victor Debs (1855-1926) was the Socialist candidate for president in 1896, 1900, 1904, 1908, 1912, and 1920. In the 1912 election he received 901,000 votes, and in 1920, though campaigning from prison because of his opposition to U.S. participation in World War I, he received 919,000 votes for president.

10. The statement on Chicago's children was based on a report by an investigator for the Chicago Board of Education in 1908 which read in part: "Five thousand children who attend the public schools of Chicago are habitually hungry. . . .

"I further report that 10,000 other children in the city—while in not such extreme cases as the aforesaid—do not have sufficient nourishing food. . . .

"There are several thousand more children under six who are also underfed, and who are too young to attend school.

"The question of food is not the only question to be considered. Many of the children lack shoes and clothing. Many have no beds to sleep in. They cuddle together on hard floors. The majority of the indigent children live in damp, unclean or overcrowded homes, that lack proper ventilation and sanitation." (*Report of Minutes, Board of Education, City of Chicago,* Oct. 2, 1908, p. 4.)

11. The first time Lincoln advanced the doctrine that "labor is prior to, and independent of capital," that "capital is the fruit of labor," and that "labor is the superior. . . greatly the superior to capital," was at a speech he delivered in September, 1859, at a State Fair sponsored by the Wisconsin Agricultural Society.

Slater, however, overlooked Lincoln's emphasis on the identity of interests of labor and capital, and his belief that because equality of opportunity existed in American society, the laborer could easily become a capitalist. While Lincoln was an advocate of the rights of labor, he was certainly no believer in socialism. (For a discussion of Lincoln's position on labor and capital, *see* Philip S. Foner, *History of the Labor Movement in the United States,* Vol. I, pp. 291-92, [New York, 1947] and Eric Foner, *Free Soil, Free Labor, Free Men: The Ideology of the Republican Party Before the Civil War* [New York, 1970], pp. 12, 16, 20, 23, 29-30, 32.)

12. Some conservative blacks in the South, to counter the charge that blacks were "criminals and rapists" who had to be deterred from such crimes by lynching, formed law and order leagues to police the black community and prove to whites that the "criminal element" did not represent the black people as a whole.

13. Reverend Slater's statement that the blacks were protected from such violations during slavery is contradicted by the simple fact that the slave woman had no protection against white rapists.

14. Reverend Slater is referring to the enthusiasm in Negro circles because Roosevelt had invited Booker T. Washington to dine at the White House, that he had appointed William D. Crum, a leading Negro citizen, to the Collectorship of the Port of Charleston, South Carolina, and when Southerners objected, had declared that unless some valid reason other than color could be brought forward against Crum, the appointment would stand, and that when the Negro postmistress at Indianola, Mississippi, resigned because of pressure of the white citizens of the town, Roosevelt ordered the post office to refuse to accept her resignation, and when she would not serve, the post office was closed. Even though the office was later reopened with a white postmaster in charge, Negroes hailed Roosevelt for his action in the Indianola affair as they had in the other two actions he took. All this changed, however, with Roosevelt's treatment of the black soldiers in the Brownsville Affair.

15. For evidence that the conditions of the Pullman porter had not changed much even by the end of World War I, *see* Philip S. Foner, *Organized Labor and the Black Worker, 1619-1973,* pp. 177-80.

16. These letters reflect both the welcome Reverend Slater received from white comrades who read his column, and a tendency toward patronizing blacks, reflected especially in the letters of Warren and Ashburn.

17. Benjamin R. Tillman (1847-1918), governor of South Carolina and United States senator, was one of the leading white supremacists in the South. He was in the forefront of the drive to disfranchise and segregate blacks.

18. The Boston *Guardian* was edited and published by William Monroe Trotter, a graduate of Harvard College and the first black to be elected to Phi Beta Kappa there. Trotter was a militant and outspoken opponent of Booker T. Washington.

19. Reverend Slater is probably referring to the movement for blacks to return to Africa, headed by Bishop Henry McNeal Turner, the chief advocate of emigration of black Americans to Africa in the years between Reconstruction and World War I.

20. The Christian Socialist Fellowship had been organized in Louisville, Kentucky, in 1906 and was one of the two active Christian Socialist organizations, the other being the Church Socialist League. While the Fellowship was interdenominational the League was formed in 1911 by an Episcopalian group.

INDEX

Abolitionists, 17,167,334-35
Abraham, 169-70,184,185
"Abraham Lincoln a Socialist," 309-11
Adams, Harland B., 35
Adultery, 321-24,356
Advantages Socialism Offers the Negro, The, 347
Africa, 249,279-80,357
African Baptist Church, 25
Agitation, 51-52
Agrarian Justice, 264
Alexander the Great, 189
Allen, Dennis V., 35
AME Church Review, 4,5
AME Zion Church, 5
American Federation of Labor, 288,290
American Railway Union, 288,290
American Revolution, 51
Ammonites, 107
Amos, 154-57
Apostles, 295,353
Appeal to Reason, 6,10,336
Ashburn, F.E., 337
Assyria, 108
Athens, 102

Babylon, 187,188,278-80
Baker, Ray Stannard, 300,355
Bankers, 129-32
"Barbarous San Diego," 30
Barnabas, 167
Bellamy, Edward, 6,15,33-34
Berger, Victor L., 24,355
Bethel, 156
Bethel African Church, 294
Bible, 16-18,42-43,44,46,88-201. *See also Bible and Socialism, The.*
Bible and Socialism, The, 16-18,88-201
Black Socialist preachers, 1,2
Black strikebreakers, 261,339-41
"Blackmen, Strike for Liberty," 316,317,327,330,347
Black-white unity, in Socialist Party, 319-20,336-38
Blatchford, Robert, 10
Bliss, William D.P., 3

"Booker T. Washington's Error," 302-04
Boston *Guardian,* 344-45,357
Brotherhood of Man, 23,244
Brown, John, 26,181,241,249,264
Brownsville Affair, 357
Bryan, William Jennings, 6,307,309,312,356

Canaan, 107-08,109,273
Canaanites, 184
Capital, 17
Carnegie, Andrew, 290
"Cat's Out, The," 305-08
Chaldea, 108
Chaldeans, 119,187
Charity, 164-69
Chicago, 241-50,309-310,355-56
Chicago Daily Socialist, 293-345
Child labor, 69-70,226-27
Children, conditions of in Chicago, 309-10; status of under capitalism, 225-28,355-56; status of under Socialism, 69-70,229-32
China, 244,279
Chinese, 22,208,287
Christ. *See* Jesus Christ.
Christian Recorder, The, 4,5,294,351-52
Christian Science, 351
Christian Socialist, The, 30-31,294,346-54
Christian Socialist Fellowship, 294,346-47,357
Christian Socialists, 3-4,260-61,353
Church, cooperative basis of ancient, 193-201; under Socialism, 72-73
Church Socialist League, 357
Citizen, The, 29-30
Citizens' Alliance, 241,264
Civil War, 59
Clark, Alexander, 4
Class struggle, 17,26,53-54,89,93,97,121,136-37
Color line, in trade unions, 282-89
Colored National Labor Union, 22
"Colored Man's Case as Socialism Sees It, The," 294

"Colored Strike Breaker, The," 339-41
Common Sense, 264
Communism, 235-39
Communist Manifesto, The, 17,101
Constantine, 276
Cooperative Commonwealth, 135,139,169,193-211,246
Coston, Reverend W.H., 5
Crisis, 264
Crum, William D., 357
Cuba, 71
Cyrus, 119

Daniel, 162,187,188
Darwinism, 290
Dawn, 3
Debs, Eugene V., 6,24,290,301,308,310,336,356
Declaration of Independence, 13,56,59
Declaration of Principles of the Christian Socialist Movement, 3
Democratic Party, 300-01
Department of Agriculture under Socialism, 60-62,; of Distribution, 65-66; of Education, 68-70; of Health, 70-72; of Intelligence, 66-68; of Manu factory, 62-63; of Transportation,64-65
Depression of 1907-08, 195,355
Distribution of Wealth, The, 18-21,203-39
Douglass, Frederick, 26,181,241,249,264

Edomite, 107
Egypt, 42,90,108,185-87,208,327
Egyptians,107
Election of 1908, 24-26,251-55,299-301,307-11,344,356
Elihu, 144
Ely, Richard T., 285,290
"Emancipation," 328-30
Emancipation Proclamation, 40,248-49,328-30
Emerson, Laura Payne, 30
Engels, Frederick, 101,263
Euell, Richard, 2-3
Exodus, 137
Ezekiel, 186,188

Farmers Alliance, 349
Fourier, Charles, 277-78,290

Free Speech fights, 27-30
Free Speech League, 29-30
French Revolution, of 1789, 276; of 1848, 278
Frick, Henry Clay, 290

Garrison, William Lloyd, 26,181,241,249,263
Germany, 53
Golden Rule, 125,163,167,173,341
Gomorrah, 154
Gould, Jay, 252,265
Government, under Socialism, 82-85
Greece, 108
Gridely, A.T., 21
Grigsby, J.H., 337
Griswold, F.H., 309

Hamilton, Alexander, 209
Hanford, Ben, 24,301
Harrison, Hubert H., 32
Hearst, William Randolph, 264
Hebrews. See Jews.
"Hell of War, The," 315-16
Herron, George D., 3
Holly, Rt.Rev. James Theodore, 1,4-5,269-81
Homestead strike, 275
"How and Why I Became a Socialist," 296-98
Howells, William Dean, 33
Huxley, Thomas Henry, 283

India, 120
Indianola affair, 357
Industrial education, 301-04,355
Industrial revolution, 282-83
Industrial Workers of the World (IWW), 27-30
Ingersoll, Robert G., 260,265
Interest, 103-19
International Socialism, 139
Iron Heel, The, 15
Iron law of wages, 102
Isaiah, 99,116,151
Israel, 158. See also Jews.

Jacob, 158
Japan, 23

Jefferson, Thomas, 209
Jerusalem, 134,151,195,277
Jesus Christ,
 3,4,42,45,46,47,51,66,72,92,94,95,96,
 97,98,100,101,110,111,119,125-26,
 139,140,141,157-64,165-66,172,173,
 174,175,176,177,178,180,181,190,191
 193,197,198,200,237,259,262,270,278,
 280,281,286,294,295,353
Jewish government, 109-10
Jewish kings, 109-16
Jewish law, 99,102-09,110-19,135
Jews,
 17,42,90,91,98,102-03,104-09,119-25,
 126-33,136-37,140,145,148,149,154,
 171,186,187,265,287-88,319,336
Job, 142-43,170
John, 94,159,163
Jones, Ellis, 24
Jones, J., 18,21,203-39
Joseph, 186
Joshua, 273
Judea, 97,142

Kidd, Benjamin, 284,285,290
Knights of Labor, 349
"Know the Truth," 321-24

LaFollette, Robert M., 264
Law of Moses, 90-91,137,140
Lazarus, 174
Lincoln, Abraham,
 13,26,40,58,59-60,249,254,309-11,
 312,314,334,348-50,356
"Lincoln and Labor," 348-50
Lloyd, Henry Demarest, 263
London, Jack, 15
Looking Backward, 6,15,19,33-34
Los Angeles Socialist, 7
Lovejoy, Elijah P., 26,181,241,249,263

Magna Charta, 247
Mammon, 175
Marx, Karl,
 15,16-17,44,92-93,95,96,121,184,204,
 263
Matthew, 101-02,130
Merrie England, 10
Miller, W.F., 337

Mills, Walter Thomas, 355
"Mine Eyes Have Seen It," 319-20
Moabites, 107
Mohammedans, 189,190
More, Sir Thomas, 124,263
Mortgages, 119-25
Moses,
 51,90-91,92-93,95,100,103,104,110,
 137,140,200,273,327
Mount Zion Baptist Church, 7
Mount Zion Church, 27

Nathan, 141
Nazareth, 158
Nebuchadnezzer, 119,142,189
"Negro and Socialism, The,"
 282-89,346-47
Negro Socialist Literature and Lecture
 Bureau, 294
"Negroes Becoming Socialists,"
 299-301
"New Abolitionists, The," 334-35
"New Emancipation, The," 26, 247-50

Ohio Socialist Bulletin, 2-3
Oriental exclusion, Woodbey opposes,
 22-23,243
Oriental immigration, 243

Paine, Thomas, 243,266
Palmyra, 189
Paternalism, 357
Paul, 110,111,196,238
Pennsylvania, 165
Persia, 108,119-20
Persians, 187
Pharaoh, 186,187
Pharisees, 165,280
Philippines, 120
Phillips, Wendell, 26,181,241,263-64
Phoenicians, 188
Poor, 136-64
Populist Party, 6
Prohibition Party, 6
Profit system, 133-36
Prophets,
 98-99,116-19,141,174,185,238
Proudhon, Pierre Joseph, 274,290
"Pullman Porter Pity," 331-33,355

362 Index

Pullman Porters, 331-33,355,357
Pullman Sleeping Car Company, 331-33
Pullman strike, 331

"Race Problem's Socialist Cure," 344-45
Ransom, Reverend Reverdy C., 5,282-89
"Reaching the 1,000,000," 317-18
Rent, 96-103
Republican Party, 6,11,242,310,312-14
Revolution of 1848, 278
Ricker, A.W., 10
Rights of Man, 264
"Robber Barons," 263,265
Rockefeller, John D., 114,134,170,263,306
Rome, 108,132,174,208,238
Roosevelt, Theodore, 297,307,325-27,356-57
"Roosevelt and the Race Problem," 325-27
Ruskin, John, 250,290

Salvation Army, 166,167
Samuel, 114
San Diego, 7,18,27-31,218,220
San Diego Union, 28-29
San Francisco, 27
Scientific Socialism, 17,93,294
Secession, 58
Second Baptist Church, 317
Slater, Rev. George W., Jr., 1,293-354
Slaveholders, 13,59
Slavery, 17,19-20,32,40,58-59,94,160,225,231, 320,323,357
Social service, 351-54
Socialism, departments under, 60-72; description of, 47-51; difference between communism and, 235-39; education under, 66-70; meaning of, 96;status of children in, 69-70; status of women in, 14-15, 79-80; superiority over capitalism of, 19-20; transition to, 232-35; what life is like under, 204-39; Woodbey describes how it will operate, 13-14,18-19,54-60
"Socialism and Social Service," 351-54
"Socialism from the Biblical Point of View," 4-5,269-81
"Socialist Agitation," 26-27,245-46

Socialist government, 82-85
Socialist Party, black-white in, 319-320,336-38; conventions, 21-24,242-44,265; religion and, 42-47,95,98; weakness of in approach to Negro question, 1-2
Society of Christian Socialists, 3
Sodom, 154,188
Solomon, 115,146,170,171
Solon, 102
Spencer, Herbert, 44,263,269
Standard Oil Company, 114,263
Steffens, Lincoln, 307,312,355-56
Strikebreakers, 339-41
Strikebreaking, 26

Taft, William Howard, 307-08,312-14,356
"Taft, the Republican Party, and the Negro," 312-14
"Texas Law and Order League," 321-24
Tillman, Benjamin R., 342-43,357
"Tillman vs. Till-Men," 342-43
Trade unions, color line in, 282-89
Trotter, William Monroe, 357
"Trust busters," 297
Turner, Bishop Henry McNeal, 357
Tweed, "Boss," 257,265
Tyre, 188,189

Unemployed, 301,355
United States, as land of liberty, 161
Universal brotherhood, 175
Untermann, Ernest, 24
Usury, 104-06,115-16,119-23,125-33
"Utopia," 124

Vanderbilt, Cornelius, 252,265

Walters, Bishop Alexander, 300,309
War, 145,315-16
Warren, F.D., 336
Washington, Booker T., 302-04,345,355,357
Watterson, Henry, 355
Wayland, Julius A., 10
Wayland's Monthly, 10
Weinstock, Harris, 29
Western Evangel, 294
What is Christian Socialism?, 3

"What the Socialists Want," 30-31,256-59
What to Do and How to Do It, 10-16,40-86
White supremacists, 357
Whitson, J.T., 347
Why the Negro Should Vote the Socialist Ticket, 24-26,251-55
"Why the Socialists Must Reach the Churches with Their Message," 30-31,260-62
"Wisconsin Idea," 264
Women, status under Socialism, 14-15,79-80,121,150-51
Woodbey, Charles, 6
Woodbey, Rev. George Washington, arrested, 27,240-41; challenges view U.S. is land of liberty, 161; delegate to Socialist Party conventions, 21-24; describes capitalism, 43-47; describes how Socialism will operate, 13-14, 18-19,54-60; describes Socialism, 47-51; description of, 35; description of wife, 35; early life, 6-8; explains why Negro should vote Socialist, 251-55; explains why Socialists must reach church, 30-31,260-62; favors unrestricted immigration, 22-23,244; influence on, 15; influence on others, 305; minister in San Diego, 7; on class struggle, 17,26, 53-54,89,93,97,121,136-37; on Socialist Party and religion, 42-43,47,95,98; on what life will be like under socialism, 204-39; on women under socialism, 2,14-15; opposes Oriental exclusion, 22-23,243-44; outstanding black Socialist, 5; placed in nomination for Vice-President of United States, 24; praised, 7; praises Karl Marx, 16-17; publishes *The Bible and Socialism,* 16-18; publishes *The Distribution of Wealth,* 18-21; publishes *What to Do and How to Do It,* 10-11; role in free speech fights, 27-30; shows superiority of Socialism over capitalism, 19-20; speaks for rights of immigrants, 22-25; speeches at 1908 S.P. convention, 242-44; tells what Socialists want, 256-59; urges Negroes to vote Socialist, 24-26; views Socialism as in American tradition, 15-16; writes for *The Christian Socialist,* 30-31
Woodbey, Rachel, 6

Zacheus, 174
Zion Baptist Church, 35

ABOUT THE AUTHOR

Philip S. Foner, a native New Yorker, has a B.A. from the College of the City of New York, where he graduated with high honors and was elected a member of Phi Beta Kappa, and an M.A. and a Ph.D. from Columbia University. He has taught history at City College, Lincoln University, Rutgers University, and Haverford College, and has lectured extensively at universities here and abroad, including Harvard, Yale, Columbia, University of Wisconsin, University of California, University of Moscow, University of Havana, Peking University, Nankai University, and University of Warsaw. Dr. Foner was the Independence Foundation Professor at Lincoln University, Pennsylvania, from 1967 to 1979, teaching Black History at the first black college in the United States, Lincoln University having been established in 1854.

Professor Foner is the author of many books, including the six-volume *History of the Labor Movement in the United States;* the five-volume *Life and Writings of Frederick Douglass;* the two-volume *Complete Writings of Thomas Paine; Jews in American History, 1654-1865; Jack London: American Rebel;* and *Mark Twain: Social Critic.* Besides his academic work, Dr. Foner is a member of the Board of Editors of *Pennsylvania History,* and contributes regularly to *Labor History* and other scholarly publications.